First World War
and Army of Occupation
War Diary
France, Belgium and Germany

14 DIVISION
41 Infantry Brigade
King's Royal Rifle Corps
8th Battalion
18 May 1915 - 30 June 1918

WO95/1895/2

The Naval & Military Press Ltd
www.nmarchive.com

Published in association with The National Archives

Published by

The Naval & Military Press Ltd

Unit 10 Ridgewood Industrial Park,

Uckfield, East Sussex,

TN22 5QE England

Tel: +44 (0) 1825 749494

www.naval-military-press.com

www.nmarchive.com

This diary has been reprinted in facsimile from the original. Any imperfections are inevitably reproduced and the quality may fall short of modern type and cartographic standards.

© **Crown Copyright**
Images reproduced by permission of The National Archives, London, England, 2015.

Contents

Document type	Place/Title	Date From	Date To
Heading	WO95/1895-2		
Heading	14th Division 41st Infy Bde 8th Bn K.R.R.C May 1915-Jun 1918		
Heading	14th Division 8th K.R.R.C Vol I May To Oct 15		
Heading	8th Rifle Bde Vol 10		
War Diary	Rushmoor Camp Aldershot	18/05/1915	19/05/1915
War Diary	Boulogne	20/05/1915	20/05/1915
War Diary	Merckeghem	26/05/1915	26/05/1915
War Diary	Nordpeene	27/05/1915	27/05/1915
War Diary	Thieushout	28/05/1915	28/05/1915
War Diary	Locre	29/05/1915	05/06/1915
War Diary	Dickebusch	07/06/1915	11/06/1915
War Diary	Reninghelst	12/06/1915	13/06/1915
War Diary	Poperinghe	14/06/1915	14/06/1915
War Diary	Hub Near Vlamertinghe	15/06/1915	15/06/1915
War Diary	Ypres	16/06/1915	18/06/1915
War Diary	Vlamertinghe	18/06/1915	26/06/1915
War Diary	B Huts	26/06/1915	29/06/1915
War Diary	B Huts/Ypres	29/06/1915	07/07/1915
War Diary	Ypres (Ramparts)	08/07/1915	08/07/1915
War Diary	Poperinghe	08/07/1915	22/07/1915
War Diary	Ypres	22/07/1915	22/07/1915
War Diary	Sanctuary Wood	23/07/1915	30/07/1915
Heading	8th K.R.R August 1915		
War Diary	G 4 D Sheet 28	31/07/1915	02/08/1915
War Diary	H Trenches Opposite Bellewaarde	03/08/1915	05/08/1915
War Diary	Rest Camp G 4 D	06/08/1915	10/08/1915
War Diary	Watou	11/08/1915	13/08/1915
War Diary	Wood Round St Jean Chateau	14/08/1915	18/08/1915
War Diary	St Jean Chateau Wood	19/08/1915	24/08/1915
War Diary	Watou	25/08/1915	31/08/1915
War Diary	Brielen Road	01/09/1915	06/09/1915
War Diary	A Sector Haymarket	06/09/1915	08/09/1915
War Diary	A Sector Haymarket White Chateau	08/09/1915	21/09/1915
War Diary	G.3.b.1.2 Bivouacs	22/09/1915	30/09/1915
War Diary	Potijze	01/10/1915	05/10/1915
War Diary	Railway Wood	06/10/1915	13/10/1915
War Diary	Huts Near Vlamertinghe H.1.d.8.8	14/10/1915	15/10/1915
War Diary	Huts Near Vlamertinghe H.1.c.8.8	16/10/1915	31/10/1915
Heading	14th Division 8th K.R.R.C Vol 2 Nov 15		
War Diary	A Huts Near Vlamertinghe H.1.D.8.8 Sheet 28	01/11/1915	03/11/1915
War Diary	Canal Bank I 7a Sheet 28	04/11/1915	11/11/1915
War Diary	A Huts H 1 D 8.8 Sheet 28 Near Vlamertinghe	12/11/1915	18/11/1915
War Diary	C 21.d.2.4 Sheet 28	19/11/1915	22/11/1915
War Diary	Huts H.1.d.8.8 Sheet 28	23/11/1915	26/11/1915
War Diary	C.21.C.2.4 Sheet 28	27/11/1915	29/11/1915
Heading	8th K.R.R.C Vol 3 Dec		
War Diary	C.21.C.2.4	30/11/1915	30/11/1915
War Diary	Canal Bank Bridge 3 C.25.d Sheet 28	01/12/1915	04/12/1915
War Diary	La Bells Alliance C.21 C.2.4 S 15 B Trench	04/12/1915	08/12/1915

War Diary	La Belle Alliance S 15 B Trench C 21.c.2.4 Sheet 28	04/12/1915	08/12/1915
War Diary	A Huts Vlamertinghe H.1 D 8.8 Sheet 28	09/12/1915	12/12/1915
War Diary	La Belle Alliance S 15 B C 21 C 2.4 Sheet 28	13/12/1915	14/12/1915
War Diary	C 21 C 2.4 Sheet 28	14/12/1915	16/12/1915
War Diary	Woods A.30 Sheet 28	17/12/1915	28/12/1915
War Diary	Elverdinghe Chateaux B 14 Sheet 28	29/12/1915	29/12/1915
War Diary	Elverdinghe Chateaux	30/12/1915	31/12/1915
War Diary	Lancashier Farm C.14.c.0.3 Sheet 28	01/01/1916	01/01/1916
Heading	8th K.R.R.C Vol 4 January 1916		
War Diary	Lancashier Farm C 14 C 0.3	02/01/1916	04/01/1916
War Diary	No 1 Camp A 16 Central	05/01/1916	07/01/1916
War Diary	Lancashire Farm C 14 C 0.3	08/01/1916	12/01/1916
War Diary	Poperinghe	13/01/1916	15/01/1916
War Diary	Lancashire Farm C 14 C 0.3	16/01/1916	20/01/1916
War Diary	No.1 Camp A 16 Central	21/01/1916	26/01/1916
War Diary	Lancashier Farm C 14 C 0.3	26/01/1916	28/01/1916
War Diary	Lancashier Farm C 14 C 0.3 Sheet 28	29/01/1916	01/02/1916
Heading	8th K R R C 14 Div Vol 5		
War Diary	Poperinghe	02/02/1916	07/02/1916
War Diary	Lancashier Farm C 14 C 0.3 Sheet 28	08/02/1916	10/02/1916
War Diary	No 4 Camp A8.b Sheet 28	11/02/1916	11/02/1916
War Diary	Winnezeele J.17 Sheet 27	12/02/1916	20/02/1916
War Diary	Amiens	21/02/1916	21/02/1916
War Diary	Naours	21/02/1916	26/02/1916
War Diary	Sombrin	26/02/1916	29/02/1916
Heading	8 K R R C Vol 6		
War Diary	Arras	01/03/1916	08/03/1916
War Diary	Blangy	09/03/1916	12/03/1916
War Diary	Simencourt	13/03/1916	19/03/1916
War Diary	Arras (Blangy)	19/03/1916	22/03/1916
War Diary	Blangy	23/03/1916	25/03/1916
War Diary	Arras	26/03/1916	30/03/1916
War Diary	(Blangy)	31/03/1916	31/03/1916
War Diary	Arras (Blangy)	01/04/1916	02/04/1916
War Diary	Blangy	03/04/1916	06/04/1916
War Diary	Simencourt	07/04/1916	12/04/1916
War Diary	Blangy	12/04/1916	18/04/1916
War Diary	Arras	19/04/1916	23/04/1916
War Diary	Blangy	24/04/1916	30/04/1916
War Diary	Wanquetin	01/05/1916	04/05/1916
War Diary	Habarcq	05/05/1916	07/05/1916
War Diary	Mont St Eloi	07/05/1916	07/05/1916
War Diary	Bethune Road	09/05/1916	09/05/1916
War Diary	Habarcq	06/05/1916	07/05/1916
War Diary	Bethune Road	10/05/1916	16/05/1916
War Diary	Chelers	17/05/1916	21/05/1916
War Diary	Mont St Eloi	22/05/1916	24/05/1916
War Diary	Maroeuil	25/05/1916	02/06/1916
Heading	War Diary of 8th Battalion King's Royal Rifle Corps From 1st June 1916 To 30th June 1916		
War Diary	Maroeuil	02/06/1916	02/06/1916
War Diary	ACQ	03/06/1916	08/06/1916
War Diary	Neuville St Vaast	09/06/1916	19/06/1916
War Diary	ACQ	20/06/1916	21/06/1916
War Diary	Duisans	22/06/1916	27/06/1916
War Diary	Roclincourt K 2 Sector	28/06/1916	29/06/1916

War Diary	Roclincourt		30/06/1916	01/07/1916
Heading	War Diary of 8th Bn King's Royal Rifle Corps From 1st July 1916 To 31st July 1916 Volume 12			
War Diary	Roclincourt		01/07/1916	03/07/1916
War Diary	St Nicholas		03/07/1916	09/07/1916
War Diary	Roclincourt		10/07/1916	10/07/1916
War Diary	Roclincourt K 2 Sector		11/07/1916	15/07/1916
War Diary	Duisans		16/07/1916	21/07/1916
War Diary	K 2 Sector Trenches Roclincourt		22/07/1916	29/07/1916
War Diary	Louez		29/07/1916	29/07/1916
War Diary	Grand Roullecourt		30/07/1916	30/07/1916
War Diary	Barly Near Doullens		31/07/1916	31/07/1916
Heading	41st Brigade 14th Division 1/8th Battalion King's Royal Rifle Corps August 1916			
Heading	War Diary of 8th (S) Bn King's Royal Rifle Corps From 1st August 1916 To 31st August 1916 Volume XIII			
War Diary	Pommiers Trench		25/08/1916	26/08/1916
War Diary	Dernancourt		27/08/1916	30/08/1916
War Diary	Heucourt		31/08/1916	31/08/1916
War Diary	Pommiers Trench		25/08/1916	26/08/1916
War Diary	Dernancourt		27/08/1916	30/08/1916
War Diary	Heucourt		31/08/1916	31/08/1916
War Diary	Longueval Alley		24/08/1916	24/08/1916
War Diary	Longueval		21/08/1916	22/08/1916
War Diary	Quarry		22/08/1916	23/08/1916
War Diary	Longueval		20/08/1916	21/08/1916
War Diary	Pommiers		19/08/1916	20/08/1916
War Diary	Carlton Trench		18/08/1916	18/08/1916
War Diary	Trenches Carlton Trench N of Delville		16/08/1916	17/08/1916
War Diary	Pommiers Redoubt		13/08/1916	15/08/1916
War Diary	Dernancourt		10/08/1916	13/08/1916
War Diary	Autheux		06/08/1916	07/08/1916
War Diary	Dernancourt		08/08/1916	09/08/1916
War Diary	Autheux		01/08/1916	05/08/1916
Heading	War Diary of 8th Bn King's Royal Rifle Corps From 1st September 1916 To 30th September 1916 Volume XIV			
War Diary	Heucourt		01/09/1916	12/09/1916
War Diary	Delville Wood		12/09/1916	15/09/1916
War Diary	Green St and Switch Trench		15/09/1916	15/09/1916
War Diary	Switch Trench		15/09/1916	16/09/1916
War Diary	Fricourt Camp & Dernancourt		17/09/1916	17/09/1916
War Diary	Dernancourt		18/09/1916	22/09/1916
War Diary	Lucheux		22/09/1916	26/09/1916
War Diary	Beadmetz and F 3 Sector of Trenches		27/09/1916	27/09/1916
War Diary	F 3 Sector of Trenches		28/09/1916	30/09/1916
Heading	War Diary of 8th Bn King's Royal Rifle Corps From 1st October 1916 To 31st October 1916 Volume XV			
War Diary	F 3 Sub Sector		01/10/1916	02/10/1916
War Diary	Riviere		03/10/1916	08/10/1916
War Diary	F1		09/10/1916	24/10/1916
War Diary	Simencourt		25/10/1916	25/10/1916
War Diary	Grand Rullecourt		26/10/1916	31/10/1916
Heading	War Diary of 8th (S) Bn King's Royal Rifle Corps From 1st November 1916 To 30th November 1916 Volume XVI			
War Diary	Grand Rullecourt		01/11/1916	30/11/1916

Heading	War Diary of 8th Bn King's Royal Rifle Corps From 1st December 1916 To 31st December 1916 Volume XVII		
War Diary	Grand Rullecourt	01/12/1916	16/12/1916
War Diary	F1	17/12/1916	22/12/1916
War Diary	Beaumetz	23/12/1916	27/12/1916
War Diary	F1	28/12/1916	31/12/1916
Heading	War Diary of 8th (S) Bn King's Royal Rifle Corps From 1st January 1917 To 31st January 1917 Volume XVIII		
War Diary	F1	01/01/1917	03/01/1917
War Diary	Riviere	04/01/1917	08/01/1917
War Diary	F1	09/01/1917	15/01/1917
War Diary	Simencourt	15/01/1917	21/01/1917
War Diary	F1 Sector	21/01/1917	27/01/1917
War Diary	Riviere	28/01/1917	31/01/1917
Heading	War Diary of 8th (S) Bn King's Royal Rifle Corps From 1st February 1917 To 28th February 1917 Volume XIX		
War Diary	Simencourt	01/02/1917	01/02/1917
War Diary	Grand Rullecourt	02/02/1917	28/02/1917
Heading	War Diary of 8th (S) Bn King's Royal Rifle Corps From 1st March 1917 To 31st March 1917 Volume XX		
War Diary	Grand Rullecourt	01/03/1917	15/03/1917
War Diary	Fosseux	16/03/1917	22/03/1917
War Diary	Arras	23/03/1917	24/03/1917
War Diary	Trenches In Front Of Beaurain	25/03/1917	27/03/1917
War Diary	Old Enemy Trenches In Front of Bearains	28/03/1917	28/03/1917
War Diary	Ronville Cellars & Caves	29/03/1917	31/03/1917
Heading	War Diary of 8th (S) Bn King's Royal Rifle Corps From 1st April 1917 To 30th April 1917 Volume XXI		
War Diary	Trenches E Of Beaurain	01/04/1917	04/04/1917
War Diary	Arras	05/04/1917	06/04/1917
War Diary	Dainville	07/04/1917	07/04/1917
War Diary	Ronville Caves	08/04/1917	08/04/1917
War Diary	Old Nos Trenches Ronville	09/04/1917	09/04/1917
War Diary	Blue Line	10/04/1917	10/04/1917
War Diary	Brown Line	11/04/1917	11/04/1917
War Diary	Wancourt	12/04/1917	12/04/1917
War Diary	Arras	13/04/1917	13/04/1917
War Diary	Monchiet	14/04/1917	14/04/1917
War Diary	Grand Rullecourt	15/04/1917	22/04/1917
War Diary	La Cauchie	23/04/1917	23/04/1917
War Diary	Ransart	24/04/1917	24/04/1917
War Diary	Ficheux	25/04/1917	25/04/1917
War Diary	Cojeul Switch	26/04/1917	28/04/1917
War Diary	Niger Trench	29/04/1917	30/04/1917
Heading	War Diary of 8th Bn King's Royal Rifle Corps From 1st May 1917 To 31st May 1917 Volume XXII		
War Diary	Niger & Nepal Trench	01/05/1917	01/05/1917
War Diary	Trenches E Of Wancourt	02/05/1917	03/05/1917
War Diary	Albatross Trench	04/05/1917	04/05/1917
War Diary	Cojeul Switch	05/05/1917	14/05/1917
War Diary	Trenches E Of Wancourt	15/05/1917	24/05/1917
War Diary	Cojeul Switch	25/05/1917	25/05/1917
War Diary	Beaurains	26/05/1917	31/05/1917
War Diary	Beaurains Rest Camp	01/06/1917	04/06/1917
War Diary	Cojeul Switch	05/06/1917	09/06/1917
War Diary	Beaurains Rest Camp	10/06/1917	10/06/1917

War Diary	Beaurains	11/06/1917	11/06/1917
War Diary	Monchiet	12/06/1917	12/06/1917
War Diary	Gaudiempre	13/06/1917	13/06/1917
War Diary	Bertrancourt	14/06/1917	10/07/1917
War Diary	Terasmenil	11/07/1917	11/07/1917
War Diary	In The Train	12/07/1917	12/07/1917
War Diary	Berthen	13/07/1917	05/08/1917
War Diary	Korton Loop	06/08/1917	15/08/1917
War Diary	Dickebusch	16/08/1917	16/08/1917
War Diary	Observatory Ridge	17/08/1917	20/08/1917
War Diary	Chateau Segard	21/08/1917	21/08/1917
War Diary	Clapham Junction	22/08/1917	24/08/1917
War Diary	Chateau Segard	25/08/1917	25/08/1917
War Diary	Halfway House	26/08/1917	27/08/1917
War Diary	Dickebusch	28/08/1917	28/08/1917
War Diary	Phinc Boom	29/08/1917	31/08/1917
Heading	War Diary of 8th (S) Bn King's Royal Rifle Corps From 1st September 1917 To 30th September 1917 Volume XXVI		
War Diary	Meteren	01/09/1917	02/09/1917
War Diary	Aldershot Camp	03/09/1917	09/09/1917
War Diary	Bristol Castle	10/09/1917	10/09/1917
War Diary	In The Line Cast of Messines	11/09/1917	14/09/1917
War Diary	In The Line	15/09/1917	18/09/1917
War Diary	In The Trenches	19/09/1917	19/09/1917
War Diary	Bristol Castle	20/09/1917	20/09/1917
War Diary	Aldershot Camp	21/09/1917	29/09/1917
Miscellaneous	Awards Referred to in Sheet 1	30/09/1917	30/09/1917
Miscellaneous	Casualties	30/09/1917	30/09/1917
War Diary	Aldershot Camp	01/10/1917	06/10/1917
War Diary	Zevecoten	07/10/1917	08/10/1917
War Diary	H.31.d.5.5	09/10/1917	10/10/1917
War Diary	Polderhoek	11/10/1917	16/10/1917
War Diary	Ridgewood	17/10/1917	21/10/1917
War Diary	Chippewa Camp	22/10/1917	22/10/1917
War Diary	Meteren	23/10/1917	31/10/1917
War Diary	Killed	10/10/1917	10/10/1917
War Diary	Wounded	10/10/1917	10/10/1917
War Diary	Killed	11/10/1917	11/10/1917
War Diary	Wounded	11/10/1917	11/10/1917
War Diary	Killed	12/10/1917	12/10/1917
War Diary	Wounded	12/10/1917	12/10/1917
War Diary	Killed	13/10/1917	13/10/1917
War Diary	Wounded	13/10/1917	13/10/1917
War Diary	Killed	14/10/1917	14/10/1917
War Diary	Wounded	14/10/1917	14/10/1917
War Diary	Killed	15/10/1917	15/10/1917
War Diary	Wounded	15/10/1917	15/10/1917
Heading	War Diary of 8th (S) Bn K.R.R.C From 1st November 1917 To 30th November 1917 Volume XXVIII		
War Diary	Meteren	01/11/1917	10/11/1917
War Diary	Tattinghem	11/11/1917	28/11/1917
War Diary	B Camp	29/11/1917	30/11/1917
Heading	War Diary of 8th (S) Bn King's Royal Rifle Corps From 1st Dec 1917 To 31st Dec 1917 Volume XXIX		
War Diary	B Camp Brandhoek	01/12/1917	01/12/1917

War Diary	California Camp	02/12/1917	02/12/1917
War Diary	Wieltje	02/12/1917	02/12/1917
War Diary	In The Line	03/12/1917	05/12/1917
War Diary	Wieltje	06/12/1917	07/12/1917
War Diary	Brandhoek	08/12/1917	22/12/1917
War Diary	In The Line	23/12/1917	26/12/1917
War Diary	Wieltje	27/12/1917	27/12/1917
War Diary	Quelmes	28/12/1917	31/12/1917
Heading	War Diary of 8th (S) Bn King's Royal Rifle Corps From 1st January 1918 To 31st January 1918 Volume XXX		
War Diary	Quelmes	01/01/1918	02/01/1918
War Diary	Sailly Laurette	03/01/1918	21/01/1918
War Diary	Mezieres	22/01/1918	22/01/1918
War Diary	Roye	23/01/1918	23/01/1918
War Diary	Berlancourt	24/01/1918	24/01/1918
War Diary	Clastres	25/01/1918	25/01/1918
War Diary	In The Line S. of St Quentin	26/01/1918	31/01/1918
Heading	8th Bn K.R.R.C War Diary From February 1st 1918 to February 28th 1918 Volume XXXI		
War Diary	Urvillers N. Sector	01/02/1918	09/02/1918
War Diary	Clastres	10/02/1918	14/02/1918
War Diary	Orvillers S. Sector	15/02/1918	28/02/1918
Heading	41st Brigade 14th Division 8th Battalion King's Royal Rifle Corps March 1918		
Heading	War Diary of 8th (S) Bn King's Royal Rifle Corps From 1st March 1918 To 31st March 1918 Volume No.XXXVI		
War Diary			
War Diary	In The Line Round Urvillers	20/03/1918	27/03/1918
War Diary	Grandvillers	28/03/1918	31/03/1918
Miscellaneous	8th Battn Kings Royal Rifles	18/12/1915	18/12/1915
Heading	41st Inf Bde 14th Div War Diary 8th Battn The King's Royal Rifle Corps April 1918		
Heading	War Diary of 8th (S) Bn King's Royal Rifle Corps From 1st April 1918 To 31st April 1918 Volume XXXIII		
War Diary	Bacoul	01/04/1918	01/04/1918
War Diary	Hourges	02/04/1918	02/04/1918
War Diary	Bois Blangy	03/04/1918	03/04/1918
War Diary	Bois de Vaire	04/04/1918	04/04/1918
War Diary	Aubigne	05/04/1918	07/04/1918
War Diary	St Fuscien	08/04/1918	09/04/1918
War Diary	Buigny	10/04/1918	11/04/1918
War Diary	Fruges	12/04/1918	13/04/1918
War Diary	Mencas	14/04/1918	15/04/1918
War Diary	Molinghem	27/04/1918	27/04/1918
War Diary	Crepy	28/04/1918	28/04/1918
War Diary	Fressin	29/04/1918	30/04/1918
Miscellaneous	Extract from The King's Royal Rifle Corps Chronicle 8th Battalion War Records	30/10/1923	30/10/1923
Heading	War Diary of the 8th Bn King's Royal Rifle Corps From 1st May 1918 To 31st May 1918 Volume XXXVII		
War Diary	Fressin	01/05/1918	01/05/1918
War Diary	Embry	02/05/1918	14/05/1918
War Diary	Near Aire	15/05/1918	31/05/1918
Miscellaneous	Extract from The King's Royal Rifle Corps Chronicle 8th Battalion War Records	30/10/1918	30/10/1918

War Diary	Boesinghem	01/06/1918	26/06/1918
War Diary	Frencq	27/06/1918	30/06/1918

M995/1895(2)

14TH DIVISION
41ST INFY BDE

8TH BN K.R.R.C.
MAY 1915 – JUN 1918

NO DIARIES

121/7594

H/16/Kurdistan
14

S.H.R.R.C.
Vol I

May to Oct 15.

June 116

8th Rifle Bde
Vol 10

Army Form C. 2118.

8 KRRC

WAR DIARY
or
INTELLIGENCE SUMMARY.
(Erase heading not required.)

Instructions regarding War Diaries and Intelligence Summaries are contained in F.S. Regs., Part II. and the Staff Manual respectively. Title pages will be prepared in manuscript.

Place	Date	Hour	Summary of Events and Information	Remarks and references to Appendices
Rushmoor Camp Aldershot	May 18		In strongly inclement weather the Transport party (1 of 107 of all ranks) leave Camp under Major C.H.M. Sequeira.	
		5.30am	Southampton where they embark for Havre. This party include Transport (under Lt Tetley) & Machine Gun Detr. (under Lt Bowring) cyclists etc.	
"	May 19	5.30 Thu	15th Entrain in Two Train loads at Govt Siding Aldershot. (1) Under Lt Col Green H.Q.² A + B Coys (2) Under Major J.L. Crum C + D Coys & proceed to Folkestone, where Embark	
	19.5(2)	6.30 pm	1st Train load on SS Invicta with Dio¹ + Bde H.Q.⁰ + 7th B⁴ 2ⁿᵈ Train load Embark on arrival	
			Folkestone later on S.S. Queen with 8th R/Bde. Both parties disembark Boulogne during night.	
			After good crossing & proceed to rest Camp at Boulogne.	
Boulogne	May 26	2.0ᵃᵐ	Parade to March to Station where Entrain 15ᵗʰ in troop train from HAVRE on which Transport had left.	
		3.20pm	already loaded. Travel in large trucks (cannot) 40 to 44 men per truck. Detrain WATTE N.W. Yvenuck,	
			to MERCKEGHEM where 15ᵗʰ is billeted & remain till Wednesday morning 26 May.	
MERCKEGHEM	May 26		March to Nordpeene. Bn Head Qrs at Armoured Cars Head Qrs.	
Nordpeene	27		March via Zuytpeene, Bavinchove, Cassel, CAESTRE to Billets at Thieushout.	
Thieushout	28		Bde split up & 8ᵗʰ B.K.R.R. Rifles attached North Midlands Brigade for instruction in	
			trench warfare at LOCRE (marched via Berthen, Westouthe) Bussing with Belgians.	
LOCRE	29		A + B	

WAR DIARY
or
INTELLIGENCE SUMMARY
(Erase heading not required.)

Army Form C. 2118.

June '15
8th V.R.C

Place	Date	Hour	Summary of Events and Information	Remarks and references to Appendices
LOCRE	30	—	A & B Coys under Instruction with 5th & 7th Bns Sherwood Foresters. Lt Williams wounded & 3 Men A Coy Gobelhard too injured whilst in Dugout with 2 Officers Sherwood Foresters by trench mortar.	
"	31	—	C & D Coys relieve A & B Coys, 3rd & 4th Bns went back through LOCRE. Rfn MORRIS A Coy killed, Rfn Davies A Coy wounded. Cpl Barnes accidentally wounded. Rfn Denison (Mean D Coy) wounded. Subsequently died in Hpl Bailleul.	
"	June 1st	—	Quiet day in trenches. 1 Man C Coy wounded.	
"	2nd	—	A & B Coys go to trenches for Adv. Instruction 24 hrs by Platoons. 1 Rfn B Coy wounded.	
"	3rd	—	A certain amount of Snipping. Rfn Wilcox B Coy killed. S.6 Shelled (B Coy)	
"	4th	—	C & D Coys relieve A & B. During Afternoon Trenches occupied by London Scottish Platoon Shelled, Trenches evacuated, Hq 3 Casualties of which Rfn Heuispaui(?) proved fatal, & in Hpt. LOCRE. Reliefs took a long time	
"	5th	—	Orders received to be prepared to move tomorrow.	
LOCRE/DICKEBUSCH	6th	—	March DICKIE BUSH via LA CLYTTE. Stay night in CANADA Hutments. Commanding Officer and Coy Officers visit Trenches Two large shells pitch in Vicinity of Camp. Shrapnell	
Dickebusch	7th	—	The Battn take over trenches from E. Surrey and Middlesex Regts. Relief delayed owing to M/Guns Reliefs going wrong. B Coy 7th K R Rifles attached in Support Adv. Bn Hq. Qrs attended Cuttelosh(?) ex-GORDON Farm near Kruis... Situation Quiet	
"	8th	—	Situation .... to a certain amount of gun fire in the afternoon. Trenches improved. One Casualties.	

A.D.S.S./Forms/C. 2118.

Army Form C. 2118.

WAR DIARY
or
INTELLIGENCE SUMMARY.
(Erase heading not required.)

Instructions regarding War Diaries and Intelligence Summaries are contained in F. S. Regs., Part II. and the Staff Manual respectively. Title pages will be prepared in manuscript.

Place	Date	Hour	Summary of Events and Information	Remarks and references to Appendices
DICKEBUSCH	June 9th	—	Mining reported in the early morning between M1 & M2 trenches. The hostile taken up by R.E. Report. Quiet day large carrying party for trench stores. 4.8" R.F.A. Bde shell HOLLANDSHE R for for Snipers Casualties	
"	10	—	Quiet. Some rain. Orders given by Bde. for new trench in support of M2 in case of burning. Relieved by 7th B.: Relief Complete by 4.30 AM (11th June). Rain during night.	
"	11th	—	Coys on Relief Disposed as under. A. B. & C Coys in RIDGE WOOD. B Coy at GORDON Farm with 2 Sections platoon in SUPPORT Fm. Casualty Rfn Ride killed in action. Hd Qrs WILTSHIRE farm	
RENINGHELST	12	—	Remain in Support till 7pm when have to Huts at RENINGHELST. Transport & M/G very late getting in.	
"	13	—	Remain in Huts at RENINGHELST.	
POPERINGHE	14	—	Start 7.30 am & march via HEKSEN to bivouak W of POPERINGHE. A Coy billeted in Brewery	
Huts Near VLAMERTINGHE	15	—	Capts Rothschild & Barton carry out reconnaissance. Brigade march from POPERINGHE about 10pm arriving huts at about midnight. Heavy intensive bombardment of HOOGE from at 2.50 am.	

Army Form C. 2118.

WAR DIARY
or
INTELLIGENCE SUMMARY.
(Erase heading not required.)

Instructions regarding War Diaries and Intelligence Summaries are contained in F. S. Regs., Part II. and the Staff Manual respectively. Title pages will be prepared in manuscript.

Place	Date	Hour	Summary of Events and Information	Remarks and references to Appendices
YPRES	16th	10.45	Leave Huts at 10.45 am & march as a Bde. via KRUISSTRAATE when Bn. sent to allotted trenches in support of 42nd Bde. On arrival at trenches 2 Bns 4/1 Inf. Bde SHR occupying trenches So delay, this Bn. eventually sent up to occupy dugouts on N. Entrenchment of Rly from LILLE GATE for 300 yds. Kist. trench activity in Back our & Enemys Artillery. Some Shrapnell in evening. Casualties one Sgt. (Bart)	5th Oxford? & 9th R/ffle
"	17th		In early morning before dawn both. moved to G.H.Q. trenches in extension of 9th R/Bde. Heavy arty. burst. Some enemy Host Shelling. (Casualties 3 wounded.)	
"	18th		Remain in same trenches in support, rather heavy shelling during afternoon, salvo of guns on our west leaving. Casualties 8 wounded (including Capt Whith.) near trenches 8.50 pm & return to Huts near VLAMERTINGHE.	
VLAMERTINGHE	19th		In Huts. Coys OH in prospect of leave M.O. 9th Bn. Shelled as they were leaving Huts. two down road.	
"	20th		Move into Huts vacated by 42nd Bde.	
"	21st		Morning occupied in digging Shelter trenches & dug-outs. About 11.30 pm the Enemy placed several 5" Shells into the vicinity of the Huts. No Casualties.	
"	22nd		Signalling M/Gun & bombing classes commenced. Ordered to stand by during night.	
"	23rd		10 Shells over during afternoon. Coys continue training. Instruction to Bomb-throwers under R.E. Officer.	
"	24th		Shelled (10) Evening (62) Coys continue training. 4 Officers Visit trenches	
"	25		Reserve W/Gun lectures delivered. Bombers exercised. No Shelling. 4 officers visit trenches	

Army Form C. 2118.

WAR DIARY
or
INTELLIGENCE SUMMARY.
(Erase heading not required.)

Instructions regarding War Diaries and Intelligence Summaries are contained in F. S. Regs., Part II. and the Staff Manual respectively. Title pages will be prepared in manuscript.

Consolidated checked on this sheet

Place	Date	Hour	Summary of Events and Information	Remarks and references to Appendices
VLAMERTINGHE B. Huts	26th June		morning Bomb Throwing Bn employed in Digging during light & tending & completing new Communication Trench. Lieutenant Rawes & Sir Rfm hit. (Rfm Hall subsequently killed leaving H/ot.)	
"	27th	Sunday	Shelled morning & early afternoon. (Lr. should to 2. Ambulance Sick) Evening M.D. + C Coys go digging. Reserve Co/s, in Section formed.	
"	28th	Mon.	morning Shelled. then carry on as usual.	
BHUTS / YPRES	29th	Tues.	Battn move into YPRES in Bde reserve Dugouts, Cellars etc. Quarters very dirty. (Fallen Sick) Rfm Pollard killed by shrapnel shelling	
"	30	Wed.	Battn remain in YPRES M/G un Section relieved by another 2nd team. Large Carrying parties etc. Rfm Harris killed by Shell carrying Trench Stores. 3 wounded	
"	1st July	Thurs	Battn remain in YPRES. Sons Shelling. Rfm Barnes killed & 1 man wounded M/G Section. more Cave about Aeroplane Scouting.	
"	2nd	Fri	" fatigue parties to clear up roads.	
"	3rd	Saturday	" Heavy shelling of ECOLE then fire opened at SALLY PORT one shell exploded in shelter in which A Coy were cooking Teas. 3 killed 15 wounded (2 subsequently died in Hospital at Hospital at Asylum)	
"	4th	Sunday	YPRES Carrying parties each night 13th also Construct Machine Dugouts. (A--------) (1 wounded & very slightly) Sgt. Hughes poisoned from drinking from a bottle found in the town.	
"	5th	Mon.	" two batches of Epsom up Sharks Helmets carried out. Bomb throwers buried. Lemerle Rfm Hutching & Rfm Freeman w/g anners killed by Shell. Rfm Andrews & Rfm Latkin wounded. (Rfm Terry & Hawken C by Coy killed on carrying party & Six wounded (afternoon) Rfm Hodges & Hanna subsequently died)	
"	6th	Tues	Battn remain in YPRES	
"	7th	Wed	Very Quiet day as regards shells. The Priminister, Lord Kitchener & Coy/party visit YPRES. Two Sick men to Hospital. Several Horses kill. Dwn coming to water 2 mm killed & 1 horse	

Army Form C. 2118.

WAR DIARY
or
INTELLIGENCE SUMMARY.
(Erase heading not required.)

Instructions regarding War Diaries and Intelligence Summaries are contained in F.S. Regs., Part II. and the Staff Manual respectively. Title pages will be prepared in manuscript.

Place	Date	Hour	Summary of Events and Information	Remarks and references to Appendices
YPRES (Ramparts)	8th July	Thurs.	Day spent through cleaning up billets & dugouts. Anoka dugout finished. Also 3 large dugouts of A Coy. Batt. Relieved by 5th K.R.S.L.I. Completed by 11.30 a.m. Coys. march back to fields near Brewery POPERINGHE previously occupied by Batt. One tram back to H/qrs. Casualties during period in Belt reserve (29th June to 8th July) Off. wd. 1/ other ranks. 15 killed 21 wounded. Both Cheese to Ahn Salience	
POPERINGHE	9th	Friday	Batt. (14th Div.) in General Jellicoe's in Corps	
"	10th	Sat.	Batt. have baths & change of clothing (not altogether satisfactory) Coy. physical & running drill. Point throw class got together again. A fresh team selected for Reserve M/Gun Sects. Bombers class commence work. V. good lecture by Officer of Border Regt. on Bombing.	
"	11th	Sun.	Service in morning. Burying officials from Fld. Cookers. 450 men by lorry Bus to dig at YPRES at Hyper Strong point & communication trench. 1 known wounded.	
"	12th	Mon.	Brigadier visits bivouacs.	
"	13th	Tues.	Bombers practiced. Reserve M/Gun Sects. made up	
"	14th	Wed.	C/marched. " 10 bodies per platoon allowed into POPERINGHE. Field Sanitary arrangements	
"	15th	Thursday	450 men under Capt. Moore go to dig cut (laying out) Motor Bus. No Casualties but V. hot Bomb trenches for practice completed. Bomb demonstration by B.M. Bomb officer.	
"	16th	Fri.	Snipers cope demonstration.	

1577 Wt. W10791/1773 500,000 1/15 D. D. & L. A.D.S.S./Forms/C. 2118.

Army Form C. 2118.

WAR DIARY
or
INTELLIGENCE SUMMARY.
(Erase heading not required.)

Instructions regarding War Diaries and Intelligence Summaries are contained in F.S. Regs., Part II. and the Staff Manual respectively. Title pages will be prepared in manuscript.

Place	Date July	Hour	Summary of Events and Information	Remarks and references to Appendices
POPERINGHE	17	Sat.	Route march cancelled owing to Rain.	
"	18	Sunday	Parade Services.	
"	19	Mon	Working party of 200 under Major Seymour proceeded by Bus to YPRES.	
"	20	Tues	A Coy Cmdrs proceed to C Sector to see trenches. Taking over of trenches postponed 24 hrs.	
"	21	Wed	Get ready for move tomorrow.	
POPERINGHE/YPRES	22	Thur	Take over of C Sector trenches from 2nd Gn. Hdrs. 8th Bde. [This was the last entry made by Capt W.J. Davis, killed in action 30/7/15]	
Sanctuary Wood	23	Friday	C Coy occupies C1. C2 right. 1 Platoon D Coy in C2 left isolated. 1 Platoon D Coy in shaft F1. 2 Platoons D Coy & A Coy at Battalion in Sanctuary Wood. B Coy at H.Q. Hooge. C2 left shelled in afternoon and damaged, built up considerably at night. 2nd Lt Henriques wounded by bullet in head. in F1. 3 men wounded	
	24	Saturday	2nd Lt Henriques died at Bailleul. C1 L+R C2L+R constantly demolished, by heavy trench mortar fire. Working party of A Company much interfered with, Every built it up at night. 1 Platoon of A Coy in 2nd Bomb. Line relieves the Platoon of D Coy C2L. 1 W. Pt Party 1 Platoon of A relieves C of Barlun and the platoon of D Coy in F1. W. Smith + 1 Platoon of D Coy to H Q. Carry rations shell at night.	
	25	Sunday	C2 L+R shelled with half of RE. Two unworkable trenches towards crater from Pt 59 in front of C3, one pace East of wall.	
	26	Monday	Bombardment all day. Exchange of trench ammunition etc in C2 L/R.	
	27	Tuesday	Bombardment recommences 4.45 am 57 mins 6.7 cm Trench Mortars fire on C3 from all sides of trench. One shelled with HE from E of Sanctuary Wood. Burnt front of C1.	
	28	Wednesday	Patrols patrol in front. 1 Pr/pr killed. German machine gun located.	

Note from 28. This sector commd. under Lt Col. from V Carter; Inches relieved J. vice C.

Army Form C. 2118.

WAR DIARY
or
INTELLIGENCE SUMMARY.
(Erase heading not required.)

Instructions regarding War Diaries and Intelligence Summaries are contained in F. S. Regs., Part II. and the Staff Manual respectively. Title pages will be prepared in manuscript.

Place	Date	Hour	Summary of Events and Information	Remarks and references to Appendices
Sanctuary Wood	July 29	Thurs	Dug outs made. Communication trenches cleared. Parapets repaired especially in F.1. 7 K.R.R. relieved 8 K.R.R. about midnight. 8 Battalion returns to Ypres. A & D Coys to Ramparts near little square. B & C Coys to dugouts near White house west of Asylum.	
	30	Friday	Enemy attack hinted roused by 9 R.B. v 7 K.R.R. at 7.0 am using liquid fire. Heavy [?] trenches opposite Zouave wood lost. Bombardment by our guns and enemy guns opens at 3·45am. 9 K.R.B. in Zouave wood. Heavy loss of Battn. 8 K.R.R. to 2 man wood at 8·30am 3/min. 8 K.R.R. ordered to reinforce 9 K.R.B. in Zouave wood. Left the Battalion a Coy at a time. Major Crum, Capt Baker. Remainder of Battalion goes to Sanctuary wood. 11.23 Platoon of D Coy reinforce a Coy of 8 K.R.B. Most of Zouave wood evidently shelled. They are withdrawn to Sanctuary wood at 12.0 noon. 1st Northants R.A.M.C. killed just past Croft. He on way up to Sanctuary wood with the battalion. Intense bombardment by our artillery opened at 2·15pm. Counter attack arranged for at 2·45 – 3·15 to support 9 K.R.B. attack the launched from Sanctuary wood. R.B. 's from Zouave wood. Every machine gun fire marked in position to keep wood; battle of Hooge wood heavily carried out. [?] Hooge was. A Coy v B Coy in particular supported by Cley, D Left, in forward in tier.[?] some way out from wood and from Sanctuary wood. About 3·15 pm a message was received by Col Green from Major Seymour saying that the 7 Battn and our own advance had stuck up & asking whether to shove again attempt to push on. Col Green seeing that the R.B. attack had also been held up, decided to look to orders – This orders were shortly received from the Brigadier not to press the attack further. Col Green intend for a trench to be dug through Sanctuary wood at the point but by one of my Coys. This was done by all available men – helped by the 8 K.R.B. who had sent 2 Coys to reinforce 7 The Battn has been very heavy including Captain WJ Davis. The Adjutant, B. Watson, Killed & 8 Officers wounded, & N.C.O.s & men. The Medical arrangements carried in not of casualty to available. Dr Hawkes had been after expressed in finding & bringing ambulances up. Dr Watson available to cope with over 500 cases good difficulty inexperienced was experienced. In the thick woods of Sanctuary wood being found in bringing them to dressing station, impossible for any ambulance up within 500 x of the front aid station main body had to remain out for more 24 hrs. This cupola with the far-line the Battn had had no rations for 36 hrs & suffered from want of water caused by the Germans lines. The Riflemen who might have been saved. At about 3 Pm a terrific rifle & MG fire opened to be a heavy rifle attack. The artillery & these efforts & routed both sides aided in this confusion of what appeared The Col Glass the 7 Battn & AdjL Coys had been relieved only B & C Coys & D position A small to develop which under Col Green on MG under Riflemen Bentley particularly distinguishing itself. Col Green worth Brigadier & Bn Gen in the 2 Coys having from below falls on he creek

8ᵗʰ KRR.

August 1915

Army Form C. 2118.

WAR DIARY
or
INTELLIGENCE SUMMARY.
(Erase heading not required.)

Instructions regarding War Diaries and Intelligence Summaries are contained in F. S. Regs., Part II. and the Staff Manual respectively. Title pages will be prepared in manuscript.

Place	Date	Hour	Summary of Events and Information	Remarks and references to Appendices
G.d. sheet.28	July 31	Saturday	Returned to Rest Camp at G4d sheet 28 from Sanctuary Wood. Capt. Blane given command of C. Company.	
"	August 1	Sunday	Church parade.	
"	2	Monday	A.B. & C Companies get bathes at Poperinghe in the morning. The battalion relieves 9th Rifle Brigade in H Sector, leaving rest Camp in Motor busses at 8.0 p.m. Capt. Campbell-Ida. (invalided to England) Command of D. Coy from 6 Capt. Baxter. Two Coys 5th Prof. Shire L.I. under Command of O.C. 9 K.R.R. The battalion is temporarily attached to 42nd Brigade. Right sector under Command of Colonel Green. A Coy occupies H16, H15. B Coy H14, H13, C Coy H12, C.S.11.	15.07 = R13" of afficers attached 9. 8th K.R.R. for 1st duty in trenches.
H Trenches opposite Bellewaarde	3	Tuesday	Communication by telephone with firing line completed, taken. D Coy S5, S6. Two Coys of K.S.L.I. in G4 & S3, A.S.11 Major Jordan Senior Officer of K.S.L.I. Damages to trenches built up at night.	13 Casualties
"	4	Wednesday	Casualties from to-day's Coys in A & D Company. During this tour of duty - A Company suffered most casualties. Major Crum writes a report to General Markham. Culvert blown in, damage to trenches built up at night.	38 Casualties
"	5	Thursday	The battalion & 2 Coys K.S.L.I. is relieved by 12th K.S.L.I. and 2nd York & Lancaster Regt. the 6th Division. A & B Coy under Major Crum are relieved through Oxford & Bucks trenches in left sector. B Coy does not get out of trenches before daylight and remains an extra day in Oxford/Bucks trenches. The battalion returns in busses to G.d. Rest Camp. A & B Coy are relieved by A & B Coy 7 K.R.R. Total Casualties during this tour of duty 101.	24 Casualties 128
Rest camp G.d.	6	Friday	Gr. rest Camp G4d.	
"	7	Saturday	G. rest camp	
"	8	Sunday	The battalion has bathes at Poperinghe. Church parade in 8 K.R.R.C field attached by 7 K.R.R.	
"	9	Monday	Running parade before breakfast. Inspection of Coys in pith helmets, order dress by C.O. at 10.30 am.	

Army Form C. 2118.

WAR DIARY
or
INTELLIGENCE SUMMARY.
(Erase heading not required.)

Instructions regarding War Diaries and Intelligence Summaries are contained in F.S. Regs, Part II. and the Staff Manual respectively. Title pages will be prepared in manuscript.

Place	Date	Hour	Summary of Events and Information	Remarks and references to Appendices
64th Rest Camp	August 10	Tuesday	50 men per Coy paraded at 6-45 a.m. and march to 1/3rd NE of VLAMERTINGHE to work on 4 redoubts. Return at 1-0 p.m. Inspection of infantry equipment by O.C. Coy with special reference to new information of thin air inflow equipment. Battn paraded at 7-0 p.m. to march to new billets at WATOU W. of POPERINGHE. Move unofficially cancelled when Battn had fallen in on the VLAMERTINGHE - POPERINGHE road. The men carried out after ½ hr delay. The others were sent on along the march, but his on arrival at WATOU at 10-15 p.m. he was felt out during the march. Three large fields allotted to Bn, bivouacing.	
Watou	11	Wednesday	Bn R.O. Nº 40 & 11, 14th D.R. O 372. 15th resting	
"	12	Thursday	Coy at disposal of Coy Officers. The following Officers joined the Bn this afternoon. Lt E.G. Kerton-Shand reported after Sick leave in England. Lt E.G.H. Armitage, 2nd Lt G.E. Ingman, 2nd Lt A.M.F. Hill, 2nd Lt J.F. Egerton, 2nd Lt C.R. Roman, 2nd Lt Cd. Munday, 2nd Lt W.R. Baird, 2nd Lt H.D. Sampson, 2nd Lt G.D. Robson. Special order by G.O.C. 41st & 9th Infy Bde 1st August 1915. "The following message has been received from the G.O.C. 2nd Army "Army Commander is glad to receive such a satisfactory report this morning. Please convey to all troops engaged his appreciation of the way in which they have held their ground and improved their position." The Brigadier is glad to be able to add to the above commendation from General Sir Herbert Plumer, his own appreciation of the gallant attempt of the 8th, for the loss of the Brigade to recover the ground lost on the morning of the 30th for the loss of the trenches	

1577 Wt.W10791/1773 500,000 1/15 D. D. & L. A.D.S.S./Forms/C. 2118.

no blame can be attributed to any officer or man of the garrison. In the attempt to recapture them, only high praise can be given to the gallant effort made by men who had already be very highly tried and who were exhausted from want of food and sleep. The attack failed owing to conditions that made success impossible for the time.

All reports received speak of the supreme devotion to duty of officers and men, of the gallant stand made by those who held the trenches, and of the courage shown as well by those who took part in the attack as by the parties who held their ground in various places of the line under great loss throughout the day. The brigade will soon be restored to strength, it is not likely again to go through a severer trial than it passed through on the 30th and the memory of a very gallant effort will always constitute but the least of the honours yet to be gained.

The Brigadier General deeply deplores the loss of so many gallant officers and men.

Army Form C. 2118.

WAR DIARY
or
INTELLIGENCE SUMMARY.
(Erase heading not required.)

Instructions regarding War Diaries and Intelligence Summaries are contained in F. S. Regs., Part II. and the Staff Manual respectively. Title pages will be prepared in manuscript.

Place	Date	Hour	Summary of Events and Information	Remarks and references to Appendices
Woeten	August 13 Friday		Battalion paraded at 6-30 p.m. & march to Potersche Square, entraining there en masse which takes at 6-H.M. central/Sheet 28 suppm guides from 1st North unfastened fourteen take companies up to the trenches. Battalion relieves 1st N. unfastened. A Coy in A6, B Coy in A5, occupy front line, C Coy in H2 D Coy in H3 occupy support line. Head Quarters in a particularly shine dug-out built for a French Brigadier in the wood near Pt Jean Chateau. Relief completed by 2.0 a.m.	
Wood near Pt Jean Chateau	14 Saturday		Telephonic communication tried everywhere. Sand bags due to men out instruments. At night trotile at Oder horses advanced trench, work on the "gap" begun.	
"	15 Sunday		Two working parties of 20 men sent up from C & D Coys to work on front parapet of A5 & A6. Strafing work 9-3.0 p.m. Draft of 100 men brought up by transport and allotted to companies.	
	16 Monday			
	17 Tuesday		Snipers collected at Head Quarters and used with effect for the remainder of the tour.	
	18 Wednesday			

Army Form C. 2118.

WAR DIARY
or
INTELLIGENCE SUMMARY.
(Erase heading not required.)

Instructions regarding War Diaries and Intelligence Summaries are contained in F. S. Regs., Part II. and the Staff Manual respectively. Title pages will be prepared in manuscript.

Place	Date	Hour	Summary of Events and Information	Remarks and references to Appendices
St Jean Chateau Wood	August 19	Thursday		
"	20	Friday	D Company relieves A Company by small parties during the day. This relief was carried out quite easily and was finished except for the Oder Lodge advanced post by 5 o'clock in the afternoon	
	21	Saturday	C Company relieves B Company by day, relief completed by 4.30 p.m.	
	22	Sunday	The "Sgt" finished also work at Oder Lodge. Captain Trevor goes on leave, 5 days, to England. B Company under command of Lt. Rawdon-Shand temporarily.	
	23	Monday	Battalion relieved by 2nd Sherwood Foresters and 8th R.B. A, B, & C Coys relieved by 8th R.B. D Coy relieved by 2nd Sherwood Foresters. 18th Inf Bde 6th Div. The 6th Division takes Opr line having its right on Crump Farm, 6th Div later taken over Bond St. communication trench entirely. The Battalion is in bivouac from H.11 central sheet 28 took to Lovatin.	
	24	Tuesday	At 2.0 a.m. when unloading rifles Rfn Matthews of 15 Coy was fatally wounded by Rfn Williams in B. Coy. Battn occupies the same bivouac ground at station. as it left on Friday 19th Aug.	

Army Form C. 2118.

WAR DIARY
or
INTELLIGENCE SUMMARY.
(Erase heading not required.)

Instructions regarding War Diaries and Intelligence Summaries are contained in F. S. Regs., Part II. and the Staff Manual respectively. Title pages will be prepared in manuscript.

Place	Date	Hour	Summary of Events and Information	Remarks and references to Appendices
Watou	25- Wednesday		Colonel Green goes on 5 days leave to England, also S/L Heaton. Major Crum in command of the Battalion.	
"	26 Thursday		Lt Zetter, Lt Bower, C.S.M. Webb, S/L Wesley on 5 days leave to England. Band of Somersetshire Infantry played in B^n field from 5:0 to 7:0 pm	
"	27th Friday		C.S.M. McGilgan. C.S.M. Powell. Cpl Brotherton on 5 days leave to England	
"	28th Saturday		Surf sent from 7-30 pm to 9-30 pm	
"	29th Sunday		Church parade 9-0 am. Heavy rains from 4-30 pm. Rfn Patrick of A. Coy. & Rfn Brown of B. Coy on 5 days leave to England.	
"	30th Monday		Battalion relieves 7th R.B. in billets in BRIELEN ROAD. B^n Conveyed on motor busses from WATOU at 6:0 pm, 7.29 strong. arrives at H.11 central Hud/28 at 7-45 p.m. 5 officers of B^n sent on ealier in the day guide B^n to billets. D Coy So 16 KAIEE SALIENT. Relief completed by 9-30 pm. Reserve M. Greeting of 7 & 8th R.B. attached to this B^n.	
"	31st Tuesday		Working parties. By day - 20 men on Bde & Batts Dugouts near Canal, under Supervision of R.E. By night 50 men on Piccadilly switch. 50 on Piccadilly Communication Trench. 50 men clearing Bellevue de Beck in Poperinghe Road. 50 men thickening parapet of Line.	

1577 Wt.W10791/1773 500,000 1/15 D. D. & L.   A.D.S.S./Forms/C. 2118.

WAR DIARY
or
INTELLIGENCE SUMMARY.
(Erase heading not required.)

Army Form C. 2118.

KRRC
Sept 1915

Place	Date Sept	Hour	Summary of Events and Information	Remarks and references to Appendices
BRIELEN ROAD	1 Wednesday		III Div Guns bombard their front & Bellewarde farm at 4.0 am. Working parties as usual. B Coy joins D Coy in KAIEE SALIENT during the afternoon.	
"	2nd Thursday		III Div Guns bombarded at 4.0 am. German reply on our guns at 5-30 am. No working parties at night owing to rain.	
"	3rd Friday		III Div Guns bombard 4.0 am. German reply at 5.0 am. No working parties by day or night owing to wet weather.	
"	4th Saturday		III Div Guns bombard. 4.0 am. Working parties as usual by day and night.	
"	5th Sunday		Working parties as usual, with an extra one of 50 men working at new Bd dugouts on Canal bank. — 8 dugouts started. There were 3 bombardments today by our artillery. — III Div at 4.0 am. XIV Div at 10.30 am. French Guns & our heavy artillery at 2-0 pm. The wire III Div at 4.0 am. of our own guns bombarding somewhat unpleasant. Neared Mill to BRIELEN Houses so got away (in German replies).	
"	6th Monday		Working parties as usual during the morning. 16 of new Bd dugouts well underway. No working parties in afternoon owing to relief. Advance party and 1 officer per Company leaves BRIELEN at 2-0 pm. 7th Bn K.R.R.C. relieves 8th Bn K.R.R.C. in BRIELEN ROAD & KAIEE SALIENT. This relief was completed at 9-0 pm. 2nd Royers and 2.5 men left in billets in BRIELEN ROAD. 8th Bn K.R.R.C. relieves 8th Bn Rifle Brigade in 'A' Sector (Haymarket) Relief begun at 7-0 pm. Completed at 10.0 pm.	

WAR DIARY
or
INTELLIGENCE SUMMARY

Army Form C. 2118.

Place	Date	Hour	Summary of Events and Information	Remarks and references to Appendices
A Sector Hooge	5/6th 6th Monday	continued	Battalion goes into trenches with 15 officers and 677 other ranks. B Coy in A & b. C Coy in A 5. A Coy in x 2. D Coy in x 5. H.O. 36, M 6 41.	In front line A Coy
"	7th Tuesday		Major Grun goes on Scotch leave. Trenches very wet. Inspected by Col. Westley. Left Lce B Coy badly wounded in back by bullet while on listening post early this morning. Shelling along our front and into Ypres from 6.0 am. Aeroplanes active. Special working party of 50 K.R.R.C. thickening parapet & wire. New dump and shelter begun for A 5. Drawing began. An enemy aeroplane dropped 3 bombs 40 yds in front of x2 about 6-30 p.m. No damage was done. Enemy Trench Mortar firing into RAILWAY WOOD from opposite Bellewarde was observed by Capt Frewen from A 5 b. This was communicated to the artillery – apparently with the desired result. Our snipers were successful in putting a stop to sniping from Enemy advanced trench during the afternoon.	
"	8th Wednesday		Large working parties on new dugouts. A quantity of bricks collected between front line and x line to floor trenches. Enemy H.E. along our front at 12·30 p.m. Rfn Goodrich, B Coy, died of wounds. Rfn Hill was wounded. Cpl Wood, C Coy, w B Coy was killed. Rfn Foubrick, B Coy, died of wounds. These casualties were all from a direct hit at the Op of Duke St	

Army Form C. 2118.

WAR DIARY
or
INTELLIGENCE SUMMARY.
(Erase heading not required.)

Instructions regarding War Diaries and Intelligence Summaries are contained in F. S. Regs., Part II and the Staff Manual respectively. Title pages will be prepared in manuscript.

Place	Date	Hour	Summary of Events and Information	Remarks and references to Appendices
A Sector Hayonet Wd & M. R. Chatham	Sept 8th Wednesday		continued. Enemy observed improving Advanced T trench,- trards were seen carried along it. Enemy observing for ½ hr with periscope from Advanced T trench, worked by an R/R fix.	
"	9th Thursday		In firing trench each man works 4 hrs by day and 2 hrs by night. 2 small trenches for listening posts have been dug and wired in front of A5. At 7.30 p.m. Loud cheering by the Enemy was heard on our left. A piercing whistle was being played in enemy advanced trench during our evening "Stand to". An enemy working party in front of Bay 9. A5 was scattered at 9.0 p.m. From observation in firing trenches following Aeroplane reports was sent in - German aeroplanes 1 passed over 5-0 a.m. " " " 7-20 a.m. 1 patrolling 9-0 — 9-30 a.m. " " 3-15 — 3-55 p.m. 1 passed over 4-15 returned 4-20 p.m. " " " 4-25 p.m. 1 patrolling 4-45 — 5-0 p.m. British Aeroplane - Nil. Wind East.	
	10th Friday		Dugouts built from 4-30 — 5-0 a.m. and again at 6-30 a.m. Enemy bombarded E. F. Dixon on left. Our post was strengthened for a short time. Two following were up opposite our lines at time this bombardment	

WAR DIARY or INTELLIGENCE SUMMARY

Army Form C. 2118.

(Erase heading not required.)

Place	Date	Hour	Summary of Events and Information	Remarks and references to Appendices
"A" Sector, Haymarket (Northern Sector)	Sept. 11th Saturday		Old dugouts dismantled - new ones built. 600 sand bags were used near parapet & parados of A.S.T. Patrol from A.S.T. reports everything quiet in front of German line. Rfn Jolly, B Coy, was hit in the head by enemy sniper from advanced trench and afterwards died.	
"	12th Sunday		VI Division Toby Mortar (Enemy advanced T'head) at 4.0 p.m. - went in gate too far. Two rounds were duds. One of our Toby's was bombed by 12th Shropshire L.I. In this performance. Probably in reply to Toby Mortar practice, enemy shelled our front line trenches with a heavy howitzer from 4.30 p.m. to 5.15 p.m. One Rfn in B Coy was slightly wounded - he was deaf and did not hear the shell coming. During the night there was no firing from enemy front trench and all enemy verey lights were fired from what appeared to be enemy support line. Officers patrol reconnoitred line of willows running up to German trenches, on return to report.	
"	13th Monday		A number of dugouts were completed, and revetting frames fired up. One of the enemy whilst moving a sheet to signal a "washout" was seen to be hit.	
"	14th Tuesday		Infantry reliefs completed by 9.0 p.m. A Coy to A.S.T., D Coy to A.S.E., C Coy to T.T., B Coy to T.S. New traverse begun Bay 14 A.S.T. Officer's patrols from one of the front bays passed enemy night. & Officers report sent in to the Division.	

WAR DIARY or INTELLIGENCE SUMMARY

Army Form C. 2118.

(Erase heading not required.)

Place	Date	Hour	Summary of Events and Information	Remarks and references to Appendices
"A" Sector Hayreneth + White Chateau	Sept 15th Wednesday		New firing steps, 2 new latrines, dugouts and revetting, breaking forty in front of "No Man's Wood" reported to R.A. and heavily shelled. A battery round heard whenever shelling began – though to be operating an order to take cover. Enemy resumed work whenever shelling ceased. Three different weapons of Oskar fawn reported: (1.) German Khaki (2.) Blue & red fa cap; (3.) Blue & white fa cap; 10 shots fired from Major Gunn's .416 Express Rifle via a periscope at loopholes in enemy advanced trench – damage done and no reply from firing bays.	
"	16th Thursday		Listening posts moved in and trip wires with cans placed in front. Our heavy artillery fired two rounds into Petite maison – firing from 12.30am to dusk. Enemy replied chiefly on Railway Wood and on our left. Enemy artillery reply observed from A.S. Support trench and written report sent into 13th A.D. This report was made by Lt C Potterwell of the Snipers, who carried out the observation of fire,— The report was commended as of considerable value by G.O.C. 14th Division. A good observation post found in roof of red roofed cottage further East of Chetwood Cottages – to be described as Rifleman's post.	

WAR DIARY
or
INTELLIGENCE SUMMARY

Army Form C. 2118.

Place	Date	Hour	Summary of Events and Information	Remarks and references to Appendices
A Sector Haymarket Whitsheets	Sept 17th Friday		Delay in work from want of material, especially corrugated iron. Parapets in front of CRUMP FARM repaired in the evening. At 7-45 a.m. two trays of parapets in A.5.6. were blown in by 4 "H.E." 5 in. – 20 Casualties – at 10-30 a.m. same place was shrapnelled. This was probably owing to the fire of our Trench Mortar earlier in the morning. It fired at MOUND with some effect. A new and well hidden loophole placed in A.5.6. commanded end of German advanced Trench & enfilade communication trench in rear.	
"	18th Saturday		Renewing Shrüts [?] loopholes in front line – where nothing is being done down by a Rfn. Skillet in the art. Handing over to officers of 2nd D.L.I. who came round during the morning. Several cases have occurred lately of men being hit on the road just outside H.Q. a screen has been erected by ruph[?] to see where the bullets fall. Too bullet-proof towels were placed by R.E. at the place where screen was hit by 6 x 6 bullets. In one of these cases a bullet [?] Pn. + 3 a track floor from fixed rifle opposite Ocher Houses. Bullet probably came from fixed rifle opposite Ocher Houses.	

WAR DIARY or INTELLIGENCE SUMMARY

Army Form C. 2118.

Place	Date	Hour	Summary of Events and Information	Remarks and references to Appendices
Aector Maynard's Watch Makers	Sept 19th Sunday		Heavy bombardment by enemy from 4.5.0 am. Enemy retaliated mostly in RAILWAY WOOD. This was observed when he halted day and until evening report sent in. BRIELEN ROAD party used as a carrying party each night bring bags at 7.0 pm. On front line, L of Rail Way Cully.	
"	20 Monday		Put in bach. Rfn Pichard was during of bomb when enemy dropped H.E. into our front line. Our snipers fired on enemy snipers who fired on after having lay bombardment of Bellewarde.	in the line
"	21 Tuesday		Lt Armitage, in charge of BRIELEN ROAD party, was wounded during Enemy of reply to our bomb bombardment. Enemy shelled our front line with H.E. at 6-30 am. 2 killed in A Coy and 4 wounded. 3 killed in D Coy. and 3 wounded. Total Casualties for this tour of duty- 9 killed & 43 wounded. 14 3 Reported Sick. They were mostly from the drafts. 41 went to Rest Camp & Field Ambulance. Battalion relieved by 2 Coys of 2nd D.L.I. Relief began at 8.0 pm finished at 9-30 pm	

Army Form C. 2118

WAR DIARY
or
INTELLIGENCE SUMMARY

(Erase heading not required.)

Instructions regarding War Diaries and Intelligence Summaries are contained in F.S. Regs., Part II. and the Staff Manual respectively. Title Pages will be prepared in manuscript.

Place	Date	Hour	Summary of Events and Information	Remarks and references to Appendices
Reddar, Haymoult, Winthchateau	Sept 1st and		B⁴. moved by companies to bivouacs at G.3.C.1.2. N.E. of Poperinghe on the ELVERDINGHE road. Battalion left trenches 7=9 7/9 1915y. Two draft waiting in bivouac camp.	
G.3.C.1.2. Bivouacs	22	Wednesday	Coys at disposal of Coy officers, resting, cleaning up. Working parties 100, 60, 50, & 50 leave by Poperinghe train at 6.0 p.m., working for 14=DW artillery, signal Coy, and 43rd & 2nd Bdes. In all cases to draw ur and in some cases to work whatever to be done. Returned by train at 4.0 am. Capt. Maclure in charge of parties on train.	
"	23rd	Thursday	Coys at disposal of Coy officers - drill etc. Strength of Battalion with addition 1 draft 993.	
"	24th	Friday	Companies inspected by Commanding Officer, a Coy lines in full marching order. Battalion has orders for the next day. Orders situating a were received and preparations made accordingly.	
"	25th	Saturday	Allowing officers joined the Battalion 2/Lieut Hyson Lt R.A. WARRY to A Coy. 2/Lt R.L. HARDY to B Coy. 2nd Lt F.G. Scott to D Coy. Row and proposhoes. bivouac	

Army Form C. 2118

WAR DIARY
or
INTELLIGENCE SUMMARY
(Erase heading not required.)

Instructions regarding War Diaries and Intelligence Summaries are contained in F. S. Regs., Part II. and the Staff Manual respectively. Title Pages will be prepared in manuscript.

Place	Date	Hour	Summary of Events and Information	Remarks and references to Appendices
G.S.6.1.2. Burnes	Sept 26		Commanding Officer inspected Borders. Batt- ready to move at a moment's notice. Following officers joined the batt- today. 2nd Lt R.M.Rogers, 2nd Lt Mackintosh to B Coy. 2nd Lt C.E.Scott to B Coy.	
"	27th Monday		B" Remaining in readiness to move Coy's at disposal of Coy. commanders, particularly for the factory of the attack. Lt Sent of an advance officers kit strictly limited to 35 lbs the use of Coy. Offers.	
	28th Tuesday 29th Wed		Coy's at disposal of Coy. Officers. Regimental court martial. President to be Major Annan, Somewhere Capt Barker, Wt Vorbourne Shand.	
	30th Thurs		Coy's at disposal of Coy. Officers.	
POTIJZE	Oct 1st Friday		Batgalion relieved 17th Infantry Bde. (2nd Leinster Regt) in A. Sector. Coys marched off from Burnes at 3.30pm in following order. B.C. A.D. A 10 mins interval. Cookers accompanied B- as far as YEAMERTINGHE. Relief began from POTIJZE at 7.30 pm Ended at 8 of 10pm. Near General (Pendennie) watched Battalion march round. Dead DEVILS ELBOW. There was considerable shelling of the road and no casualties. Two Coys of 10th D.L.I on X1, 9 X2 attached to Bn. A Coy in A5, B Coy in A3, C Coy in A4. Trench very wet. D Coy carrying for rest of Battalion. Officers patrols sent out and along enemy's front from I 6 C 2.3 to OSKAR found only small parties at work on wire.	

1875 Wt W593/826 1,000,000 4/15 J.B.C. & A. A.D.S.S./Forms/C. 2118.

WAR DIARY or INTELLIGENCE SUMMARY

Army Form C. 2118

8 KRR 10/15

Place	Date Oct	Hour	Summary of Events and Information	Remarks and references to Appendices
POTIJZE	2nd Sat.		A good deal of firing from M.G. at BEGWAARDE FARM enfilades our line. A new large enemy airplane reported.	
	3rd Sunday		Trench mortar firing on RAILWAY WOOD chiefly. It seemed by Major CRUM it was on firing until dusk. Reported at 4:30 p.m. that enemy fired on by our guns. Their second cascadions on wood outside Btn HQs.	
	4th Mond.		Enemy infantry appears to lay about by night by night officer's patrols out every night — one from A3 to a wound opposite enemy trenches of Duffield and works of light trollies. Enemy end of patrol to within 30 of a trolley post in front of A3.	
	5th Tues.		Considerable shelling on POTIJZE WOOD and our lines to left of A5 and to enemy to small enemy attack on OBER LODGE. The fog gives to left were bombarded by very heavy much mortars some of which were used in shelling the trenches. Enemy entered Sap head by OBER 20 D96 at very queue and after making further a wounded Pte of SHERWOOD FORESTERS.	
	6th Wedn. 7th Thur.		Officer's patrol from A3 whilst waiting outside German trench, and being was challenged by some working party emerging from trench, and fired upon. Lt Callanon adjutant gone sick. Temporarily replaced by 2nd Lt Egerton. Relief from occupying A. Sector to Coy over H. Sector from YR RB completely and successfully Battalion relieved by 2nd LEINSTER Regt. and moved now as relieve battalion generally goes into support a the usual. Enemy has been remarkably quiet of late so that even KATES RAIL	
RAILWAY WOOD	8th Friday	at 3.0 pm	HAT HOOD trenches are comparatively healthy. Lt BIRD 2nd Lt looking over the parapet of crater only 30+ off was hit in head by sniper. Through faulty sandbag. He died at once. A good officer and	

WAR DIARY or INTELLIGENCE SUMMARY.

Army Form C. 2118.

(Erase heading not required.)

Place	Date	Hour	Summary of Events and Information	Remarks and references to Appendices
RAILWAY WOOD	8th	(P.M.)	a great loss to the Regt	
	9th	(a.m.)	The position of enemy M.G. BIRD having been located, it was heavily crumped by our Trench Howitzers. Fire observed to be effective. Working party discovered to enemy observation post about 1300x away behind PRINCE OSCAR FARM. Guns were turned on to it to keep fire from the 67 BOWEN. Scattered them with two machine guns. The battalion having just had a great deal of hard work in the A sector has now to resume its labours in the H trenches, which were heavily damaged by the affair of the 25th September; it is fortunate in having Company officers experienced in engineering, and a good lot of new to work. It was had to post up with a good deal of hardships having their kept in the trenches to reform properly intervals of rest, and no time to refresh properly Thanks to battalion having most efficient officer regular NCOs — under Lt Col GREEN, it keeps up its high standard of efficiency.	
	10th		Good progress in trenches turning off night within 30 yds of Crater and in front of H.22 to mend turned in rifle fire and very light. Lt. SIMPSON wounded in the Sully. Enemy working party again located. Artillery fire called for. The is obtained eventually but is built, about 80 yds out. Fire is a great difference between the P.O.O's of our army batteries. Those that proved themselves to be of most use were men who had risen from the ranks.	
	11th	mod	Continued progress. Working party again to call and on M.G. again and Satire looking party. First after gun was put in (10 salvos) hangs fixed; to two twenty yards — first to find it bearing. That afternoon again the German deliberately searched to the gun position, and after firing about 40 rounds, only succeeded the observation post. This is a lesson in the efficiency of the German system of observation as compared with ours. Our batteries in keeping up almost loud above, failed to get answer from 800 yds, and it was an easier shot to range on than the Germans had.	

Army Form C. 2118.

WAR DIARY
or
INTELLIGENCE SUMMARY.
(Erase heading not required.)

Place	Date	Hour	Summary of Events and Information	Remarks and references to Appendices
RAILWAY WOOD	11th (cont)	Mod.	The enemy's trench mortars are very active & try to far have inflicted three hits on two occupied points. Heavy artillery bombardment of communication trenches that lie in rear of our line from 8.0 am to 9.0 am. 9 in. & S.A. Gun S.A. very ham [?] distant bombardment from direction of front. Also clouds of smoke seen.	
	12th	Tues.	Enemy snipers and trench mortars active. Difficulty in locating enemy working parties as not fire on them. Considerable damage to trenches and annoyance from enemy at 7.15 pm. The German started a very heavy bombardment of RAILWAY WOOD, starting with their heavy howitzers. It was at first thought that they intended to attack. After 5 minutes all communication with front line companies was cut. The bombardment continued into a hell till 8.15pm, when it eased. At first enough very explosive but towards the end mostly whizz-bangs, and mostly shear shrapnel. Considering its heaviness the fire little damage was done. The front line was badly knocked, but the communication trenches were fairly well cramped in up to & from A'. We did not suffer at all. 2 of our machine guns were burned. Casualties say eight & killed & to wounded. After the bombardment the night was quiet, and everything was quiet in that everything was stood up again by the next morning.	
	13th	Wed.	Relief 5th OX & BUCKS to come up to RAILWAY WOOD Battalion to go back in reserve in huts by YUAMERTINGHE. That evening enemy's heavier began to give severe bombardment of and behind YPRES. The continues & till 10.0 pm so that relief which should have arrived by 8.0pm begun at 10.0 pm. The Platoon came in at 11.0 pm, having come the right way and lost the Battalion. The remainder instead of coming through the MENIN GATE, came by two routes north round the N. of the town and by & line This battalion suffered very heavy casualties in about 8 2nd Sgt. and consequently consisted chiefly of recruits.	

WAR DIARY or INTELLIGENCE SUMMARY

Army Form C. 2118.

Place	Date	Hour	Summary of Events and Information	Remarks and references to Appendices
HqS near Vlamertinghe K.1.d.8.8	14	Thursday	Battalion kept the u/c fortnight's tour of duty in trenches at Potyze & Railway Wood. Casualties – 1 officer killed, 3 wounded, Other Ranks 9 killed and 36 wounded. Lt. Cullinan returned from hospital, Lt Egerton Captain FREWEN sick in Camp. Carried on duties of adjutant.	
"	15th	Friday	Large working parties, 45 men B Coy, 45 C Coy, under 2/Lt Mackaulay went on field defences covered by train to Asylum 9.0 pm return by train 4.30 am. Coy at disposal of O.C. Corps. Following complimentary order was published last night: — "The Commanding Officer is pleased to announce that the Brigadier has written thanking the battalion for the cheerful and dogged way they worked in the trenches during their tour of duty, especially the way they stuck to it and squared things up after the bombardment."	
"	16th	Sat	Coy at disposal of O.C. Corps. Battn has bivouacked baths at POPERINGHE for the day. Working parties 150 men & 2 offs by night and 100 men by day.	

Army Form C. 2118.

WAR DIARY
or
INTELLIGENCE SUMMARY.
(Erase heading not required.)

Place	Date	Hour	Summary of Events and Information	Remarks and references to Appendices
Hut near VLAMERTINGHE H1. C.8.8.	16th Oct Sat		Night working parties 1 officer 100 men on ECOLE defences, 1 officer and 50 men work at L10a 6.8 N. of Ypres MENIN GATE 10-0 p.m. Night working parties are conveyed to ASYLUM by train and brought back by train at 4-30 am. Day working party, 2 officers and 100 men work on defences of Ypres rendezvous BRIDGE 7 at 9-30 am. Like housewage return about 5-0 pm. Infact Bright v Day working parties are often poor on early to inspect work to be done with R.E officer. These working parties continue to be found by battn. until 22nd October.	
"	17th Sun		Parade service in field. North of Camp at 10-45 am working parties by day and night as usual.	
"	18th Mon		Coy at disposal of O.C. Coys, working parties as usual. Lt. Col. H.R. GREEN goes on 3 days leave to England. Major F.M. CRUM in Command of Battn.	

Army Form C. 2118.

WAR DIARY
or
INTELLIGENCE SUMMARY.
(Erase heading not required.)

Instructions regarding War Diaries and Intelligence Summaries are contained in F.S. Regs., Part II. and the Staff Manual respectively. Title pages will be prepared in manuscript.

Place	Date	Hour	Summary of Events and Information	Remarks and references to Appendices
1st Army VLAMERTINGHE H.1.c.8.8.	19.	Tues	Coys at disposal of O.C. Coys. Working parties by day & night. Formed as usual.	
"	20	Wed	Coys at disposal of O.C. Coys. Working parties as usual.	
"	21	Thurs	Coys at disposal of O.C. Coys. 1 N.C.O. and 5 men from each Coy carrying out still in construction of dug outs tomorrow under direct supervision of R.E. 2nd Lt Hardy in charge of this party. The wire defences, loopholes, drains, revetments etc. at H.Q. 8 2nd Field Coy R.E. inspected by Officers and R.C.O.S.	
"	22	Friday	Last day working party. No night working parties. Coys at disposal of O.C. Coys.	
"	23rd	Sat	Route March. C & D Coys in the morning. A & B in the afternoon. Route - VLAMERTINGHE - WULFSEVLE & home via HAZEBROUK about 6 miles.	

1577 Wt. W10791/1773 500,000 1/15 D.D.&L. A.D.S.S./Forms/C. 2118.

Army Form C. 2118.

WAR DIARY
or
INTELLIGENCE SUMMARY.
(Erase heading not required.)

Place	Date	Hour	Summary of Events and Information	Remarks and references to Appendices
Hut near VLAMERTINGHE H.1.c.8.8.	October 24	Sun	Parade Service 12-0 noon in field north of Camp.	
"	25 Mon		Coys at disposal of O.C. Coys to carry out programme of work as follows - 8-30 am to 12-30 pm — 7-0 am running drill. and 2 pm to 3-0 pm. Instruction in Company & Platoon drill, Extended order drill, Care of arms, practice in rapid loading etc. Battalion armed Company snipers report to Major Crum at 8.30 am — The nave at the disposal of snipers during the afternoon — and at the disposal of Companies as follows — D Coy — 8-30 am C Coy — 9-30 am B Coy — 10-30 am A Coy — 11-30 am Bomber report to Bombing Officer at the bombing trench as follows — A Coy — 8-30 am B Coy — 10-0 a Instruction for 1½ hours, C Coy — 11-30 a During other periods bombers D Coy — 2-0 pm at the disposal of Company Officers.	

WAR DIARY
or
INTELLIGENCE SUMMARY.

Army Form C. 2118.

Place	Date	Hour	Summary of Events and Information	Remarks and references to Appendices
Huts after WLAMERTINGHE appx^m H1C8.8.	October 25th	9 am	Each Coy send 5 N.C.Os at 10 am and 11.0 am to report to Sgt-Major for instruction in Commanding Drill. Signallers report to Signalling Sergeant for instruction during allotted time for work. Machine Gun teams and Reserve Machine Gun teams at the disposal of the Machine Gun Officer. The Specimen at the disposal of Companies for exercise in trench placing and tactics as follows — A Coy - morning. Construction and tactics as follows — A Coy - morning. B Coy - Afternoon. 2nd Lt TYLER in charge of the Coy^d Companies communicate with 2nd Lt TYLER before using it. Men marked for drill and hired stores from 3-0pm to 4-0pm. parade under Sgt-Major Instructors. Owing to wet weather this programme of work will be carried out to-day and to-morrow instead. Common: F.G.C.M. of which Major Crum was president assembled in Farm here at 10-30 a.m.	

WAR DIARY
INTELLIGENCE SUMMARY
Army Form C. 2118.

Place	Date	Hour	Summary of Events and Information	Remarks and references to Appendices
INTERN VLAMERTINGHE HIC.8.8	26 Tues		2nd Lt. J.J. Egerton goes to 2nd Army Grenade School. Orders of signal O.C. Coys to carry out yesterday's programme of work. G.O.C. & Brig.Gen. inspects Coys at work. 2nd Army Commander inspects companies at work at 3.15 p.m.	
"	27th Wed		Major C.H.N. Seymour and 25 picked men go to inspection by H.M. KING GEORGE V. beyond POPERINGHE. Battn. Route march in morning cut short owing to rain. B Coy marches at 7.30. Stood all ranks on parade under Bombing officer at 2.0 p.m. for instruction in bombing.	
"	28th Thurs		Programme of work as issued on 25th inst carried out. Specimen trench being used by C & D Coys. G.O.C. 41st Bgde inspects battalion at work at 10 a.m.	

Army Form C. 2118.

WAR DIARY
or
INTELLIGENCE SUMMARY.
(Erase heading not required.)

Instructions regarding War Diaries and Intelligence Summaries are contained in F. S. Regs., Part II. and the Staff Manual respectively. Title pages will be prepared in manuscript.

Place	Date	Hour	Summary of Events and Information	Remarks and references to Appendices
	Oct			
Between VLAMERTINGHE & HICES	29th Friday		Carried out disposal of O.C. Corps to carry out programme of work	
"	30th Sat		Battalion route march - 8 miles - in the morning. Baton marched on 810 strong with cookers.	
"	31st Sunday		Parade Service 10-30 a.m. Strength of Battn - all ranks = 988. A canteen and coffee bar has been started under direction of Major Crum in the Recreation Farm.	

1577 Wt.W10791/1773 500,000 1/15 D. D. & L. A.D.S.S./Forms/C. 2118.

8th K.R.R.C.
Vol. 2

12/
776

14th Kwazan

Nov. 15

WAR DIARY or INTELLIGENCE SUMMARY

Army Form C. 2118

Place	Date	Hour	Summary of Events and Information	Remarks and references to Appendices
A. Huts near VLAMERTINGHE H.I.D.8.8. Sheet 28.	November 1 Monday		14th Divisional Baths at POPERINGHE allotted to the battalion. Scouts Lecture at POPERINGHE by Major J.M. Crumm 2nd Field Coy. and 5-R.C.O.8 and men of 7-R.B. Rifle Brigade are attached for instruction in Sniping.	
"	2nd Tuesday		CNs at disposal of O.C. Coys to carry out Programme of Work	
"	3rd Wednesday		Coys at disposal of O.C. Coys. May orders received. Weather very wet. Specimen trench full of water. The Battalion relieves East Yorkshire Regt. in dugouts on Canal bank I.17.a sheet 28. near Prison of YPRES. B. Coy. and two M.Gs. Coy. to KAAIE SALIENT. Two M.Gs. Coy. b- + two (A.S.) Battalion attached to 16th Infantry Brigade. Relief completed by 9.0 p.m. Working parties of total 120 formed. Battns. marches out to see Church Major Crum remaining at Huts near VLAMERTINGHE in charge of details of 8th K.R.R.C. and 8th R.B. men instructing. Lt. Rogers left to unstruck in Sniping.	

Army Form C. 2118

WAR DIARY
or
INTELLIGENCE SUMMARY
(Erase heading not required.)

Place	Date	Hour	Summary of Events and Information	Remarks and references to Appendices
Canal Bank I 7a sheet 28	Nov 4	Thursday	Weather clears after yesterday's heavy rain; fine warm day. Rec'd working parties for RAILWAY WOOD and POTIJZE. Company on wiring.	POTIJZE
"	5	Friday	Working parties according to table annexed. The dug outs are very badly constructed, evidently made for summer use and not for the winter. The dug outs along the canal practically all fallen in. Heavy shelling during the evening in BRIELEN ROAD and neighbourhood.	BRIELEN ROAD
"	6	Saturday	KAAIE SALIENT shelled during the night. One M. Gunner hit by shrapnell. Working party returning from POTIJZE at 8.0pm shelled – 5 men in D Coy wounded. D Coy goes up to F.48+ and is attached to 6 Queens Westminsters. ½ A Coy under Lt WARRY goes to POTIJZE defences. B Coy is relieved by 7th K.R.R. in KAAIE SALIENT and returns to D Coys dug out.	

1875 Wt. W593/826 1,000,000 4/15 J.B.C. & A. A.D.S.S./Forms/C. 2118.

Army Form C. 2118

WAR DIARY
or
INTELLIGENCE SUMMARY
(Erase heading not required.)

Place	Date	Hour	Summary of Events and Information	Remarks and references to Appendices
Canal bank I7a Sh28	November 7	Sunday	The Battalion is now attached to 18th Infantry Brigade. Notice of D Coy goes down with trench fever. The heat wet. Feb last month — also. Party of munition workers and Labour MP come round.	
"	8th	Monday	Working parties in wet weather. Impossible to dig owing to floods.	
"	9th	Tuesday	Orderman killed by a shell. A Coy. D Coy relieved by 11th Essex Regt. returns to A Coy's dug out in Canal bank. Remainder of A Coy goes up to POTIJZE. Very heavy shelling normal fires in BRIELEN ROAD. Some of the shells falling close to Hd. dug outs. Strange piece of shell former and sent through HD to II Army.	
"	10th	Wednesday	Orderman killed in A Coy by bullet. Curious message conveying an expected attack on YPER, and tube delivered, received at 11-30 pm	

WAR DIARY
or
INTELLIGENCE SUMMARY.

Army Form C. 2118.

Place	Date	Hour	Summary of Events and Information	Remarks and references to Appendices

Camel Farm
170 Northmoor
28
| 11th Thursday | | Sergeant Pollit, C Coy, fatally wounded in the head by shell when on working party in t.2, died at No 10 Field Ambulance at VLAMERTINGHE; and 2nd A. Corporal in C Coy wounded, and a man in C. Coy killed on same working party in t.2. Lieutenant J.D. ROBSON wounded in the legs by bullet when with working party at night. The Battalion is relieved by 10th Division Light Infantry, but we have to leave working parties for tonight - 130 men returned. Relief also begins about 9-0 pm - Battalion marches back to "A" hut A.I.D.S.S. Sheet 28. | |

A Hut
A.I.D.S.S
Shed 28
near VLAM-
ERTINGHE
| 12th Friday | | Major Crum goes on leave to England, but is detained at Boulogne by Armies. Corps at disposal of O.C. Corps. Weather very wet. One officer from each Coy sent to reconnoitre roads towards DICKEBUSCH with a view to reinforcing if necessary. Sgt Pollit buried during the afternoon in Cemetery just behind the Field Ambulance at Vlamertinghe. | |

WAR DIARY
or
INTELLIGENCE SUMMARY.
(Erase heading not required.)

Army Form C. 2118.

Place	Date	Hour	Summary of Events and Information	Remarks and references to Appendices
A Hut C H.1.B.8 Sheet 28. near VLAM-ERTINGHE	November 13.		Saturday. Coys at the disposal of O.C. Companies clearing drains etc. 7th Bn at "B" Hut. G.O.D. 8th Rifle Brigade at 5th Jan-tea-BESEN. QMS Draper leaves for England, having been given a commission. adj M. in 18 North'berland Fus. Two divisional chaplains on leave.	
"	14th		Sunday. Church Parade at 12 noon.	
"	15.		Monday. Battalion Route March, Bivy BRANDHOEK to POPERINGHE and back. Batt⁵ parades 738 strong for route march.	
"	16th		Tuesday. O.C. Coys, Platoon Section Commanders rendezvous at R.E. dump for the purpose of laying out entrenchments. Coys parade to Inspect H.O. special wire treasures at the same place later - B. & C. Coys at - 1-45 p.m. A & D " - 2-45 p.m. This working is interfered by the Engineers. Carried out in very inclement weather. One platoon of A and one platoon of D Coy carry out drill and rifle exercise wearing both helmets before Major-General Cooper.	

WAR DIARY or INTELLIGENCE SUMMARY

Army Form C. 2118

Place	Date	Hour	Summary of Events and Information	Remarks and references to Appendices
Huts Sheet 8 Sheet 28 near VLAMER-TINGHE	Nov 17th	Wednesday	Companies at the disposal of O.C. Companies. Commanding Officer visits Head Quarters of 2nd Yorks Lancs during the morning at C21 c2.4 Sheet 28 near La Belle Alliance Farm. The Company Officers also, and adjutant go up at night to take over from Yorks Lancs. Very wet weather.	
"	18th	Thursday	Roman Catholics parade Service at 9 am 7th K.R.R. H.Q. The Battalion relieves 2nd Yorks Lancs, 16th Inf Bde in trenches from junction B15—B16 to junction D18—D19 between Forward Cottages and Turco Farm. Battn. H.Q. at C21 c2.4 Sheet 29 near LA BELLE ALLIANCE farm. C Company in B16. B Company in WILLOW WALK, S18A, & MORTELDJE SALIENT. D Company 2 Platoons at Batt H.Q. in S15-6. One Platoon at FRASCATI, one Platoon at La BRIQUE. A Company 6 in outer Canal Bank close to bridge 4. Fine moonlight night. Trenches in very bad condition. Relieved on left of 8th K.R.R. 5th West Yorks Territorials agst Division. Relieved on right 11th Suffolks 16th I.B. 6th Dwgies 7th R.B. on Canal Bank near bridge 3. 8th R.B. in Huts H1 D8 8. 7th K.R.R. also not more.	

Army Form C. 2118

WAR DIARY
or
INTELLIGENCE SUMMARY
(Erase heading not required.)

Place	Date	Hour	Summary of Events and Information	Remarks and references to Appendices
C21d24 Sheet 28	November 19th		Friday. At 5 o'clock in the evening Captain T.P. BLANE was very seriously wounded by a trench bomb on the left of 13.16 Trench. This officer was a very serious loss to the battalion.	

Army Form C. 2118

WAR DIARY
or
INTELLIGENCE SUMMARY
(Erase heading not required.)

Instructions regarding War Diaries and Intelligence Summaries are contained in F. S. Regs., Part II. and the Staff Manual respectively. Title Pages will be prepared in manuscript.

Place	Date	Hour	Summary of Events and Information	Remarks and references to Appendices
C2 IC 2.4 Sheet 28	November 20th		Saturday. Much shelling in the neighbourhood of Batt's H.Q. during the morning. Clear, frosty, moonlight nights. Seven men, 5 in B Coy, 2 in C Coy driven from their posts. Three were Battn's trench feet cases. D Coy relieves B. A Coy relieves C Coy. Lieut R.L. BOWEN in command of C Company. 2nd Lieut RA. RODWAY Machine Gun Officer.	
	21st		Sunday. Work concentrated on drawing trenches and erecting cover for trench. Fire is no communication with the front line trenches by day.	
	22nd		Monday. Sgt Williams badly wounded by bullet when returning from bombing post in the morning. 8th R.K.R. is relieved by 7-19th R.B. 8th K.R.R. returns to Huts J.4.1 & 8.8 near Hamertinghe.	
Hut H.1 N 8.8 Nee/26	23rd	12.35 am	Tuesday. Companies at the disposal of O.C. Companies. Captain T.P. BLANE died of wounds this morning at No 10 Casualty clearing station near POPERINGHE.	
	24th		Wednesday. Batt'n has divisional latrines POPERINGHE.	
	25th		Thursday. Very hot weather, Considering pool of O.C. Coys.	

WAR DIARY
or
INTELLIGENCE SUMMARY

(Erase heading not required.)

Army Form C. 2118

Place	Date	Hour	Summary of Events and Information	Remarks and references to Appendices
Huts H.10.B.8.8 Sht 28	November 26th Sunday		Battn. relieves 7th R.B. at C.21.c.2.4, B Coy to Willow Walk, C Coy to B.16. B Coy to M.H.Q. Brascah & La Brique. A Coy two platoons Natural Canal bank, 2 platoons in 9. Coy march off at 6.30 p.m. 7th West Yorks, 49th Div. relieves the relief completed at 8.30 p.m. 7th K.R.R. on the right. 8th R.B. on Canal bank, 7th R.B. left. 7th K.R.R. on the right. ad Hut H.1.d.8.8	
C.21.c.2.4 Sht 28.	27	Saturday	Took considerably in fact ow owing to kindness of the 7th Ground wire parks of 50 men each night aiming S.16.T. under R.E. supervision.	
	28	Sunday	On leaves shelled German sap head in front of B.16 and machine guns fired all night. A Coy relieving C., D Coy holding B.	
	29th	Monday	At 9.15 a.m. a German working party was observed by our snipers ad hair 82 Figure 15 and knocked out by our artillery, which put several hits, a stretcher was been carried away from the place.	

8th K.R.R.C.
Vol: 3
A

WAR DIARY
or
INTELLIGENCE SUMMARY

(Erase heading not required.)

Army Form C. 2118

Place	Date	Hour	Summary of Events and Information	Remarks and references to Appendices
P21C 2.6 Canal Bank BRIDGE 3 C.2.5.d Sheet 28	November 30th Tuesday		8th K.R.R. relieved by 7th R.B, and goes to Canal Bank. KAT FARM and Burgomaster FARM, BnH.Q. at BRIDGE 3.	
	Dec 1 Wednesday		At night working parties up 320 men.	
	2 Thursday		Working parties around C Coy at KAT FARM, ½ B Coy at BURGOMASTER FARM, ½ B Coy; A Coy & D Coy along Canal bank near BRIDGE 2. Heavy shelling around Bn. H.Q. at 7-0 p.m. some gas shells.	
	3 Friday		Working parties 300 men. 100 x 2 Offs to work with Liverpool Regt	
	4 Saturday		8th K.R.R. relieve 7th R.B. in trenches junction P.15-P.16 to Junction D 18 D 19. Weather very hot.	

Army Form C. 2118

WAR DIARY
or
INTELLIGENCE SUMMARY
(Erase heading not required.)

Place	Date	Hour	Summary of Events and Information	Remarks and references to Appendices
La Belle ALLIANCE C.21.C.2.16 S.15.B finish	Dec 4-8th		During this period of duty 4–5 Dec – 8th Dec the weather was very bad and there was no moon. It was highly difficult to get through much mud in the trenches beyond draining. Captain Brewer? Scheme for Willow Walk was continued, and wire was put up along the willows between the swamp and BOUNDARY ROAD. There was considerable shelling, especially round B⁺ Headquarters, though we actually fell in Headquarters. On the morning of the 5th S.16.C was heavily shelled. Its machine gun dugout of the 7th Rifle Brigade and three machine gunners of 7th Rifle Brigade was blown in and three machine gunners of 7th Rifle Brigade were killed. On the morning of the 7th our 8th Line bombarded from 5 a.m. to 5:30 a.m., which caused retaliation on the S line, and BOUNDARY ROAD. Casualties one man killed in S.16.C. At 11:0 a.m. the German heavy guns began a systematic bombardment of our support trenches and of Boundary Road, – this lasted one hour. Our heavies retaliated on Can̅ adian Farm.	

WAR DIARY
or
INTELLIGENCE SUMMARY
(Erase heading not required.)

Army Form C. 2118

Place	Date	Hour	Summary of Events and Information	Remarks and references to Appendices
LaBelle ALLIANCE S15-b.10.4. C21.c.2.4. Sheet 28	Dec 4-8-		Just before we had relieved the 7th R.B. on the night of 6th Dec. a patrol of 7th R.B. in Mortelolje Salient captured a German prisoner of the 235th Res 9th Regt. aged 63. He was one of a burying patrol of 10 men, and was slightly wounded by one of our bombs. On the right of us during this tour was the 7th Bn. K.R.R. and on the left the 5th West Yorks 49th Division. The 7th Bn. Rifle Brigade relieved us on night of 8th Dec. The battalion marched back to "A" huts VLAMERTINGHE. Casualties during this tour of duty were 3 killed and 9 wounded, — these occurred mostly in x.9.	

WAR DIARY
or
INTELLIGENCE SUMMARY

(Erase heading not required.)

Army Form C. 2118

Place	Date	Hour	Summary of Events and Information	Remarks and references to Appendices
"A" Hutt WINNER- TINGHE H/38.8. sheet 28	Dec 9th Thursday		Companies at the disposal of O.C. Companies. Health very bad. general work everywhere.	
"	10th Friday		Companies at disposal of O.C. Companies. Weather still wet.	
"	11th Saturday		Colonel Green goes on leave, Major J.M. Cure is in command of the battalion.	
"	12th Sunday		Lt. Sharrard commanding A Coy - Major Seymour away on leave. Lt. Hardy commanding B Coy - Captain Trevelen acting as 2nd i.c. command. The battalion relieved 7th Rifle Brigade in trenches, C2.1, C2.2.4, Coy's A Coy to T316, C Coy to T319, B/b Canal bank, D Coy to WILLOW WALK. Battalion seeing trenches 650 short. The relief was carried out early.	
La Belle ALLIANCE S.15.6. C2.1.C2.4 sheet 28	13th Monday		During the morning there was considerable heavy artillery activity on both sides. BOUNDARY ROAD and S line were heavily shelled and also CORN HILL communication trench.	

Army Form C. 2118

WAR DIARY
or
INTELLIGENCE SUMMARY
(Erase heading not required.)

Instructions regarding War Diaries and Intelligence Summaries are contained in F.S. Regs., Part II. and the Staff Manual respectively. Title Pages will be prepared in manuscript.

Place	Date	Hour	Summary of Events and Information	Remarks and references to Appendices
La Belle ALLIANCE 21st C21C2 & Sheet 28.	Dec 13th Monday		He wires to all companies were taken. At 1-0 p.m. a big enemy bombardment began in the direction of ST JEAN and POTITZE. At 3-45 p.m. Shelling began to concentrate round Batt: Head Quarters - heavy black shrapnel and 5-9 enemy howitzer. At 4-0 p.m. We had six officers in the head Quarters Meer du Port - Major Cuiver, Captain FREWEN, Capt MILLER R.A.M.C., Lieut PURDON machine gun officer of 7th Rifle Brigade, Lt Evans R.A. forward observing officer and J. Cullinan, - when the dug out was crumped in by a 5-9 howitzer shell. Lieut Purdon was buried and severely injured. Captain Miller was also buried, but as soon as he was extricated, rendered invaluable assistance in getting Lieut Purdon out to another dug out, and looking after him while the shelling continued and the head quark trenches had been evacuated. At 4-30 p.m. the bombardment	

Army Form C. 2118

WAR DIARY
or
INTELLIGENCE SUMMARY
(Erase heading not required.)

Place	Date	Hour	Summary of Events and Information	Remarks and references to Appendices
La Belle ALLIANCE C.21.c.2.4 Sheet 28	Dec 13th Monday		of Battalion Head Quarters ceased. 100 men of 11th King's Liverpool Regiment (Pioneer Battalion) and 50 men Essex Regt came up to Bn: H.Q. at 8.30 p.m., and made a new Head Quarters adjacent near the old aid post and dug an emergency head. Returned La Belle ALLIANCE farm and moving down to CONEY. They worked splendidly until 11-o'clock. and then men finished off the work at the dug out.	
"	14th Tuesday		Head Quarters was moved down to dressing station and new dug out at 7-o'clock a.m. At 11-0 a.m the trenches normal HQ were closed and the emergency bench occupied. five signallers remaining in signalling dug out. They were relieved in signalling dug out every hour. Wires to front line Companies were broken At 1-0 p.m.	

WAR DIARY
or
INTELLIGENCE SUMMARY

Army Form C. 2118

Place	Date	Hour	Summary of Events and Information	Remarks and references to Appendices
C.2.C.2.4 Sheet 28	Dec 14th Tuesday		Enemy aeroplane reports boarder advent of ST JEAN, Y POTIJZE, ending up with an old Battalion H.Q., which was shelled at 2-0 pm and again at 4-20 pm. Considerable damage was done, but there were no casualties. Wiring continued with an emergency trench.	
"	15th Wednesday		Very quiet night. Patrols reported that Germans had no patrols out and appeared to be doing no work. At 10.0 am our Lewises began shelling in neighbourhood of CANADIAN FARM, MOUSE TRAP FARM, and point 82. Where working parts in communication trench was scattered. Enemy retaliated first on TURCO FARM and S16a and later on S16C and BOUNDARY ROAD. A few whizzbangs on B16, no damage, except officer's kitchen blown in. Bn. H.Q. was shelled as usual during the afternoon.	

WAR DIARY
or
INTELLIGENCE SUMMARY

(Erase heading not required.)

Army Form C. 2118

Place	Date	Hour	Summary of Events and Information	Remarks and references to Appendices
C21c24 Sheet 28	Dec 16th Thursday		During this tour of duty the 7th K.R.R. have been on our right, and the 7th West Yorks 49th Division on our left. Considerable artillery activity on both sides, were broken 6 Willow Walk Bn. Headquarters Shelled during the afternoon. The battalion was relieved tonight by 12th Bn. K.S.L.I. 17th Divn — the relief was completed at 8-15 p.m — unusually early. On relief the battalion marched back to Camp B. Woods A.30. Sheet 28. The battalion is now in 5th Corps Reserve.	
hood A.30 Sheet 28	17th Friday		Companies at the disposal of O.C. Companies. All warm clothing handed in. Weather very wet, — mud extraordinary.	
"	18th Saturday		Was attack expected on 6th Corps front. Emergency orders sent from 4th I.R. Battalion to be in readiness to occupy defences at B 23 central Sheet 28.	

Army Form C. 2118

WAR DIARY
or
INTELLIGENCE SUMMARY
(Erase heading not required.)

Place	Date	Hour	Summary of Events and Information	Remarks and references to Appendices
Trench A.3.0. Sheet 28	Dec 18th Saturday		The following Special Order was published last night — "The O.C. Battn wishes to put on record the good work done by all ranks during the last tour of duty in the trenches. It was a most trying time in every way, and the way the Battn stuck it and came through with flying colours shows them to be second to none in the whole regiment. The valuable work of the Signallers calls for special mention."	
"	19th Sunday		Heavy shelling was heard about 5-30 am and soon after a message arrived from 41st I.B. that the Battalion was to hold itself in readiness to move at short notice.	

WAR DIARY
or
INTELLIGENCE SUMMARY
(Erase heading not required.)

Army Form C. 2118

Place	Date	Hour	Summary of Events and Information	Remarks and references to Appendices
Woods A.20 Sheet 28	Dec 19	Sunday	The Germans had opened their Gas cylinders on 6th Div and 49th Div front. No serious infantry attack was made though a few German infantry advanced opposite the MORTELDJE SALIENT and were driven back. The battalion was ready to move within half an hour of the alarm, the transport, officers' ponies etc had arrived from the transport camp and the men had had some water. Eventually no move was made and the order to 'Stand down' came through.	

Army Form C. 2118

WAR DIARY
or
INTELLIGENCE SUMMARY
(Erase heading not required.)

Place	Date	Hour	Summary of Events and Information	Remarks and references to Appendices
Wood A.20.d. Sheet 28	Dec 19th	Sunday	Brig-General Tendwine The following Special Order from 41st Inf Bde is published with orders tonight — — 41st Infantry BRigade Special Order 19th December 1915 — "I have received the following message from the Major General Commanding the 14th Division: — The G.O.C. wishes to thank Brig-General TEUDWINE, the Officers and men of the 41st Brigade for the work done during the past month. They took over the trenches in a deplorable condition;— by then constant and cheery work in bad weather, and often under heavy shell fire, we have been able to hand over the trenches in a much better state than we took them over." It is a great pleasure to me, on the last day of my command	

Place	Date	Hour	Summary of Events and Information	Remarks and references to Appendices
Army A.3.0 Sheet 28	Dec 19th Sunday		— of the G.1st Infantry Brigade, to be able to make known this expression of the Major General's satisfaction. I wish to add my own most sincere thanks to the Commanding Officers, Warrant Officers, Non-Commissioned Officers, and men of the Brigade, including the Signal Section and Headquarters, for the loyal and ready support they have always given me in circumstances of real hardship, difficulty, and danger. They have every reason to look back with pride on the strenuous days of the last few months, and to feel that by their cheeriness, fortitude, and self-sacrifice	

Army Form C. 2118

WAR DIARY
or
INTELLIGENCE SUMMARY

(Erase heading not required.)

Instructions regarding War Diaries and Intelligence Summaries are contained in F.S. Regs., Part II. and the Staff Manual respectively. Title Pages will be prepared in manuscript.

Place	Date	Hour	Summary of Events and Information	Remarks and references to Appendices
Woods A.30 Sheet 28	Dec 10th Sunday		they have established a right to share in the high reputation of the famous Regiments to which they belong — a reputation won by fine deeds in many great campaigns. I am glad to have had the privilege of commanding this Brigade, and hope it may soon meet with the opportunity, to which I know all ranks look forward, of leaving its mark upon the enemy. sd. H.S. Jeudwine. Brig-General, Commanding 41st Infantry Brigade.	

1875 Wt. W593/826 1,000,000 4/15 J.B.C. & A. A.D.S.S./Forms/C. 2118.

WAR DIARY
or
INTELLIGENCE SUMMARY
(Erase heading not required.)

Army Form C. 2118

Place	Date	Hour	Summary of Events and Information	Remarks and references to Appendices
Woolf A.30. Sheet 28.	Dec 20 Monday		POPERINGHE shelled in the early morning. Colonel Green returning from leave. Two Companies go to 49th Div trenches in the afternoon. Heavy rain in the evening. POPERINGHE again shelled at night.	
"	21 Tuesday		Very wet morning. New Brigadier Lord BINNING visits Camp in morning.	
"	22 Wednesday		Frequent heavy showers. No mails arrived.	
"	23 Thursday		Wet evening. No mails.	
"	24 Friday		Again frequent showers and no mails.	
"	25 Saturday		Christmas Day. Church of England parade service at 12-15pm in church. Army hut in the WOODS. Rev Neville Talbot took the service. Warning order received in the morning from the 41st I.B. transport to be prepared to move by road to NORDAUSQUES in the neighbourhood of LOOMER on 26.	

WAR DIARY
or
INTELLIGENCE SUMMARY.

Army Form C. 2118.

Place	Date	Hour	Summary of Events and Information	Remarks and references to Appendices
WOODS A.30.d.30.e.30	Dec 25th Saturday		The Battalion to go to the same place by rail from POPERINGHE on 27th. All preparations for this move had already been made, - worn clothing etc had been returned to Ordnance - Officers kits reduced to 35 lbs - quantities of orderly room stuff destroyed, - maps handed over to 11th Division & destroyed; the Battalion had been brought up to 2 officers and 16 O.R. short of War Establishment, - whilst heavy draft horses had been exchanged for mules, - in fact everything that had been done with a view to leaving Flanders and going to another theatre of war in a warm climate. At 5-o'clock in the evening Operation Orders came from 4. I.B. giving time table of trains, arrangements for	

Army Form C. 2118.

WAR DIARY
or
INTELLIGENCE SUMMARY.
(Erase heading not required.)

Instructions regarding War Diaries and Intelligence Summaries are contained in F. S. Regs., Part II. and the Staff Manual respectively. Title pages will be prepared in manuscript.

Place	Date	Hour	Summary of Events and Information	Remarks and references to Appendices
Nostra A 30 Neat 28	Dec 25th Saturday		Advance parties — orders for the move on Dec 27th in detail. At six o'clock there came a wire from 41st I.B. saying that all orders for the move were in abeyance and that we were to stand fast, — at 8-30 p.m. another wire came from 41st I.B. saying that operation orders were cancelled and the move of the Brigade definitely off. — So much for Christmas Day 1915.	

WAR DIARY
or
INTELLIGENCE SUMMARY.
(Erase heading not required.)

Army Form C. 2118.

Place	Date	Hour	Summary of Events and Information	Remarks and references to Appendices
Woods A 26 Sheet 28	Dec 26 Sunday		Jaskated of leaving this country for a warmer climate, we are to remain in the YPRES SALIENT and relieve the 49th Territorial Division in the BOESINGHE Sector just the French. It has rained mostly the last few days	
"	27 Monday		Colonel Green spends the day at YPRES hunting out from 49 I.B. to move to ELVERDINGHE, and Canal Bank. Machine Guns relieve West Yorks Machine Guns, no further arrangements made for this relief. Major Cruse goes to ELVERDINGE CHATEAUX to see accommodation for 600 men which accommodation scarcely existed.	

WAR DIARY
or
INTELLIGENCE SUMMARY.
(Erase heading not required.)

Army Form C. 2118.

Place	Date	Hour	Summary of Events and Information	Remarks and references to Appendices
Wood Dp A35 Sheet 28	28 December		Colonel Green and Company officers go to ELVERDINGHE to take over accommodation. — B Coy to Canal bank between Bridge 4 and Bridge 6. 3rd Monmouth pioneer Batt. & 5 West Yorks R.E. all at ELVERDINGHE. A For d Berks and R.E. all at ELVERDINGHE. Chateau and not leaving there until 29th with considerable difficulties, accommodation is found for 5-30 men. About the Batt. moves up — A, B & C Coy to ELVERDINGHE 4-30 pm the Batt moves up — A, B & C Coy to ELVERDINGHE CHATEAU. D Coy to canal bank	
ELVER-DINGHE CHATEAU B.14 Sheet 28	29 Wednesday	1-0 p.m.	Take over from 3rd Monmouths during the morning, about there was considerable shelling in the vicinity, of the CHATEAU, — some gas shells — about 1-30 P.M. a very heavy shell — probably from	

Army Form C. 2118.

Instructions regarding War Diaries and Intelligence Summaries are contained in F. S. Regs., Part II. and the Staff Manual respectively. Title pages will be prepared in manuscript.

WAR DIARY
or
INTELLIGENCE SUMMARY.

(Erase heading not required.)

Place	Date	Hour	Summary of Events and Information	Remarks and references to Appendices
ELVER- DINGHE CHATEAU B14 Sheet 28.	Dec 29th Wednesday		A 12 inch Naval Gun killed 38 of 3rd Monmouth's in the wood about 200 yds South of Chateau and wounded 12. They were formed up near their huts, collecting their kitt ready to move off. In 12 minutes another shell fell near the first. After the same interval a third smashed the church. Army hut, about 150 yds from Chateau, and then a fourth fell about 10 yds from the third. The Pioneers & Stretcher bearers front one OS crew with the Medical officer and rendered all assistance possible. The burial was arranged and carried out by this Battn. 4th I.B. Chaplain taking the service	

WAR DIARY or INTELLIGENCE SUMMARY

Army Form C. 2118

Place	Date	Hour	Summary of Events and Information	Remarks and references to Appendices
ELVERDINGHE CHATEAU	Dec 30	Thursday	Quiet day. No accommodation now that Monmouth Regt. has left. 9th R.B. arrive in evening. Operation orders for relieving 7th R.B. received. First batch of warm clothing arrives.	
"	31	Friday	Battn. relieved 7th R.B. in trenches. Night Quiet.	
Lancashire Farm C.14.c.O.3 Sheet 28.	Jan 1916 1	Saturday	Just after 12 midnight 31st-1st our heavy guns began a short bombardment in direction of C⊥.E.01 where the Canadians are working party of enemy opposite E24 dispersed at 2.0am and again at 2.30am after which work was discontinued. B Coy are in E23 & E24 & night support trench. C Coy are in E25 & E26 and left support. A & D Coys in Canal Bank	

8th K.R.R.C.
Vol: 4
JANUARY 1916

1A

41.Pyde

Army Form C. 2118

WAR DIARY
or
INTELLIGENCE SUMMARY
(Erase heading not required.)

Place	Date	Hour	Summary of Events and Information	Remarks and references to Appendices
LANCASHIRE FARM. C14c 0.3	Jan 2 Sunday		Quiet night except for enemy machine gun fire. Lieut McKinlay wounded in hand - when going up to front of E 25. Canal bank heavily shelled, causing 4 casualties in "B" Coy & casualties in "A" Coy. Men on working parties with 7th King's Liverpool Regt. Weather very bad. Wind Northerly.	
"	3 Monday		On right are 43rd Brigade, on our left 7th K.R.R. One German observer with glasses in front of E 24 was hit twice with telescopic rifle, another who kept popping up to see where shells were bursting was hit by one. Ens- Many Germans were seen in front. Both Blue and khaki green - with red bands or caps.	
"	4 Tuesday		8th R.B. relieving 8th K.R.R. relief slow owing to darkness of night and condition of the ground. Relief complete 12·30am.	

WAR DIARY
or
INTELLIGENCE SUMMARY
(Erase heading not required.)

Army Form C. 2118

Place	Date	Hour	Summary of Events and Information	Remarks and references to Appendices
Rest Camp Nr Abeele	5	Wednesday	Battalion when relieved marched to Rest Camp. Kits & gum-boots were carried in 9 G. waggons. The Batt. did not get into camp until 6.30 a.m.	
"	6	Thursday	Companies at the disposal of O.C. Companies. All companies went to the 49th Divisional Baths	
"	7	Friday	Companies at the disposal of O.C. Companies. B Company moved up to the Canal Bank & went into Brigade Reserve	
"	8	Saturday	The Batt. relieves the 9th R.B. in the trenches. "A" Coy front line left, the 7 K.R.R.C. were on our left and the 7 S.L.I on our right. D Company relieves E. 3, A Coy Reformany by bus. D Company relieves B. the road forming remaining for the night on the Canal Bank.	
LANCASHIRE FARM.				
CITTEBOS			has been much improved by the 8th R.B	

WAR DIARY or INTELLIGENCE SUMMARY

Army Form C. 2118

Place	Date	Hour	Summary of Events and Information	Remarks and references to Appendices
LANCASHIRE FARM C14 c 0.3	Jan 9 Sunday		Day quiet. Enemy transport very loud about 6 p.m. At night A coy took over D22 & Dawson City from 6th S.L.I. The last road supply is from Bridge 4 to Pont Ferry, thence along Pekeem Road. Relief was started by early light, not midday — very long time. Work is ?? from M E23. D rainage & New Rd hole up in E23 enfilades several points in German line V Pekeem Road.	
"	Jan 10 Monday		Inability to use rifle flares. The enemy shelled D22 & Dawson City & M7A & M7B. These are isolated trenches, cut off from HQs and others by day & hard to approach by night owing to mud. Communication is needed between E23 & D22.	
"	Jan 11 Tuesday		Enemy's guns again active. Enfilading D22, Dawson City & Canal Bank. Our flares seem to retaliate with effect. Getting direct hits on dugouts C14 a 4.3 — C 14 9 1.0. HMs little grouping in front of E24 — Our hare 13.7 & 24.15 are constantly under fire.	

1875 Wt. W593/826 1,000,000 4/15 J.B.C. & A. A.D.S.S./Forms/C. 2118.

WAR DIARY
or
INTELLIGENCE SUMMARY
(Erase heading not required.)

Army Form C. 2118

Place	Date	Hour	Summary of Events and Information	Remarks and references to Appendices
LANCASHIRE FARM C14.C.3	Jan 11th		Enemy's searchlight reported C.15.b.25. Info. by pigeon messenger returned to the R.A. but no communication was possible. Enemy busy trucking up the parapet. Reached M/gs fired in E.23.	
"	Jan 12		At 7:30 a.m. we bombarded the HpR [rectangle] between the enemy retaliated with whizzbangs on [?] trenches [?] dwellings and hangars C.14.b.5.9 on DAWSON CITY from direction PILKEM caused five casualties. Heavy shell bombardment on DAWSON CITY at 2:30 p.m. [?] very few strays [?] little aircraft. The R.F.C. very [?] in the evening. One of our planes flew very low [?] machine gun fire in [?] from the Hn. system. After a short [?] along the railway [?] followed up by [?] from the [?] S.K. H.Q. on the log square.	
POPERINGHE	Jan 13		Battn. [?] Continues at Divisional H.Q. (legs). Weather cold and [?] high. The patrol likely to end in pre-[?] on the ground in which [?] shortly to yield strong results in which [?] [?] [?] was [?] The recruits were ready as very	

WAR DIARY
or
INTELLIGENCE SUMMARY
(Erase heading not required.)

Army Form C. 2118

Place	Date	Hour	Summary of Events and Information	Remarks and references to Appendices
POPERINGHE	Jan 14	Friday	Companies at the disposal of O.C. Coys. The 4th Divisional Baths were again allotted to us. Inspection of billets in the morning by the C.O.	
POPERINGHE	Jan 15	Saturday	Companies at disposal of O.C. Coys. A Coy left by train in the evening to go into Brigade Reserve on the Canal Bank. A lively contest against the 7th KRRC was held in the evening ending in a victory for the 8th Batt by a single event.	
LANCASHIRE FARM C14 C.3	Jan 16	Sunday	There were services for C of E. Roman Catholics & Wesleyans in the morning. In the afternoon the 3 remaining Coys detrained at the Asylum en route to the trenches where we relieved the 7th R.B. A.D. remaining on the Canal Bank. The relief was completed 8 P.M., but was not assisted by our artillery opening fire from behind the Canal Bank & drawing immediate retaliation while the road and bridge B were thronged with men.	

WAR DIARY
or
INTELLIGENCE SUMMARY

(Erase heading not required.)

Army Form C. 2118

Place	Date	Hour	Summary of Events and Information	Remarks and references to Appendices
LANCASHIRE FARM C14 C93	Jan 17 Monday		A quiet night 16/17th. Germans working on their parapet in front of D22. About dawn two of the enemy came over & threw 2 bombs at a post in this trench, unluckily our rifle fire did no damage. Snipers busy on an observation Post in C trenches. The day was quiet except for a few shells near Dawson City and an intermittent bombardment of Caesar's Post. Our aeroplanes very active in the morning, 12 being up together at 10 a.m.	
"	Jan 18th Tuesday		The night of the 17/18th was again quiet, except for a M.G. which was turned on to a wiring-party of C Coy in front of D22, wounding 5 men slightly. There seem to be 2 M.G.'s in front of D22 and fires from the High Redoubt. Romely customarily fall in front of the E22 D22, but always short. Most[?] there are a [?] of thrown by a catapult, as in spite of bright moon our enemy was seen except now & before in front of D22. Our patrols tried to waylay them when they went out. The day was quiet owing to bad weather & the comparative inactivity of our guns.	

WAR DIARY
or
INTELLIGENCE SUMMARY
(Erase heading not required.)

Army Form C. 2118

Place	Date	Hour	Summary of Events and Information	Remarks and references to Appendices
LANCASHIRE FARM C.14.c.3	Jan 19th	Friday Wednesday	The night of the 18/19 was quiet & patrols found & heard no movements. One party our men lay out for several hours in front of the wire, but their presence was unrewarded. Artillery very active on both sides, the Canal Road & Shelton Road being the usual targets for the enemy's fire; a good many shells also to the right of Dawson City.	
"	Jan 20th	Thursday	There were 3 casualties from rifle bullets during the night, the 19/20 the bat more from exceptionally heavy M.G. fire during four or five hours, answered by our M.G's & Rifle batteries. Enemy guns detected by flashes at twilight or near which the R.A were registered. Aeroplanes busy in the morning, the weather being favourable. Evening was intermittent. The 7th R.B. relieved us in the evening. The battn returning by bus to rest camp. During this tour of duty the 7th KRRC were on our left, the 43rd Brigade on our right. Much progress was made with wiring, drainage etc. Our Snipers have now got loopholes in F.3. Dr., as have the 7 H KRRC. 3 Germans with grey caps and white ducks observed at one point. Fixed battery to let off H.E. manned by 2 men, but found to be out of order.	

WAR DIARY
or
INTELLIGENCE SUMMARY

Army Form C. 2118

Place	Date	Hour	Summary of Events and Information	Remarks and references to Appendices
Nel Camp A=6 Central	Jan 21st Friday		Coy's at disposal O.C. Coy's. A small rifle range is being built to give men practice with superrifles. A working party for Canal Bank and Shipton Road leaves by bus at 4hr.m returning at midnight. Reliefs will take place in future every sixth day instead of every fourth	
"	Jan 22nd Saturday		The 49th Divisional Baths at our disposal. Another working party for the Canal Bank in the evening. They report that a MG is now added to the inconveniences that beset the RE dump at Bridge 6: the trains but (?) 7th R.B. hit there in the evening. Shortly before midnight one or more hostile Taubes raided POPERINGHE & dropped about a dozen bombs: some loss of life, but the accounts conflict	
"	Jan 23rd Sunday		Another fine day. Parade Service in the morning at the Church Army Hut. Another party of 150 men to work on Canal Bank in evening	

WAR DIARY or INTELLIGENCE SUMMARY

Army Form C. 2118

Place	Date	Hour	Summary of Events and Information	Remarks and references to Appendices
No 1 Cunt A:6 Central	Jan 24	Monday	Weather remains good. A hopeful work march towed enfiriods owing to the numbers men taken for working parties and refugees. A training contest against the 7th K.R.R.C in POPERINGE the Brigadier gave away the prizes.	
"	Jan 25	Tuesday	C Coy relieves a Coy of the 7th R.B. on the Canal Bank. A Coy to trained over POPERINGHE, but dropped no bombs. In spite of bright clear day an artillery strafe threatened for several days against the German line opposite the 42nd Brigade — No R/g our sector — was again postponed.	
"	26	Wednesday	Bn relieves 7th Rifle Brigade in trenches in PILCKEM Rd. A Coy to D22, 'DAWSON CITY', B Coy to E23, 'HEADINGLY Rd', and 'SPAH', F.M. B.v.C Coys Canal Bank. B.H.Q. Lancashire FM dugouts. 6th K.O.Y.L.I. on right, 7th K.R.R on left.	

Army Form C. 2118

WAR DIARY
or
INTELLIGENCE SUMMARY
(Erase heading not required.)

Instructions regarding War Diaries and Intelligence Summaries are contained in F. S. Regs., Part II. and the Staff Manual respectively. Title Pages will be prepared in manuscript.

Place	Date	Hour	Summary of Events and Information	Remarks and references to Appendices
LANCASHIRE FARM C14.C.0.3.	Jan. 26 Wednesday		Drive to rid lake about Enlefeg relief not completed till about 3-0 a.m. Troops continued to expect some celebration of the Kaiser's birthday.	
	27th Thursday		Kaiser's birthday. Enemy's artillery very active from daybreak, but chiefly clear of our lines. Canal bank heavily shelled.	
	28th Friday		Rather more rifle fire than usual. Trench mortar flew in E.23 on our left exposing our only daylight approach via Skipton Rd. very heavy. Shelling of Canal bank in afternoon. Snipers at new O.P. C.11 found it an excellent view of High Command Redoubt – parties of men were observed and rifle slugs moving D.22 – seemed often alarmed and continued observing and apparently trying to order in direction of D.2.2.-21 – Light blue caps and white cotton. They seemed new to their surroundings. One German his from E.23 WAITY SEE Cookshot.	

Army Form C. 2118

WAR DIARY
or
INTELLIGENCE SUMMARY
(Erase heading not required.)

Instructions regarding War Diaries and Intelligence Summaries are contained in F. S. Regs., Part II. and the Staff Manual respectively. Title Pages will be prepared in manuscript.

Place	Date	Hour	Summary of Events and Information	Remarks and references to Appendices
LANCASHIRE FARM. C14.C0.5. Sheet 28	Jan 29th Saturday		Very quiet day owing to mist. Parts working on parapet at C14 a 6.2. They were fired at with 4 steel bullets viz: inches below top of parapet with idea of penetrating; this was widely successful for the working party stopped at once and ceased work for the day. From rear new O.P. a German officer at C14 b4.6. looking over his parapet was killed. Wind moderate N to E. Work done on new PILCKEM R? Nights Quiet — issued new type P.H. little wheel turret new gun.	
"	30th Sunday		Exceptionally quiet day — thick mist and very little break. Wind East variable.	
	31st Monday		Wind S. Bearable — dull observation difficult. Very little movement of enemy of any kind. Two officers	

1875 Wt. W593/826 1,000,000 4/15 J.B.C. & A. A.D.S.S./Forms/C. 2118.

WAR DIARY or INTELLIGENCE SUMMARY

Army Form C. 2118

Place	Date	Hour	Summary of Events and Information	Remarks and references to Appendices
LANCASHIRE FARM C1 & C.O.3 Nwg	Jan 31	Monday	— And a black day. Seen in direction of Von Kluck's Chapel. They had carried very strongly over a few lines — Laid Cpl on parapet and proceeded to observe — one shell at 650 yds Suspended their operations — the officer picked up his cap and wore a Fowell did not reappear. Three hostile Bears burst just over Bn.H.Q. at dusk	
	Feb 1st	Tuesday	Mostly morning — Bombardment of High Comm and redoubt postponed — cleared late — very little movement in enemy lines — No sentries even being visible from O.P. which is in contact with the last few days. Bn.H.Q. relieved by 7th R.B. and returns by train to POPERINGHE billets.	

84 KRR
3 P 4
Vol 5

Army Form C. 2118

WAR DIARY
or
INTELLIGENCE SUMMARY
(Erase heading not required.)

8th K.R.R.C.

Place	Date	Hour	Summary of Events and Information	Remarks and references to Appendices
PEPERINGHE	Feb 2nd Wednesday		Major CRUM is command of Battn: — Commanding Officer on leave. — Copy of the defence of O.C. Corps. Following letter received from 46th Division — once more "The G.O.C. desires to express his high appreciation of the excellent work which has been done by troops under your command since the Division took over the left sector of the 6th Corps front. He is well aware of the conditions which prevailed on taking over and of the great change which has been wrought during the past month. He is also aware that this has only been accomplished by working units at high pressure, to which they have responded most willingly. He feels certain that all ranks will continue their efforts to improve the defences, so that they may be handed over, whenever the Division is relieved, in as satisfactory a state as possible." RLA	

Army Form C. 2118

WAR DIARY
or
INTELLIGENCE SUMMARY
(Erase heading not required.)

Instructions regarding War Diaries and Intelligence Summaries are contained in F. S. Regs., Part II. and the Staff Manual respectively. Title Pages will be prepared in manuscript.

Place	Date	Hour	Summary of Events and Information	Remarks and references to Appendices
POPERINGHE	Feb 3 Thursday		Companies at the disposal of O.C. Coys. Billets inspected by Commanding Officer at 11·0 a.m. R.L.H.	
"	4 Friday		Battn. has baths in Convent Rue de Reninghe[?] POPERINGHE. R.L.H	
"	5 Saturday		Lecture to artillery & infantry officers at BAILLEUL at 2·0 p.m. by Major CRUM. Battn. Concert at 6·0 p.m. in 14th Division Soldiers Club. R.L.H.	
"	6 Sunday		Church of England parade service in the "Javries" Hall at 10·30 a.m. Roman Catholic service Notre Dame Church 11·0 a.m. Non Conformists at T.B. Coys. HQ. at 3·30 p.m. D Coy. leave for the Canal bank by train at 4·15 p.m. to go into Batt. reserve R.L.H.	
"	7 Monday		Battn. entrained at 6·45- for the trenches. A Coy. shelled as train arrived near Asylum. Relief complete at 8·30 p.m. night quiet. R.L.H.	

Army Form C. 2118

WAR DIARY
or
INTELLIGENCE SUMMARY
(Erase heading not required.)

Instructions regarding War Diaries and Intelligence Summaries are contained in F.S. Regs., Part II. and the Staff Manual respectively. Title Pages will be prepared in manuscript.

Place	Date	Hour	Summary of Events and Information	Remarks and references to Appendices
LANCASHIER FARM (14 co 3 Hust 28.	Feb. 8 Tuesday		B22 & DAWSON CITY intermittent shelling. Aeroplanes active - 2 German planes over our lines. At 10.15 am 7 of our aeroplanes crossed over going E.N.E. The enemy have covered with sandbags or filled in most of their loopholes. Since our last tour of duty - this is probably due to elephant gun and new steel bullets. There is no sign of fresh loopholes. One enemy periscope broken and any movement sniped. On all peered very quiet along the front which was under observation from three points. There were interchanges of rifle grenades. B Coy in E 23, HEADINGLY LANE and SPAH1 - commanded by 2nd Lt. Dodd-Naylor. C. Coy in D22 and DAWSON CITY commanded by 2nd Lt. Hill. And Corson Canal Bank. 7th K.R. Rifles on the left and 5th K.O.Y.L.I. 43rd I.B. on the right. R.L.H	

1875 Wt. W593/826 1,000,000 4/15 J.B.C. & A. A.D.S.S./Forms/C. 2118.

WAR DIARY or INTELLIGENCE SUMMARY

Army Form C. 2118

Place	Date	Hour	Summary of Events and Information	Remarks and references to Appendices
LANCASHIRE FARM (H.Co 5) Sheet 28	Feb 9 Wednesday		Some exchange of rifle grenades from F.2.3 and with KRUPP FARM trenches. Our grenades seemed to burst well. The Dunnolliue Company Officer agreed to cover up new communication trench from Bt. H.Q. to F.2.5. This is very important as it forms a conspicuous mark for aeroplane observation and is likely to draw shelling on Bt. H.Q. Enemy aeroplane very active observing in the morning, Canal Bank and Skipton Road were heavily shelled. About 2.30 p.m. two pigeons were released from Bt. H.Q. and while circling were evidently observed,— Bt. H.Q. being which? Carzeal almost immediately. Considerable artillery activity throughout the night. Canal Bank and Skipton chiefly coming in for shelling — A few over Bt. H.Q. and Highland Farm about 10 pm. Lees rifle and M.G. fire. Patrols found enemy's wire intact and a few small working parties. Sound of transport, hammering and voices audible 5-6 am 10 unit.

R.L.H. | |

Army Form C. 2118

WAR DIARY
or
INTELLIGENCE SUMMARY
(Erase heading not required.)

Instructions regarding War Diaries and Intelligence Summaries are contained in F.S. Regs., Part II. and the Staff Manual respectively. Title Pages will be prepared in manuscript.

Place	Date	Hour	Summary of Events and Information	Remarks and references to Appendices
LANCASHIER FARM C14 c 03 Sheet 28	10th Thursday		Canal bank heavily shelled at intervals also Skipton Road. At 1-30 p.m. enemy trench mortar fired at the right of E 23 from C14 a 61. but was quickly silenced by R.A. directed by snipers from O.P. Snipers Butt in C Line to the top of B.H.Q. heavily crumped in afternoon. Snipers report enemy appear to have been relieved as they took more liberties - they lost on the day with here sniping, but our snipers soon got it under. Battn. relieved at 8-30 p.m. by 10th D.L.I. Goes by Bridger huts corner to Pop Camp A8.b. Sheet 28. During this tour 2 N.C.Os & 5 Officers of 11th Rifle Brigade 25th Division were attached to the Battn. to get to know the trenches. RLH	
Pop Camp A8.b. Sheet 28	11th Friday		Lt Colonel HR Green returns - Battn. leaves Camp at 11-20 a.m. to billets round WINNEZEELE J 17 Sheet 27 via ABEELE and STEENWORDE 13 miles. Transport accompanies Battn. Dinners on the march at 1-0 p.m. just past POPERINGHE. Battn. arrives Winnezeele at 5-30 p.m. C.O.'s Coys & Transport some 2½ miles off - A & B at farms about 1 mile distant. B.H.Q. in WINNEZEELE. RLH	

Army Form C. 2118

WAR DIARY
or
INTELLIGENCE SUMMARY
(Erase heading not required.)

Place	Date	Hour	Summary of Events and Information	Remarks and references to Appendices
WINNEZEELE J.17 Sheet 27	Feb			
	12 Saturday		Coys at the disposal of O.C. Coys. Office at 12 noon. Billets visited by Commanding Officer. The 7th Rifle Bde are also billeted in Winnezeele. 41st Bde H.Q. in WINNEZEELE. Heavy shelling in the direction of the Canal. heard German attack near PILKEM. R.L.H	
"	13 Sunday		Heavy shelling continues. Coys at disposal of O.C. Coys. R.L.H	
"	14 Monday		Coys at disposal of O.C. Coys. Commanding Officer inspects A & C Companies in full marching order. Machine Gunners return from the trenches. R.L.H	
	15 Tuesday		Commanding Officer inspects B Company. Bde Machine Gun Company formed under Major Evans 7th K.R.R. from this Battⁿ. The Machine Gun section under 2nd Lieut RODWAY and 2nd Lieut RODDICK. Machine Gunners march off to Bde Billets at 3-0 p.m. D Coy moves to two farms near cross roads J.12 & 8.7 Sheet 27. R.L.H	

WAR DIARY
or
INTELLIGENCE SUMMARY

(Erase heading not required.)

Army Form C. 2118

Place	Date	Hour	Summary of Events and Information	Remarks and references to Appendices
WINNEZEELE I 17 Sheet 27	Feb 16 Wednesday		Commanding Officer inspected D Coy at 11.0 am and C Coy at 12 noon. The following is an extract from battalion orders by Lieut Colonel H.C.R Green of today's date:— "The Commanding Officer wishes to express his appreciation of the good work done by the snipers during the last tour of duty in the trenches. The battalion occupied a section where the enemy had entirely the upper hand, and by the time the battalion left, the enemy had sand bagged up his loopholes and sniping from the trenches in front of the battalion was practically dead. The observation of the snipers also often enabled the supporting batteries to do good work in shelling enemy working parties and trench mortars; while the information of enemy's movements and uniforms obtained by the snipers was forwarded to Corps Head Quarters." R.L.M	

Army Form C. 2118.

WAR DIARY
or
INTELLIGENCE SUMMARY.
(Erase heading not required.)

Instructions regarding War Diaries and Intelligence Summaries are contained in F.S. Regs., Part II. and the Staff Manual respectively. Title pages will be prepared in manuscript.

Place	Date	Hour	Summary of Events and Information	Remarks and references to Appendices
WINNEZEELE J.17 Sheet 27	Feb 16 Wednesday		"The commanding officer much regrets that the Battalion machine Gun Section left today, under orders to join the Brigade Machine Gun Company and may this sever connection with the Battalion. The Machine Gun teams have always supported the Battalion with their fire regardless of the fire to which they themselves were subjected, and there was always a feeling of security amongst all ranks when they knew that they were supported by their own machine gunners." R.L.H	
"	17 Thursday		At 2.0 p.m. the Battalion was inspected by the Commander in Chief – Sir Douglas Haig. The 7th R.B. 61st Field Coy R.E. and Both Machine Gun Coys were inspected at the same time. The Battalion afterwards marched passed the Commander in chief. R.L.H	

Army Form C. 2118.

WAR DIARY
or
INTELLIGENCE SUMMARY.
(Erase heading not required.)

Instructions regarding War Diaries and Intelligence Summaries are contained in F.S. Regs., Part II. and the Staff Manual respectively. Title pages will be prepared in manuscript.

Place	Date	Hour	Summary of Events and Information	Remarks and references to Appendices
WINNEZEELE I.17 Sheet 27	Feb 18 Friday		Companies at the disposal of O.C. Coys. Regimental Court Martial held – Captain Prewen president – members Revd F.G. London-Shand and Lieut R.L. Hardy. B Company inoculated today. R.L.H.	
"	19 Saturday		Companies go for route marches – Brekers with D Coy. Billeting party under Captain Prewen leave at 8.30 am. Orders to move South arrive. R.L.H.	
"	20 Sunday		The battalion parades at 9.30 pm less 3 platoons of C Coy and marches to railway station at Bavinchove just beyond Cassel. The transport and D Coy leave at 7.40 to entrain before arrival of battalion at 12.30 am. The three platoons of C Coy left behind come on with Brigade H.Q. on morning of 21st.	
AMIENS & NAOURS	21 Monday		The battalion arrives by train at AMIENS at 10.30am on 21st and marches out through Amiens to village of NAOURS 14 miles – packs carried in motor lorries. Battalion arrives at NAOURS at 4.30 pm and is billeted there. R.L.H.	

Army Form C. 2118.

WAR DIARY
or
INTELLIGENCE SUMMARY.
(Erase heading not required.)

Instructions regarding War Diaries and Intelligence Summaries are contained in F. S. Regs., Part II. and the Staff Manual respectively. Title pages will be prepared in manuscript.

Place	Date	Hour	Summary of Events and Information	Remarks and references to Appendices
NAOURS	Feb 22 Tuesday		7th K.R. Rifles and 7th Rifle Brigade also billeted in NAOURS. 4th Bde and 14th Div H.Q at Vaucelles also 8th R.B. Commanding Officer inspect billets at 10-30 am	R.L.H
"	23rd Wednesday		Very cold. Frosty weather. C & D Coy inoculated	R.L.H
"	24th Thursday		Order obtained of O.C. Coys. Heavy snow fall.	R.L.H
"	25th Friday		At 2-0 am telegram from 41st T.I.B ordering Bn to be prepared to move at short notice. Horses and mules rested. Battalion leaves NAOURS at 10-45 am and following 7th KRR marches to DOULLENS — 12 miles; arrive at DOULLENS at 3-0 pm and billeted there one night. Frost and snow continue.	R.L.H
"	26th Saturday		Battalion leaves DOULLENS at 11-0 am and marches to SOMBRIN — 11 miles in heavy snow storm — roads hilly and very difficult for transport. Cookers however manage to

Army Form C. 2118.

WAR DIARY
or
INTELLIGENCE SUMMARY.
(Erase heading not required.)

Place	Date	Hour	Summary of Events and Information	Remarks and references to Appendices
SOMBRIN	FEB. 26 Saturday		6 Sect in poor offs: the Battalion, which arrived between 2.30 and 3.0 p.m. Newhold transport gets in by 9.30 p.m. earlier than that of any other regiment:- Lorries with blankets do not arrive until evening of 27th. The supply wagons arrive until afternoon of 27th. RLH	
"	27 Sunday		No food or forage as supply wagons are held up on the road by snow, party of 40 men sent to dig them up. Slight thaw sets in. RLH	
"	28 Monday		Considerable thaw. - Colonel and Major Crum go to inspect new trenches. RLH	
"	29th Tuesday		Battalion leaves SOMBRIN at 12 noon and marches to BERNEVILLE arriving at 4-30 p.m. Dinners on the march. BERNEVILLE very crowded, full of French troops and the 43rd Brigade. D Company marches on to ARRAS with 7th K.R.R. and is under their orders. Officers mess cart company went ahead early in the day to go round the trenches with the French. RLH	

14

8 KRRe

Vol 6

8th K.R.R.C.

WAR DIARY
or
INTELLIGENCE SUMMARY

(Erase heading not required.)

Army Form C. 2118

Instructions regarding War Diaries and Intelligence Summaries are contained in F. S. Regs., Part II. and the Staff Manual respectively. Title Pages will be prepared in manuscript.

Place	Date	Hour	Summary of Events and Information	Remarks and references to Appendices
ARRAS	March 1 Wednesday		BERNEVILLE. The Battalion leaves BERNEVILLE at 5-0 p.m. and marches to ARRAS getting into billets there soon after 7-0 p.m. D Coy goes up into front line trenches on night of 1st K.R.R. A Coy in BLANGY support billets. C Coy in St Sauveur support billets. B Coy in RUE DOMINIQUE also Bn. H.Q.	
"	2 Thursday		Reconnoitring trenches of 7 K.R.R. D.L.H.	
"	3 Friday		C/pl OTTERWELL – the best sniper – killed when observing in the BLANGY sector on the left. R.I.H.	
"	4 Saturday		Battalion Officer is held every morning for A.B.+ C Coys. Very cold – heavy snow. R.I.H	
"	5 Sunday		D Coy is relieved by 8th R.B. and comes back to billets in Grande Place. A Coy relieves 5th Oxford+Bucks.L.I. in Retou Rou to Scarpe defences. Two platoons of C Coy relieve Oxford+Bucks on Railway defences, two platoons come back to Grande Place. R.I.H.	

WAR DIARY or INTELLIGENCE SUMMARY

Army Form C. 2118

Place	Date	Hour	Summary of Events and Information	Remarks and references to Appendices
ARRAS	March 6 Monday		Snow and cold continue. Divisional front was rearranged last night, so that all three brigades are in the line. The 41st I.B. has two batts. in the line, one in Arras and one back in Divisional reserve at ~~BERNEVILLE~~ SIMENCOURT. Our transport camp is at BERNEVILLE.	R.L.H.
"	7 Tuesday		The battalion relieved 7th K.R.R. in left sector Blangy. Bn. H.Q. in Rue de DOUAI. D Coy in support in Rue de Douai. A Coy on the left in BLANGEY. B Coy in the centre, and C Coy on the right. On our right the 8th R.B. and on our left across the river – the Cheshire Regt, 13th Bde V. Div.	R.L.H.
"	8 Wednesday		Very quiet night. A few shells at B Coy in the morning. The Blangy Pectn. is in among houses and ruined walls – the present position is distinctly unsafe.	R.L.H.

WAR DIARY
or
INTELLIGENCE SUMMARY
(Erase heading not required.)

Army Form C. 2118

Instructions regarding War Diaries and Intelligence Summaries are contained in F. S. Regs., Part II. and the Staff Manual respectively. Title Pages will be prepared in manuscript.

Place	Date	Hour	Summary of Events and Information	Remarks and references to Appendices
BLANGY	March 9. Thursday		There was more rifle fire at night. The Boch has two fixed rifles on an important corner in A Coy's dist. which are annoying us. The salients to the top of B Coy's line was fairly heavily shelled with 4.2 c.m. Our guns retaliated, but put 8 shells behind our own trenches before they got on to the Boch. R.C.H.	
"	10 Friday		D Coy relieves A Coy in the BLANGY Sector. A Coy in support. A bombing encounter took place in the early morning, resulting in 4 casualties - seriously wounded - on our side. A few small shells along the front of C Coy and the right by B Coy. R.C.H.	
"	11 Saturday		D Coy lose their C.S.M. CLARK and a Corporal wounded by rifle fire. The result of injudicious attempts to snipe. Good work by the Kings Liverpools (Pioneers) on the new support line in BLANGY	

WAR DIARY
or
INTELLIGENCE SUMMARY

(Erase heading not required.)

Army Form C. 2118

Place	Date	Hour	Summary of Events and Information	Remarks and references to Appendices
BLANGY	11 Saturday		Snipers report a rifle band playing in the morning about ½ mile behind German line. Movement of their transport also plainly heard during the night a very short distance away. Our own transport & their general situation in ARRAS too exposed to make retaliation for our artillery to intervene. R.I.H.	
"	12 Sunday		Sniping persistent in the BLANGY sector. Our snipers report closing several German loopholes & opening others. About 50 shells between our right Coy's support line and the cemetery during the afternoon. Artillery have orders not to give retaliation unless serious damage is sustained; in there were cases intensive retaliation by all batteries is promised. The batt'n is relieved by the 7th KRRC and marches to billets in SIMENCOURT tracked by 7th R.B. R.I.H R.C.H	
SIMENCOURT	13 Monday		Bright, warm weather. Companies at disposal of O.C. Coy's. R.C.H	

WAR DIARY or INTELLIGENCE SUMMARY

Army Form C. 2118.

Place	Date	Hour	Summary of Events and Information	Remarks and references to Appendices
SIMENCOURT	March 14th Tuesday		A party of 150 men attended a FLAMMEN WERFEN demonstration held at WANQUETIN under VIIth Corps arrangements to watch the effect of having the flammenwerfer of liquid fire. The demonstrator burnt himself. Limited opportunity for bathing in the village; but this is the first opportunity trained for the troops to have some. Feb 5th. R.L.H.	
"	March 15 Wednesday		Arrangements made to train reserve Bombers, Lewis Gunners and Stretcher-Bearers. Weather bright & warm; some hostile aeroplanes about driven off by our own M.G. by aircraft fire. Word of a draft of 57 N.C.O. & men, including several old members of the Battalion. This draft had been sent in error from the 4th Entrenching Batt to the 13th K.R.R.C. R.L.H.	
"	March 16th Thursday		It is decided to form a "Communication Section" as a coherente unit consisting of signallers, guides & orderlies under command of Lieut Wrygell. & Lieut	

Army Form C. 2118.

WAR DIARY
or
INTELLIGENCE SUMMARY.
(Erase heading not required.)

Place	Date	Hour	Summary of Events and Information	Remarks and references to Appendices
SIMENCOURT	March 17th Friday		Another draft of men arrives composed chiefly of old members of the Battalion. Companies at disposal of O.C. Coys.	R.L.H.
"	March 18th Saturday		Training of Reserve bombers & Lewis gunners continues. The number of garrison fatigues that have to be found tends to interfere with company training.	R.L.H.
SIMENCOURT, ARRAS (Blangy)	March 19th Sunday		The battalion leaves billets & relieves 7th K.R.R.C. in front line. During our week's stay we found much lacking in the comfort & cleanliness of the billets. Complaints were forwarded to the Brigade. A.D.M.S. arranges 8th R.B. are on our right & the 5th division across the River La Scarpe on our left. A heavy bombardment on the 42 Brigade on the right by the 8 R.B. compelled them to evacuate some front line trenches. Enemy great always suspected, except for the usual guns & trench bombs on BLANGY. The trenches have been much improved by the 7 K.R.R.C. during their tour of duty & the weather has cured them	R.L.H.

Army Form C. 2118.

Instructions regarding War Diaries and Intelligence Summaries are contained in F. S. Regs., Part II. and the Staff Manual respectively. Title pages will be prepared in manuscript.

WAR DIARY
or
INTELLIGENCE SUMMARY.
(Erase heading not required.)

Place	Date	Hour	Summary of Events and Information	Remarks and references to Appendices
ARRAS BLANGY	March 20th Monday		There have been several duels during the day in BLANGY. The enemy using rifle grenades and rifle grenades against our catapult bombs. Flaks grenades; we had one or two casualties. Much work is needed on our wire, especially in front of the centre Company, (I15 – I 67) where it has been broken by the grenades. Our own Lewis guns have also damaged our wire. R.L.H	
"	March 21st Tuesday		All front-line dug-outs have to be blocked & closed by 3rd Army order. A party from the Battalion in Bgde. Reserve 7th R.B. is working at the provision of temporary shelters for our right company. In future this party will work under the King's Liverpools upon the I.S line, which will become ultimately the main line of defence, be provided with dug-outs; the present front line being held with Hurdivipers. Several casualties from bombs in BLANGY. Our snipers observed there some Germans dressed in apparently English uniform, also several officers observing our line, including a general. R.L.H	

1577 Wt.W10791/1773 500,000 1/15 D. D. & L.   A.D.S.S./Form/C. 2118.

Army Form C. 2118.

WAR DIARY
or
INTELLIGENCE SUMMARY.
(Erase heading not required.)

Instructions regarding War Diaries and Intelligence Summaries are contained in F. S. Regs., Part II. and the Staff Manual respectively. Title pages will be prepared in manuscript.

Place	Date	Hour	Summary of Events and Information	Remarks and references to Appendices
ARRAS (BLANGY)	March 22nd	Wednesday	A prolonged bombing duel in BLANGY in early hours of Wednesday morning, answered by our shooting a German wiring in front of the salient in our line. During the day our guns registered on a fruit store opposite BOILER House, where a rifle grenade stand has been located. Snipers were active. Opposite the Germans in their front line, N. of the railway, where footballs being kicked up & new wire erected. D relieves A Coy in the evening in BLANGY, A Coy returning to Batt'n Reserve. R.C.H.	
BLANGY	March 23rd	Thursday	Our guns registered on a machine throwing various trench mortars from a point opposite the nearest salient in our centre Company. These caused several casualties. A quiet day, except for a few whizzbangs on hamlet of IBa. R.C.H.	
"	March 24th	Friday	Much less activity on the part of the German bombers in BLANGY, due probably to our guns having registered on one or two of their machines. The new T.S. line in BLANGY and by HQ's adjoining it were wholly ruptured during the day; the enemy was very accurate and hit no ? on them. Our snipers	

1577 Wt.W10791/1773 500,000 1/15 D. D. & L. A.D.S.S./Forms/C. 2118.

WAR DIARY
or
INTELLIGENCE SUMMARY

Army Form C. 2118

(Erase heading not required.)

Instructions regarding War Diaries and Intelligence Summaries are contained in F. S. Regs., Part II. and the Staff Manual respectively. Title Pages will be prepared in manuscript.

Place	Date	Hour	Summary of Events and Information	Remarks and references to Appendices
Neuville BLANGY	Friday March 2?	Friday	Red Whistler fired their number four track and otherwise support who was carried out casualties in our own no further. One in front of Red M.T. the railway. A sudden move is to smoke & cold weather keep causing some damage to the trenches & made general mischief. R.W.C.	
" "	March 4 25	Saturday	A few shells during the night died down enough to leave a lot of men from Douai Road between Petit H? and Coy H.Q. to BLANGY Station. This is unlikely to be due to enemy movement in daytime as we hear the members of field mortar battery situated above. They have to find routed living-places. A dummy movement from the dug-out. Hung by the hunter's scarce weather. Our my the four much hungry the B? was done in BLANGY upon sending rivulets & soldiers from trenches. The four lives were in front of our Coy's was also much strengthened when it was ordered to its trays the b-t-t is relieved by the T. R. R.R.C. from SIMENCOURT the relief completed 11.30 p.m. R.L.H.	

1875 Wt. W593/826 1,000,000 4/15 J.B.C. & A. A.D.S.S./Forms/C. 2118.

WAR DIARY or INTELLIGENCE SUMMARY

Army Form C. 2118

Place	Date	Hour	Summary of Events and Information	Remarks and references to Appendices
ARRAS	March 24th Sunday		The Battalion is in Brigade Reserve. C.O's Coys find the Nominal quorum of the CEMETERY ST. SAUVEUR. The two men supplying each house in the B in reserve billet lines. Rum & coffee find fights to work on the defences day & night in Rest or Markets; however enough ammo is kept in the pouches to be found ready in the trenches. A & B Coys are billetted in the trench streets adjoining the DOUBT road. A & B Coys' H.Qs. are billetted in the Rue's "Ronville" the women & children... The R.E. left Bank up & men working such a Normally, on in up off to their underground excavation into the sanitary cellars. R.L.H.	
"	25 Monday		We visit the many excellent Pataca Rs, no hay found Company Many that when filled in clothes are available including kitchen and washing. With the R.E. on defences, the CEMETERY ST. SAUVEUR, we find 300 men for working parties the 24 hours, including two bakery. It is the hospital for Battalion. R.L.H.	
"	March 26 Tuesday		Easy. Full wet Hen. The C.O. inspects billets in Ronville	

Army Form C. 2118.

WAR DIARY
or
INTELLIGENCE SUMMARY.
(Erase heading not required.)

Instructions regarding War Diaries and Intelligence Summaries are contained in F. S. Regs., Part II. and the Staff Manual respectively. Title pages will be prepared in manuscript.

Place	Date	Hour	Summary of Events and Information	Remarks and references to Appendices
Hulce ARRAS	March 28	Wednesday	Ref to Hintz. Fck men directionist captured technical meanings as stand by for firing. The subaltern & one returned to duty from the F.A. (two sharp). The neww elephant tripod with the sighting gears all correct. Very disturbed night on the left [?] (the heavy artillery to NW) enemy aeroplane enemy dumps on the CAMBRAI RAIL were far from willing to our south.	
"	March 29	Wednesday	Now batteries continue their operations in BLANGY by horsemen at the R.F.C. A German sniper who has claimed several victims in the last day or two from B.P.T. M.R.H. was shot through the loophole after hours of patient watching by one of our men. R.L.H.	
"	March 30	Thursday	Fine bright weather, suitable for aeroplane activity. Several captive German balloons made an appearance. Three balloons have a commanding view of the [illegible] sectors the west side of the front Place? R.L.H.	
(BLANGY)	March 31	Friday	Heavy firing early in the morning to the north beyond the faubourg. The Germans had 2 guns in a wood, which made an attack, which appeared most heavy. We [illegible] the N.R.R.C. in the load. As often enemy shelling our during the key alley R.L.H. Ref Arras Road near But. H.Q.S. [illegible]	

WAR DIARY
or
INTELLIGENCE SUMMARY.
(Erase heading not required.)

Place	Date	Hour	Summary of Events and Information	Remarks and references to Appendices
ARRAS (BLANGY)	April 1st	Saturday	Trenches in excellent condition owing to the warm, dry weather. Two men hit unluckily while on duty on the Mound in the salient Jn I.68. This is a marked place and needs the greatest caution. A quiet day & hostile sniping much ↓. A lot of work has been done by the 7th Battn in BLANGY, but very dangerous places still need building up. This work is being done. RLH	
"	April 2nd	Sunday	Twenty rev ball-grenades fired from N.West Bomb Thrower provoked heavy retaliation with urgent bombs. Our out-post unfortunately broke; the STORES trench-mortar was called upon for retaliation. After a new one her alarming experiments the final shots reached the German trenches & drew a rapid service rifle bangs upon coy HQs. This is the first time the wired front has been fired since our guns registered on it a week ago. As regards on the shell Mound opposite I.65 N.of the Railway still continued, our guns fired salvoes of shrapnel over this shop during the night true gunners fired at it intermittently. A stray bullet hit 2nd Lt. EGERTON while on return early in the Evening. He had only just returned from acting as A.D.C. to the G.O.C. 4th Divn & would probably have joined the Battn. in a week. The wound is very serious. RLH	

Army Form C. 2118.

WAR DIARY
or
INTELLIGENCE SUMMARY.
(Erase heading not required.)

Instructions regarding War Diaries and Intelligence Summaries are contained in F. S. Regs., Part II. and the Staff Manual respectively. Title pages will be prepared in manuscript.

Place	Date	Hour	Summary of Events and Information	Remarks and references to Appendices
BLANGY	April 3rd	Monday	D Coy relieve A Coy in BLANGY after listening to a lecture on the evacuation of the line from Major CRUM. The party for leave is cancelled at the last moment owing to the boat to HAVRE being closed. Much movement of rifle fire turned on was noticable during the early morning; stray shots continually passed over the road. One man was hit near the station. The Germans afforded BLANGY were evidently nervous & fired constant Very Lights. 2nd Lt EGERTON died at 10.45 p.m. at the 42 nd C.C.S. DOULLENS. He rejoined the Battalion has lost a very honourable, as well a popular officer. RL"	
"	April 4	Tuesday	Snipers report a new loophole in the wall opposite SCARPE Corner. They fired at various loopholes which the enemy may use, but observed no movement in their lines. During the early part of the evening our Lewis guns fired a parties working on the railway. Funeral of 2nd Lt EGERTON of DOULLENS, attended by 2nd Lt HOLT & HARDY. RL"	

Army Form C. 2118.

WAR DIARY
or
INTELLIGENCE SUMMARY.
(Erase heading not required.)

Place	Date	Hour	Summary of Events and Information	Remarks and references to Appendices
BLANGY	April 5th	During day	A German Rifle-grenade which had been troubling with I 67 and carrying men but tonight was located in the White Chateau behind the village behind their lines. Two field guns silenced it by firing shrapnel & H.E. shells. The medium trench-mortar in BLANGY came into action for the first time and fired at the sap on the N. of the railway where work has been in progress for some time. From the Boiler house in BLANGY 'shermouses' observed enemy working parties & sounds, apparently of winnowing an M.G. emplacement at the ruin to windowing our O.P. in the Boiler House. Two sentries were hit (one killed) in the ulean-post, BLANGY 76 meilhat fired from across the river.	R.L.H.
"	April 6th	During day	The apparent M.G. emplacement mentioned above was kept under continual fire from our rifle grenades, and intermittent the howitzer. a shower of travel bombs in response, to which Hostiles Howitzer replied. Rifle-grenade finally called upon their artillery, & the dual	

1577 Wt. W10791/1773 500,000 1/15 D. D. & L. A.D.S.S./Forms/C. 2118.

Army Form C. 2118.

WAR DIARY
or
INTELLIGENCE SUMMARY.
(Erase heading not required.)

Instructions regarding War Diaries and Intelligence Summaries are contained in F. S. Regs., Part II. and the Staff Manual respectively. Title pages will be prepared in manuscript.

Place	Date	Hour	Summary of Events and Information	Remarks and references to Appendices
BLANGY	April 6		ended with a strenuous whizzbang remark by H.Q. in BLANGY in answer to our field guns. No casualties incurred. The battalion is relieved by the 7 R.D.F. & marche back to billets in SIMENCOURT. R.L.H	
SIMENCOURT	April 7 Friday		The billets have been much improved both as regards comfort and sanitation since my last visit. The usual quiet day. 2/Lt. Bate arrived. R.L.H	
"	April 8 Saturday		another Flammenwerfen demonstration for the whole Battalion. Two officers & 100 men have to be detailed daily to work at HAMPSTM our future rest-billets. Training of Junior Bombers Lewis gunners begun. R.L.H	
"	9 Sunday		Church parade in the morning. The C.O. leaves to attend a 3rd army conference of commanding officers at the army school at VR-LE CHATEAU. Captain FREWEN in command. R.L.H	

1577 Wt. W10791/1773 500,000 1/15 D. D. & L. A.D.S.S./Forms/C. 2118.

WAR DIARY
or
INTELLIGENCE SUMMARY.
(Erase heading not required.)

Army Form C. 2118.

Place	Date	Hour	Summary of Events and Information	Remarks and references to Appendices
Sirencourt	April 10th	Midday	Two Companies go for a Route March in full marching-order. Baths at men disposal. Fine, warm weather. RL+	
"	April 11th	Tuesday	Drath Hard for remaining two Companies. In the afternoon an inter-platoon shooting competition was arranged in spite of wet weather. The standard of shooting was surprisingly good. RL+	
"	April 12th	Wednesday	A wet, cold day. The battalion returns to the trenches. The relief being very late owing to Companies being held up on the road and divided, settled into platoons. This may have been in extra returning to bombardment by enemy Div. artillery on the enemy's front line. The weather compelled its postponement. During our absence the line has been much except for some large trench-mortars thrown into BLANGY. RL+	
BLANGY				

WAR DIARY
or
INTELLIGENCE SUMMARY.
(Erase heading not required.)

Army Form C. 2118.

Place	Date	Hour	Summary of Events and Information	Remarks and references to Appendices
BLANGY	April 13.	Thursday	Everything exceptionally quiet. Even the shooting of a man from the Boiler House and the firing of a Lewis gun on a party crossing the SCARPE River by the front produced no retaliation. The wet weather has again stopped the completion of the trenches. Gradual progress is being made with the I.S. line by the Lockhards + further bent to them. Until this line is built, the scheme of blocking features of the front line is in abeyance. A bullet + pamphlets were found to-day in the lines opposite I 65, apparently written by a malcontent Social Democrat. The title was "Drei Feldpost". R.L.H.	
"	April 14th	Friday	Wet weather has made return to field works necessary. Enemy still very unresponsive to provocation. There has been no relief left to the firing of a man opposite the Mound in I 63 Salient. The harrying when over the Lochnar he was no longer visible; a screen having been erected. R.L.H.	
"	April 15	Saturday	The Mound itself in the morning opposite I 65, as well as that opposite I 63 were continuously + very emphatically crossed by our snipers in answer to compliments + heavy trench mortars shells ... H.E.Hudson's efforts hurried us to by D Coy relieved A Coy D.L.H.	

WAR DIARY or INTELLIGENCE SUMMARY

Army Form C. 2118.

Place	Date	Hour	Summary of Events and Information	Remarks and references to Appendices
BEAM?	April 16th Sunday		Trenches D.6-9. Too foggy to observe the morning to permit a bombardment on the memorial of the enemy D.6 retrenchment. In the afternoon 6.4 Corps Heavy Artillery, 14 Div Artillery & French 8 inch Howitzers fired on trenches. The shooting was good, especially that of the French. Three direct hits on the work and 10 yards of wire blown up and then a few informing rounds severely damaged. Had all been in retaliation of hostile H.E. at Amiens, or the right, the Division. There was considerable return to a similar bombardment by ours. One or two bombs in our F— ibernail? bombard post in BEAM? Name was our best wounded. RLH	
"	April 17th Monday		The enemy attempts to return the damage of our wire. He intended caught by Lewis-gun fire & fallen to hospital. Their salvos were not at iclea— as enemy to reply to... later fire on by our troops. The hour to proceed evening as usual manner for German attempts at ballons, by which on aeroplane thought to have been driven came. Gun has been removed to Verdun. RLH	
"	April 18 Tuesday		The sector (b. Fonday) trench-mortar & rifle fire on the large dull pound opposite D.18. The enemy retaliated with trench mortars of the same type. RLH	

Army Form C. 2118.

WAR DIARY
or
INTELLIGENCE SUMMARY.
(Erase heading not required.)

Instructions regarding War Diaries and Intelligence Summaries are contained in F.S. Regs., Part II. and the Staff Manual respectively. Title pages will be prepared in manuscript.

Place	Date	Hour	Summary of Events and Information	Remarks and references to Appendices
BLANGY	April 9	Tuesday	The Division was successful here in their main operation to-day, attacking at 5.30 a.m. Reports received a short time later greatly encouraging. Divisry. H.Qrs. left BLANGY unofficially left for our present HQrs. at BLANGY unfortunately wounded 2nd Lt Mackay & 2 men of 52nd Canad. Inf. Bn. Ran for medical help at BLANGY OTTERPOOLS finding Lt. R. Colonel Hopkins left the Bearer Party behind as looked after RAMC. Units were under the [illegible] as Royal trained men at the present time — preservation of horses being kept up in the present situation appears to give satisfaction to enemy. H.Q.s was considered [illegible] to the waiting. Arrangements to receive wounded from a battery at [illegible] as the situation 145 ammunition from Batteries moved into ARRAS 10 & 11 will elsewhere in CORNERY. not to take animals any nearer to ARRAS. RCH	
ARRAS	10th	Wednesday	Some improvement to-day in weather, but we have A.B. been very frequent CCB from a divisions hospital, in comparing OCS. Coming [illegible] to ask [illegible] Div. has been found in St Saveurs Rue de [illegible] two entry to valley [illegible] filling up platoons in front. Coal [illegible] from Rue 13/16 RCH	

WAR DIARY
or
INTELLIGENCE SUMMARY.
(Erase heading not required.)

Army Form C. 2118.

Place	Date	Hour	Summary of Events and Information	Remarks and references to Appendices
ARRAS	April 18th		Continuing to improve our quarters by temporary scaffolding &c. &c. As a relief was hoped for tonight. But as our night gun fell yesterday only a hundred rounds allotted us today, ammunition was hurried back to gun to RLH	
"	April 19th Thursday		On the march the enemy shelled ST SAUVEUR near by the time you return start. The RD infantry Bll's Hd Quarters &c & on Rue de Douai. Shelling of Arras Batteries from HN on ARRAS railway opened fire probably on retaliation on our batteries. Luneteer Sgt. S.F. Sanborne was wounded. There was nothing seen on HD which had removed RLH	
"	April 21st		About an attempted bombardment on the enemy of heavy shells for suburban especially Germans came down on ARRAS and several houses by Two on the Crinchon Road. A Belgian who was under suspicion knocked. Remain nothing on ARRAS could be located. RLH	
"	April 23rd Sunday		Very busy on enemy much to our employment to recently RLH	
"	April 24th Sunday		Eastersday, Fine bright weather. Enemy exceptionally quiet & take no notice of patrols to snipe which they generally oblige. No heavy fire, a few rifle. RLH	

Instructions regarding War Diaries and Intelligence Summaries are contained in F. S. Regs., Part II. and the Staff Manual respectively. Title Pages will be prepared in manuscript.

WAR DIARY
or
INTELLIGENCE SUMMARY
(Erase heading not required.)

Army Form C. 2118

Place	Date	Hour	Summary of Events and Information	Remarks and references to Appendices
ARRAS	April 23rd	[illegible]	but a Communion Service for members of this Battalion has been arranged. The battalion runners take part in a relay-race organised by the officers [illegible] of 3rd Army. Communication by flash-signals is [illegible] between some house in ARRAS and TILLOY on the ARRAS-CAMBRAI Road. RLH	
BLANGY	April 24th	Morning	The number of German [illegible] [illegible] makes movement [illegible] difficult. The following [illegible] has been published by Brigadier General Lord BINNING in handing over command of the 41st Inf. Brigade to Brig. Gen. SKINNER. "The late Brigadier in saying good bye to the Brigade wishes to thank all ranks for the way in which they have worked during his command. He will always feel proud to have had the honour to command such a Brigade even for so short a time. His thoughts will ever be with it & his best wishes for all who accompany it." We relieved the 7th KRRC in the evening. The [illegible] ([illegible]) [illegible] and 8th R[ifle Brigade] on our left & right. RLH	
"	April 25th	Morning	At 3.45 a.m. at stand-to the enemy opened suddenly a heavy concentrated bombardment with big trench mortars of the 'rum-jar' type on the front line BLANGY especially on the BOILER HOUSE ARCADE. The first of these buildings was destroyed and the second damaged. RLH	

1875 Wt. W593/826 1,000,000 4/15 J.B.C. & A. A.D.S.S./Forms/C. 2118.

WAR DIARY
or
INTELLIGENCE SUMMARY
(Erase heading not required.)

Army Form C. 2118

Place	Date	Hour	Summary of Events and Information	Remarks and references to Appendices
BLANGY	April 24th Tuesday	10 a.m.	No news was wanted or received on the others. Both the Stokes the 18 pdrs. Trench howitzers etc. the 18 prdr. fired a few rounds, but no real harm had been given to the batteries by L. [illegible]. The most serious effort came from the [illegible] howitzers who fired 4 six inch rounds. The other BLANGY [illegible] bombardment changed its front known there up to the westward. [illegible] 5435 CUL [illegible] small arms [illegible] live ammunition [illegible] & [illegible] making it quite uneasy. They did not [illegible] now the wireless stations & [illegible] began to [illegible] brew [illegible] which [illegible] kept lying in the [illegible] long up to [illegible] R.L.H.	
	April 25th Wednesday		A party [illegible] to [illegible] field was dispatched to deliver the [illegible] in BLANGY at [illegible] [illegible] being very [illegible] during the day; a few [illegible] small HE shells were sent over at intervals along the [illegible] station Rd. By night there had been some reply. HQ Pm [illegible] D.L.H	
"	April 26th Thursday		Enemy snipers rather more active, 4 men sniped at SCARPE Grove, the [illegible] to the bridge [illegible] our men now engaged by the enemy. The afternoon rather [illegible] heavy bombardment by the 5th Division on our left	

WAR DIARY or INTELLIGENCE SUMMARY

Army Form C. 2118

(Erase heading not required.)

Place	Date	Hour	Summary of Events and Information	Remarks and references to Appendices
BLANGY station	April 27	Thursday	...the SUFFTS by Lens - Number 1 H.E. shrapnel Rifle fire & green Very lights at night, & forward O.P. and frequency by spots T.B.'s in the intervals. Large Huns were observed by aerial observers working on old trench near opposite D.H. The large gun reported at ... Good work is being done in the new front line in BLANGY. Old ruins of AROYDE MILL & HUT are being removed. The remains of the trench Place being built more roughly. But the drainage may the field being ... The enemy we evidently don't know my whereabouts. He has much believes in BLANGY where damage was done to both the known buildings by his plans. A great part of his bombing munition must be large quantities seemed of no service by being known under bombing line.	
"	April 28	Friday	Enemy used to extreme of rain was kept heaviest in BLANGY. My ... over came over & were heard to execute by saving ... by savings Hills Bank's my firstly ... My HQ sphere T.B. is every seen to be seen my... a building every to Anex. N.1 was ...	
"	April 29		Not much to report H.E. shells were burst on the WHITE CHATEAU slope few to ... and other ...	

WAR DIARY
INTELLIGENCE SUMMARY
(Erase heading not required.)

Army Form C. 2118.

Place	Date	Hour	Summary of Events and Information	Remarks and references to Appendices
BETHUNE	April 29th		the Hows went to F10. The trenches were more dry as it has not been raining. Germans bombarded Cuinchy and front line trenches right forward of our men to Nout Brewed up early with 9 am attack. Lord of the captain or men at Souchez. Early in the night a searchlight was required opposite I.0.3.7/80. Battn in the trenches as before. R.L.H.	
"	April 30th Sunday		Very little movement or snipers or enemy lines. Constant enemy shelling. The whole of our front line in BETHUNE and vicinity a heavy bombardment took place. Our artillery will active up to 9 when our to Munro hus cut noted by on continuous fine, such the whole chateau the Trench and the Farthern. The Battalion is relieved by the 7th K.R.R. and goes back to new rest billets in Quadu WANQUETIN. R.L.H.	

J. Beveh. Call.
for O.C. 5th R.R.C.

WAR DIARY
or
INTELLIGENCE SUMMARY

Army Form C. 2118

8/15 R.R — Vol 8

Place	Date	Hour	Summary of Events and Information	Remarks and references to Appendices
WANQUETIN	May 1st Monday		Weather very hot and sultry. All the Companies billeted in large unventilated rooms. A good parade ground and rifle-range are at our disposal close to the outskirts of SIMENCOURT. R.L.H.	
"	May 2nd		Reveille at 6 a.m. Work arranged to settle in details so to minimize for each Company the very little to do. Parade ground never the less kept busy. The turn up of reinforcements are being used to complete establishments of Companies. Reported to Brigade late. Wondered what would a Battalion Reserve of 32 or more for R.L.H.	
"	May 3rd Wednesday		A football and shooting competition by every Company. Indents received that the 1st Inf Brigade is to be attached to the XVII Corps to be employed on work connected with machine etc. R.L.H.	
"	May 4 Thursday		The Battalion moves to HABARCQ, a small village 2 miles N.W. of WANQUETIN. Two Coys (A and B) in farms and two in huts. We then very shortly go to N.R.W. R.A. File few places in W. & N. of POETIN, have already been taken up to the line. Weather hot wither. Future movements uncertain, another move is probable in a few days. R.L.H.	
HABARCQ	May 5 Friday			

WAR DIARY
or
INTELLIGENCE SUMMARY
(Erase heading not required.)

Army Form C. 2118

Place	Date	Hour	Summary of Events and Information	Remarks and references to Appendices
H.Q. Bn. & Neuve St Eloi	May 9	Monday	Battalion arrived at HINT ST ELOI at 12 noon on its way to the new trenches. We are being used for in under shelter of the woods & take message to Companies & relieve the line by two Coys in CAVE near RITZ, in NEUVILLE ST VAAST & Br.D line in CROSS Street & FERRIER Street respectively, rather nearer to the front line. The front & supports were held by 2 a.m.— Each Coy finds 3 men on slip 6 & each of 1 hr. During this they were again bombarded. The men stuck it in number of small hostile employed in carrying away hostile posts in sandbags. Some of the money bombarder for whom we used our English form French till about 9 P.M. Two men were put up between the lines. (?)	
139 Route Road	May 9	Tuesday	The Bn. HQ arrived on Bethune Road last night and the Coys arrived in their new positions where they immediately took over the evening fatigues from the Lincoln Regt. After the war was A large mine was sprung near the left of our new front. One German jumped to our trench and was captured by "D" Coy. He belonged to the Guards. And was on outpost in the crater.	

1875 Wt W593/826 1,000,000 4/15 J.B.C. & A. A.D.S.S./Forms/C. 2118.

WAR DIARY
or
INTELLIGENCE SUMMARY

Army Form C. 2118

Place	Date	Hour	Summary of Events and Information	Remarks and references to Appendices
HABARCQ	May 1st Saturday		The whole Brigade is busy carrying the Guns, Brigade HQ having moved to AGNEZ lez DUISANS. The 2 GO Divisional Guns Batteries are now formed. Italy. The officer deputed to the GO Division is moving in the line. 6 telegram has been received from the Division asking in the C.M.D.R. to draw rewards military rank to 10716 Cpl. G. Pollen, SAYSELL, 6123 LCpl S. LANG, y 10224 Sgt. Gr. E. MASON, Sgt B/H Actn R.R. and Mess, were quite doing/Corps a Regr. Jorgens't interpretation to received. "No orders reach the Brigade until the 2 o clock to 7 H Division y XVI Corps to Army was announced aerial messay.	RHA RHA
"	May 2 Sunday		An exceedingly Hot After noon after Hunt St Lug. HQ 7th 2nd Bde & Heavy the Battalion wet to attacks for workk. They then walk to Bath He F/V to G Leicester Reg. the HQ division to the w. eats- moving night. HQ now on the BETHUNE Rd, a well ahead from NEUVILLE St VAAST y mile from MONT ST ELOI. Two officers the country between with the trenches & telephones. Verqut & Alborecht bryffe.	

WAR DIARY
or
INTELLIGENCE SUMMARY

(Erase heading not required.)

Army Form C. 2118

Instructions regarding War Diaries and Intelligence Summaries are contained in F.S. Regs., Part II. and the Staff Manual respectively. Title Pages will be prepared in manuscript.

Place	Date	Hour	Summary of Events and Information	Remarks and references to Appendices
Bethune Road	15 May Saturday		It seems Jerries had all lost his light but was fine today, and the Turkies all ready by again. This evening received high explosive shrapnel shells were put over Bn. HQrs without going any damage. The 8 hour innings was shifts or mining fatigue as going on as usual. JNW	
Bethune Road & Bn HQ	16 May Sunday		'B' Company were shelled this morning. A stone & Stokes Mortar bombs were exploded by the Coy Headquarters which knocked in the entrance but came to no casualties. Pure men were slightly wounded in other parts of the trench. High explosive shrapnel was again put over Bn. HQrs this evening with no result. Weather fine. JNW	
"	17 May Friday		Mining fatigues as usual. In the evening 4 of 'A' Coy's sergeants. Stories made prisoners a man who is supposed to have been a spy. He was dressed in Dragoons uniform without putties or rifle and asked questions as to dispositions of troops, casualties etc. He was taken to 75th Bde HQ. Today a 4.2" Howitzer shell explosive exploded in the doorway of 'B' Coy HQr Dugout. The Dugout was knocked in, causing 10 casualties. JNW	

Army Form C. 2118

WAR DIARY
or
INTELLIGENCE SUMMARY
(Erase heading not required.)

Instructions regarding War Diaries and Intelligence Summaries are contained in F.S. Regs., Part II. and the Staff Manual respectively. Title Pages will be prepared in manuscript.

Place	Date	Hour	Summary of Events and Information	Remarks and references to Appendices
Bethune R.D	May 13 Saturday		Nothing of any importance happened — A shower ~ 3rd runner was put up to our B/F front. The Germans made two attempts to the westwards but our troops still hold the near E/P of the Crater. AFW	
"	May 14 Sunday		Another attempt to be another attempt to get the crater this morning began failed. A and B Coys are now working for pistol hand to the trench. relief our men from the French today. An officer M Saunders joined to Bedfn today. He was wounded at 1005 for the 4th Battn. AFW	
"	~~May 15~~ May 16 Tuesday		A very fine day. "A" Coy HQ were shelled with 6" howitzer shells this morning. In the afternoon LA TARGETTE was shelled. A Fokker brought down and one of our aeroplanes this afternoon just behind LA TARGETTE. The 7th R.B. took over from us this evening and the Battn took a long walk of about 15 miles to CHERERS. The Coys arrived about 5 am. AFW	

Place	Date	Hour	Summary of Events and Information	Remarks and references to Appendices
CHELERS	May 19th		Two new officers joined the Battn. viz. Capt Russell from the 5th Battn. and Lt Clairmont who was wounded with the 2nd Battn. Both posted to "A" Coy. CHELERS is the best village we have yet seen. The H.Q. is in an old Chateau with a garden and grounds. The Coys are in the usual barns etc. The Coys are doing the usual peacetime work i.e. morning parade before breakfast, 4 Parades between breakfast and lunch and nothing in the afternoon	
CHELERS	May 20th Thursday		The Company's carried on with the ordinary routine. In the evening the inter-platoon football competition was continued.	
CHELERS	May 21st Friday		B and C Coys went for a route march from 6-9 a.m. to avoid the hottest part of the day. Today being the anniversary of the Battalion's arrival in FRANCE & the original officers who are still with us las Dinner together at headqrs. Mess. Major Crum rest our from his Shipping School for the occasion. The Colonel unfortunately was still in hospital. After Dinner the Officers went round and joined in a Sing Song & were by the Sergeants to commemorate the occasion	

WAR DIARY
or
INTELLIGENCE SUMMARY

Army Form C. 2118.

Place	Date	Hour	Summary of Events and Information	Remarks and references to Appendices
CHELERS	May 27th Saturday		The Brigadier inspected the Battalion on the football ground this morning, after which he visited the incinerators etc & finally going carefully to the matter of Parade States in the Orderly Room. He then went all Headquarters and rode back to the Brigade afterwards. Some were piss in the football league were played off in the evening. CRW	
CHELERS	May 28th Sunday		No parades today except our Church Parades. Some more football was played. In the evening the A.S.C. billeted in a neighbouring village held a boxing show, at which some of our men performed. The best performer in the A.S.C. was defeated by Pte Stephens of this Batt. CRW	
MONT ST. ELOI	May 29th Monday		At 11.15 pm last night the Batt. received orders to move all over to SAVY where fresh orders were received to push on to MONT ST ELOI to wait there in support owing to an attack by the Germans on the VIMY ridge. Leaving CHELERS at 2 am the Batt. arrived at MONT ST ELOI at 5.15 am the [illegible]	

WAR DIARY or INTELLIGENCE SUMMARY

Army Form C. 2118.

Place	Date	Hour	Summary of Events and Information	Remarks and references to Appendices
MONT ST ELOI	May 27 Monday		The march distance being a good 12 miles – The men were put in huts and all the Officers in one large hut. The Baltn was ordered to be ready to move at 20 minutes notice. The day was spent by all ranks chiefly in sleeping.	
MONT ST ELOI	May 30 Tuesday		The Battalion was still standing to do nothing was done except Rifle & kit inspection by Coys. Capt Gossen and Coy Officers visited the front line in the morning.	
MONT ST ELOI	May 31 Wednesday		Still standing to from 8.45 P.M. 11.30 P.M. The Baltn was ready to move DB all over, owing to an attack being made by our people to retake some trenches lost 2 days before, which was apparently captured from the Germans.	
MAROEUIL	May 28 Thursday		This afternoon the Baltn took over from the 7th K.R.R. Two Companies are billeted in MAROEUIL, one and a half Coy in ANZIN and One & the half in ROCLINCOURT. We sent out fatigues for the Tunnelling Coys R.E. are being carried on as the last tour of duty before going to CALAIS.	

WAR DIARY
or
INTELLIGENCE SUMMARY

(Erase heading not required.)

Army Form C. 2118

Place	Date	Hour	Summary of Events and Information	Remarks and references to Appendices
Maroeuil	26 May Friday		Mining fatigues. Fine warm weather. The Battalion is now attached to the 51st Highland Division in 17th Corps.	
"	27th Saturday		Fine warm weather. At MAROEUIL there are excellent baths for the troops — also Divl baths — a cinematograph — and Sgts Club — so that inspite of the long marches to and from the mines, people — the troops are very comfortable. The billets are good. In event of operations the Bn has to hold left sector of Corps line.	

WAR DIARY or INTELLIGENCE SUMMARY

Army Form C. 2118

Place	Date	Hour	Summary of Events and Information	Remarks and references to Appendices
MAROEUIL	MAY 28 Sunday		In the early morning the Germans set off a mine in the ROCLINCOURT sector close to where C Coy mining shift was working. A barrage was put up on both sides continuing for an hour. Captain Frewen in bed with fever and high temperature. We had no casualties.	MMPC
"	29 Monday		Weather continues warm and fine. Brig-Gen SKINNER goes round 17th Corps line with Capt RIXON. Captain Frewen in bed still.	MMPC
"	30 Tuesday		Colder wet morning. Turned out fine later on. Capt Miller R.A.M.C. returned to Bt. from England, where he had gone to be inoculated with Military Cross.	MMPC
"	31 Wednesday		Working parties as usual with L.M. & N. Subsectors. The B⁰ is attached to the 51st Highland Division, and works in the part of the line held by 5/12" Div. The 8th R.B. are working on our left.	MMPC
"	June 1 Thursday		Casualties so far in this sector 3 men in D Coy wounded. From 4·0 pm until midnight heavy bombardment by both sides on VIMY RIDGE.	MMPC
"	2 Friday			

J. Frewen - Captain
O.C. 8th Bn. Kings Royal Rifles

C O N F I D E N T I A L.

W A R D I A R Y

- of -

8th Battalion, KING'S ROYAL RIFLE CORPS.

From: 1st June, 1916.
  To: 30th   "   "

WAR DIARY
or
INTELLIGENCE SUMMARY

Army Form C. 2118

(Erase heading not required.)

Place	Date	Hour	Summary of Events and Information	Remarks and references to Appendices
MAROEUIL	June 2	Friday	The batt. when is relieved by the 7th Bn Rifle Brigade and marched back by Companies to billets in A.C.Q. Mar off the hostile one a Company in French huts.	
A.C.Q.	3	Saturday	The battalion had baths and change of clothing. Drafts inspected and inoculated.	
"	4	Sunday	Parade Service C.of.E. in all. The R.C.s behind HQ at 11.30 a.m. Captain Boston takes the parade. Captain Trevor goes to Commanding Officers Conference at Brigade HQ. Weather fine & warm.	
"	5	Monday	Commanding Officer inspects A.C & D Coys. A & C Coys in full marching order. D Coy in emergency marching order. B Coy have to find fatigue party of 100 to unload stores at R.E. station near ECOIVRES. C Coy find working party of 150 to do work on Reserve line of N. Sector for 5th Div.	

30 men R of field up D Coy

WAR DIARY or INTELLIGENCE SUMMARY

Army Form C. 2118

(Erase heading not required.)

Place	Date	Hour	Summary of Events and Information	Remarks and references to Appendices
ACO	June 6 Tuesday		2nd Lieut Cook is appointed B.S. Bombing Officer. Wire demonstration by a party of 1 officer and 12 O.R. from H.Q.I. 5/12 Div at 5.0 p.m. A Coy provide fatigue party of 3 offrs and 100 O.R. The remaining Offrs in Coys B Coy to wire an artillery org. Find an artillery org. Lecture by Medical Officer on Gas at 9.0 p.m. Wire fatigue of 3 offrs and 100 O.R. found by B Coy.	MWJCw MWJCw
"	7 Wednesday			
"	8 Thursday		Lieut Colonel H.C.R. GREEN to be a companion of the Distinguished Service Order. Lieut E.G. LOUDOUN-SHAND promoted temporary Captain. 2nd Lieut C.L. DOMVILE promoted temporary Lieut. 2nd Lieut P. CONNON promoted temporary Lieutenant. D Coy find wiring party of 3 offrs and 100 O.R. C Coy find carrying party of 10ff and 80 O.R. for carrying supplies and tools to FORT GEORGE in East Lines	MWJCw

WAR DIARY
INTELLIGENCE SUMMARY
(Erase heading not required.)

Army Form C. 2118.

Place	Date	Hour	Summary of Events and Information	Remarks and references to Appendices
NEUVILLE-St VAAST	June 9 Friday		8th Bn K.R.R.C. relieved 7th Bn K.R.R.C. in NEUVILLE-St VAAST and Companies in AUX RIETZ CAVE. D Coy and Coy leaves A.C.Q. at 10.15 p.m. Relief Complete at 12.30 Am. The Bgr is now attacked to the 152nd Bde. Commanded by Brig. General ROSS (of CROMARTY), this side of the Bde of 5-1st Highland Division relieving the front line from ROCLINCOURT to N.E of NEUVILLE St VAAST. The 8th R.B. are furnishing mining fatigues for 5-1st Div on Hill 9C on right, then St.O being at MAROEUIL.	
NEUVILLE-St VAAST	10 Saturday		Bakalian finding Cave working parties for 175th Coy R.E. 172nd Coy R.E. 182nd Coy R.E. and 1/8 Bn Royal Scots. Every available man on the work — mining. Capt FREWEN O.C. 8th Bn K.R.R.C. is also O.C NEUVILLE Defences and the H.Q. of O.C NEUVILLE Defences are called WINCHESTER HOUSE, — the Coole have for O.C defences in WINCHESTER — these have were selected by 152 Brigade.	

WAR DIARY
or
INTELLIGENCE SUMMARY.

Army Form C. 2118.

Place	Date	Hour	Summary of Events and Information	Remarks and references to Appendices
NEUVILLE – St. VAAST	June 11 Sunday		Wet – cold – day. Many Bangs round B.H.Q. at 3.0 p.m. – probably fire for artillery O.P. which is about 50 yds away – a cone shaped heap of ruins – very conspicuous and scarcely used at all. B, C, and D Coys take over accommodation vacated by 1/6 Argyle & Sutherland Highlanders who go to S. Surgin. The accommodation is most by dugouts See those about NEUVILLE – St. VAAST, for preferable to the AUX RIETZ Cave. A Coy remains in AUX RIETZ Cave which is much better than there is here room in the cave. Two enemy mines sent up in the evening –	↑ M.O.C.U. ↑ M.O.C.U.
"	12 Monday		Rain all day. one with an artillery barrage for a short time.	↑ A.D.C.U.
"	13th Tuesday		Still wet & cold. 3 German mines at night and a bit bombed shafts at 11.0 p.m. GENERAL ROSS was stopped by H.Q. party and sent in to report to room H.Q. Daily took him for a spy.	M.O.C.U.

1577 Wt. W10791/1773 500,000 1/15 D. D. & L.   A.D.S.S./Forms/C. 2118.

WAR DIARY
or
INTELLIGENCE SUMMARY.
(Erase heading not required.)

Army Form C. 2118.

Place	Date	Hour	Summary of Events and Information	Remarks and references to Appendices
NEUVILLE - St VAAST	June			
	14 Wednesday		Hot morning, fine afternoon. Lt Colonel Green D.S.O. has returned and came up to tea. About 5.30pm some large calibre shells near H.Q.	mh RCH
	15 Thursday		Hot day, rain. Enemy shell O.P. stand no. 10 with 4.2.s.	mh RCH
	16 Friday		Major Crump directing demonstration at A.C.Q. Two men in B.Cy. interfering with French Aerial Torpedoes when they had found. Cy.g. start - cause an explosion - both men seriously wounded and one man standing near wasteless. At 10.30pm one of our guns pass up successfully.	mh RCH
	17 Saturday		Fine showery day. B. suffered to be relieved by 7th Syph MRC. and then advance parties arrive - relief cancelled at 8.0pm.	
	18 Sunday		Air fight about midday near Bn H.Q. one of our aeroplanes brought down in our lines. Such a day.	

Army Form C. 2118.

WAR DIARY
or
INTELLIGENCE SUMMARY.
(Erase heading not required.)

Instructions regarding War Diaries and Intelligence Summaries are contained in F. S. Regs., Part II. and the Staff Manual respectively. Title pages will be prepared in manuscript.

Place	Date	Hour	Summary of Events and Information	Remarks and references to Appendices
NEUVILLE-ST-VAAST	June 19 Monday		Lt Colonel NEWNHAM Commanded composite battalion of 19th LANCERS, 6th JACOBS HORSE, 36th INDIAN CAVALRY — with his adjutant and six other officers come up to take over. They have transport at Bde. Hd. Q. and Coy Hd. Q. 2/6 Rifles arranged for. 3 Squadrons of Indian Cavalry thus relieve 4 Coys of Infantry — 600 men. Relief 750. The relief goes off quite smoothly, and the Bt Bn K.R.R.C. marches back to A.C.Q. billets. Casualties during this tour 2 killed, 11 wounded, 4 suffering from fumes gas troops. The Br. has baths in the afternoon.	MWCK
ACQ	20 Tuesday			MWCK
"	21 Wednesday		The Bn. takes over accommodation from 1/4th R. Warwick Regt. in DUISANS — marching by Coys at 10 minutes interval and arriving there at 4 o'p.m. The troops are billeted in huts — the Officers in the village.	MWCK

Place	Date	Hour	Summary of Events and Information	Remarks and references to Appendices
DUISANS	June 22 Thursday		Very fine warm day. General disposal of O.C Coys. Lt C.E. Scott appointed Bt. Lewis Gun Officer. 2nd Lt P.A. Cooke has already been appointed Bt. Bombing Officer.	MWK
"	23 Friday		"A" Company inspected in full marching order, everything in route march asking as possible with colours. Fine warm day.	MWK
"	24 Saturday		"B" Company inspected by the Commanding Officer in full marching order and go for small route march in the morning. Heavy showers throughout the day.	MWK
"	25 Sunday		Fine day. Church parade at 10.0 am taken by 5th Division Chaplain, with 14th Divisional Band present.	MWK
"	26 Monday		Commanding Officer, Adjutant and 2nd Lt C.o's go to demonstration of Co-Operation between Infantry and aeroplanes at Warlus, and Divisional arrangement C&D Coys go to route march in the morning.	MWK

Army Form C. 2118

WAR DIARY
or
INTELLIGENCE SUMMARY
(Erase heading not required.)

Place	Date	Hour	Summary of Events and Information	Remarks and references to Appendices
DUISANS	June 27 Tuesday		The following copy of letter rec'd from 41st Inf/Bde was published in Battalion orders for 23/6/16. — I To 8th Bn K.R.R.C. The Brigadier is proud to be able to publish the following correspondence, which will be communicated to all ranks. (sd) E. Wilson Capt. for Brigade Major 41st Inf/Bde 22/6/16 — II — To VI Corps Now that the 41st Infantry Brigade is returning to its Division, I would like to express my thanks and appreciation of its services whilst with the XVII Corps. Officers and men have given their best work, and their energy and soldier-like qualities have been noticed and appreciated by all. I hope you will convey to the Officers and men of this Brigade, and to its Commander, our gratitude for the help which they have given us during the last few weeks. (sd) Charles Ferguson, Lieut General 19/6/16 Commanding XVII Corps.	MJCh

WAR DIARY
or
INTELLIGENCE SUMMARY.
(Erase heading not required.)

Army Form C. 2118.

Place	Date	Hour	Summary of Events and Information	Remarks and references to Appendices
DUISANS	June 27 Tuesday	continued	III. To 14th Division. The Corps Commander has received the attached and forwards it with very great pleasure. He wishes you to inform the 41st Inf. Bde. how pleased he is to have received such a good report. 20/6/16. (sd) J Loch. B.G. G.S. VI Corps. IV. To 41st Infantry Brigade. The G.O.C. is happy to be able to forward the above report. He hopes you will convey his congratulations to your Commander. 20/6/16. (sd) G.D. Bruce, Lt. Col. General Staff 14th Light Division. V. 2 Sector Trenches Right b trenches 112-13-14-15-16 Athens. The battalion relieves the 7th Bn. K.R. Rifles in No. 2 Sector Trenches at ROCLINCOURT. C Company on the right b trenches 112-13-14-15-16. D Coy in the centre in trenches 116-17-18-19 & 20. A Coy on the left in trs. 121-125. B Coy in Battalion reserve in ROCLINCOURT. One platoon detached C Coy in G. work. McMSr	

WAR DIARY
or
INTELLIGENCE SUMMARY.
(Erase heading not required.)

Army Form C. 2118.

Place	Date	Hour	Summary of Events and Information	Remarks and references to Appendices
ROCLINCOURT K2 d/Picton	June 28	Wednesday	The 8th Rifle Brigade are on our right and the 1/4 GORDONS are on our left. The Tunnelling Coy have reported at some S1.a'3ia about the junction 113 & 1114, but they say it is with us so far as we know. The tunnels about the junction 113 & 1114 have been taken and the up to another midnight — precautions have been taken and the heat has been cleared. Some of the right & left of the place is there not have been cleared. Some right & left of the place where the Tunnellers say the mine with 50 up. Pieces of sand bags, wreck &c have been among it. There is a disused trench in front of our line hastily filled with wire; but the wire along our front is not good. Forty fired day. Some rain. S1.a'3.D.W. Shaffer morning & afternoon.	
"	29th	Thursday 4-30 am to 5-30 am	enemy shelled the left Coy A. Coy heavily with Shrapnel and 4.2 cm gun, one man killed two wounded. Bombarded by an heavy artillery fire in the afternoon. About 5.0 p.m. Enemy replied by shelling L. work and Thorgdad Avenue	

WAR DIARY
or
INTELLIGENCE SUMMARY

Army Form C. 2118

Place	Date	Hour	Summary of Events and Information	Remarks and references to Appendices
ROCLINCOURT	June 30		The enemy artillery was all our Communication trenches throughout the R. O. Office held to the trenches at 11 a.m. and 1.30 p.m. Our organised shells by our artillery in morning & afternoon. 5" Du put over smoke cloud 4.2 B.O.R. we received "Machine Gun Cy have one smoke cloud. 4.2 B.O.R. we received Pour CO Operated throughout the night. organised 5. M., Trenches & Lewis Guns Cos operated throughout the night.	
"	July 1 Saturday			

M Green Lieut-Colonel
Commanding 8th (S) 4th K.R.R.C.

CONFIDENTIAL.

WAR DIARY

- of -

8th Bn., KING'S ROYAL RIFLE CORPS.

From: 1st July, 1916.
To: 31st " 1916.

Volume 12.

Army Form C. 2118.

WAR DIARY
or
INTELLIGENCE SUMMARY.
(Erase heading not required.)

Place	Date	Hour	Summary of Events and Information	Remarks and references to Appendices
ROCLINCOURT	July 1 Saturday		For day, fairly quiet until 10-50 p.m. when the enemy exploded a mine under trenches No 113 and 114, K2 sector, and at the same time opened a heavy artillery fire with 5.9, 4.2, pros and 77 mm trench mortars, rifle bombs, etc. on the front and communication trenches. The enemy came out of his trenches, and also a party came close to our trench on the N side, at the same time another party of enemy entered trench No 115 - and bombed two dugouts, which were empty. This party was turned out by trench bombs. A party of bombers under 2nd Lieut COOKE was sent out to the N side of the crater and at the same time CAPTAIN RIXON took another party to the W side and turned out the enemy. 2nd Lieut COOKE then worked his way round the far lip and was reinforced by another party of bombers, and held the far lip. Captain RIXON then put up a Lewis gun, under 2nd Lieut. C.F. SCOTT to assist 2nd Lt COOKE. working parties were then organized to open communication with the crater and a breastwork was	Appx N[?]

Army Form C. 2118.

WAR DIARY
or
INTELLIGENCE SUMMARY.
(Erase heading not required.)

Instructions regarding War Diaries and Intelligence Summaries are contained in F. S. Regs., Part II. and the Staff Manual respectively. Title pages will be prepared in manuscript.

Place	Date	Hour	Summary of Events and Information	Remarks and references to Appendices
ROCLINCOURT	July 1 Saturday	cont'd	had made the position possible to hold. Much credit is due to the prompt way reinforcements were brought up with shovels and sand bags. This work was also made heavy fire from machine guns and Trench mortars, under parties in charge of 2nd Lieut F.G. SCOTT, 2nd Lt. R.C. HARDY, and 2nd Lieut M.T. SAMPSON. All the officers, N.C.O's and men worked extremely well and with great coolness. The above description is taken from the memorandum on the subject of the crater raid to H.Q. 4th and 2nd Bde by Lt. Col. GREEN and it continues as follows —— I consider that great credit is due to Captain RIXON who was in the front line trenches at the time of the explosion, for his prompt action in immediately organising a counter attack under very difficult circumstances and	
"	2 Sunday			

Army Form C. 2118.

WAR DIARY
or
INTELLIGENCE SUMMARY.
(Erase heading not required.)

Place	Date	Hour	Summary of Events and Information	Remarks and references to Appendices
ROCLINCOURT	July 2 Sunday	cont	to 2nd Lt COOKE and the Bombers for seizing and holding the far lip of the crater under a very heavy shell and machine gun fire. At 4.0 a.m the enemy shelled the new crater with a large trench mortar. Casualties were as follows :— 2nd Lieut. R.M. ROGERS reported missing. 2nd Lt ROGERS was in the Crater before 3.0 a.m and was then seen in BOSEY Trench going towards C. Company's H.Q.: he was seen after that, search parties were immediately organized but were unable to discover anything. At night the ground outside the trenches round the crater was thoroughly searched but nothing could be found.	

Army Form C. 2118

WAR DIARY
or
INTELLIGENCE SUMMARY
(Erase heading not required.)

Place	Date	Hour	Summary of Events and Information	Remarks and references to Appendices
ROCLINCOURT	July 2	Sunday	Casualties continued. 2nd Lieut. R.L. HARDY, bullet wound in right shoulder, serious. 2nd Lieut. M.T. SAMPSON wounded by hand mortar in head and back - not serious. 2nd Lieut. C.F. SCOTT slightly wounded in left back, remains at duty. Eight O.R. killed and 25 O.R. wounded. 8 O.R. missing. Sergeant Moore and Sergeant Richardson of C Company were both killed. The mine did not go up where the Tunnelling Company had fused it, would, consequently, one of our posts was blown up with it, it was also a far larger mine than had been expected, - 160 feet across - probably the largest mine ever blown up on the British front. The 8th Bn. Rifle Brigade and 7th Bn. K.R. Rifles assisted us by	MunMC

Place	Date	Hour	Summary of Events and Information	Remarks and references to Appendices
ROCLINCOURT	July 2 Sunday	cont	Rendered debris parties with shovels, picks and ghouls, wire etc. Two trickers Machine Guns under the Bn Machine Gun Company, were sent up immediately to the flanks of the crater. Two shifts of 60 men each came up at night from 7th Battalion as unable to do much work owing to continuous trench mortaring of the enemy. We have 3 killed and 8 wounded during this night of 2/3rd all working near the crater.	M⁄C
"	3 Monday		Quiet fine day. 1st Bt. K.R.R.C. relieves the 8th Bt K.R.R.C. which returns to Brigade reserve in St NICHOLAS. A Coy of the 7th Bt KRRC relieves C Coy of 8th Bt KRRC - early about 7-8pm in the crater sector on the night. Our C Coy is billeted in St NICHOLAS, D Coy and two Platoons of A Coy in THE U.S. Redoubt A.R.RAS. 1 Platoon of A in Rue des Auquettes - Wounded 2nd Lieut C.R ROMER.	
St NICHOLAS				

WAR DIARY or INTELLIGENCE SUMMARY

Army Form C. 2118

Place	Date	Hour	Summary of Events and Information	Remarks and references to Appendices
ST NICHOLAS	July 4 Tuesday		One platoon of "A" Coy. in OBSERVATORY holds 2nd Lt. C.H. WOOD. "B" Company remains in ROCLINCOURT as the Garrison of ROCLINCOURT, and Captain RUSSELL O.C. "B" Coy is Town Major. Kept mining shifts and working parties found by the Battalion. Bombers, Snipers and Lewis Gunners used for Carrying. etc.	
"	5 Wednesday		Enemy Aeroplane dropped 5 bombs near ST NICHOLAS at 10 a.m. Working parties as usual. Control Company is the mining caves of those reported missing including 2nd Lieut R.M. ROGERS is held at Bn.H.Q. at 10.30 a.m. Captain N.F. BARBER presided.	
"			Lieut S. CONROY & 2nd Lieut F.G. SCOTT members. The following Brigade letter No 2987/23 is published in Battalion orders — "The Brigadier desires to express his admiration at, and his gratitude for, the behaviour of all ranks of the Brigade on the occasion of the springing of a mine by the enemy under the trenches of the 8th Bn. K.R.R.C. last night. Especially does he appreciate the promptness and presence of mind displayed by the Officers of the 8KRRC.	

WAR DIARY
or
INTELLIGENCE SUMMARY
(Erase heading not required.)

Army Form C. 2118

Place	Date	Hour	Summary of Events and Information	Remarks and references to Appendices
M NICHOLAS	July 5th Wednesday	cont'd	were taken at once, and the skill with which the most suitable measures were taken at once, and the skill with which He is impressed, too, with the willingness, readiness, and alacrity with which all ranks have hastened to carry out their work, and he is especially pleased with the co-operation which existed between the various units, and the way in which mutual assistance was asked and given." The Brigadier considers that the events of last night are of hopeful augury for the future operations of the Brigade, and affords him every reason to feel proud of his command. (sd) H.S. ALTHAM Captain. for Brigade Major, 41st Inf. Bde	MMc

Army Form C. 2118.

WAR DIARY
or
INTELLIGENCE SUMMARY.
(Erase heading not required.)

Instructions regarding War Diaries and Intelligence Summaries are contained in F. S. Regs., Part II. and the Staff Manual respectively. Title pages will be prepared in manuscript.

Place	Date	Hour	Summary of Events and Information	Remarks and references to Appendices
ST NICHOLAS	July 6 Thursday		Wet day. Mining patrols and carrying parties in both sectors as usual. The following Officers and N.C.O.s were mentioned in despatches, in the London Gazette dated 16th June 1916. — Lieutenant Colonel H.C.R. GREEN. D.S.O. Major F.M. CRUM. Captain L. FREWEN Lieut Adjt CULLINAN " C.L. DOMVILLE 9/439 Sjt STONE, A. (Since killed in action) 9/3736 Q.M.S. (O.R.S) G POTIER. 8270 C.S.M. R. HUNTER. A, C & D Companies have baths during the day	
"	7 Friday		Very wet day. Court Martial held at Bn H.Q. Major CRUM President.	

WAR DIARY or INTELLIGENCE SUMMARY

Army Form C. 2118

(Erase heading not required.)

Place	Date	Hour	Summary of Events and Information	Remarks and references to Appendices
M^NICHOLS	July 8 Saturday		Fine warm day. Working parties as usual.	Maj J.C.H.
"	9 Sunday		Fine sunny day. 8th R.B. relieve 7th K.R. Rifles in K.2 Sector. ROCLINCOURT. Relief carried out largely in daylight — D Coy on the right with the new craters. B Coy in the centre, A Coy on the left. The 8th R.B. and C Coy back in ROCLINCOURT as Bn. Reserve. The 8th R.B. are on our right. In Sector, and the 1/6 Seaforths 51st Div. are on our left. 7th R.B. have one Company the Garrison of Maj J.C.H. opposite 116A.	
ROCLINCOURT	10 Monday		ROCLINCOURT. A German mine is expected to go up opposite 116A, this necessitates considerable clearance of front line trenches north and south of BOGEY Communication Trench — held by Red Caps.	
		10.30 am	Enemy shell US and BOGEY with whizzbangs and 4.2cm. Special retaliation asked for from artillery — this heard however as well as field guns. Too little from each battery fired over a period of 10 minutes — effect distinctly feeble.	Maj J.C.H.

Army Form C. 2118.

WAR DIARY
or
INTELLIGENCE SUMMARY.
(Erase heading not required.)

Instructions regarding War Diaries and Intelligence Summaries are contained in F. S. Regs., Part II. and the Staff Manual respectively. Title pages will be prepared in manuscript.

Place	Date	Hour	Summary of Events and Information	Remarks and references to Appendices
ROCLINCOURT K2 c.6.6	July 11 Tuesday		R.E. report that mine shaft in 116A sunk 5o of up a drift on slanes any day now. The Germans have not worked in it for 48 hrs. At 11-30 a.m. enemy flew a camouflet into our sap K10 opposite 116 trench. Very little damage to our gallery – no trench damage. Promiscuous shelling by the Germans throughout the day.	
	12 Wednesday		During the night the enemy fired a few rifle grenades and much french gunfire over the crater. He shelled every working party opposite crater as fired in bursts with stokes mortars and being fired several trench mortars. Aeroplanes apparently ours – passed over early in the night – at 12-30 a.m. enemy had 3 searchlights playing vigorously to the North, and was using anti-aircraft guns fo? to? on him.	
"	13 Thursday		During the night the enemy fired over two salvoes of shrapnel over ROCLINCOURT in the direction of enemy trench steadily on H trench – BOGEY Comm patrol K100k trench with 77 mm.	

1577 Wt.W10791/1773 500,000 1/15 D. D. & L. A.D.S.S./Forms/C. 2118.

Army Form C. 2118.

WAR DIARY
or
INTELLIGENCE SUMMARY.
(Erase heading not required.)

Instructions regarding War Diaries and Intelligence Summaries are contained in F.S. Regs., Part II. and the Staff Manual respectively. Title pages will be prepared in manuscript.

Place	Date	Hour	Summary of Events and Information	Remarks and references to Appendices
ROCLINCOURT K2 Sector	July 14 Friday		During the night A Coy's patrol was spotted owing to the bareness of the ground and in the hospital first which resulted in one of A Coy's parties being killed. Enemy unusually quiet during the day except for sniping. The German line opposite 113 Crater is now heavily in width — the mound of chalk is part of it has been increased at least a foot during the night. A party of 100 cyclists have been coming up each night to dig second line and spoil trench behind Crater in 113.	[sketch]
"	15 Saturday		During the night enemy sniping, rifle fire and artifice has increased noticeably. It seems probably him & new ahus and other somers that a German relief took place on the night of 13/14th — The snipers report new kind of peaked cap opposite us. Enemy shell spook trench and works lines steadily during the day. The Batt. is relieved by 7th & 8th R. Staffs — relief not complete until 5am — and marches made to BOISANE. [signature]

1577 Wt.W10791/1773 500,000 1/15 D.D.& L.   A.D.S.S./Forms/C. 2118.

WAR DIARY
or
INTELLIGENCE SUMMARY.

Army Form C. 2118.

Place	Date	Hour	Summary of Events and Information	Remarks and references to Appendices
DUISANS	July 16 Sunday		Hot day. Voluntary services in the evening at Polishers Club. Evening Officers joined the Bn from England yesterday. 2nd Lt F.E. HOTE, 2nd Lt F.J. BENDLE, 2nd Lieut R.H. GARRARD, 2nd Lieut E.F. PEACOCK.	
"	17 Monday		2nd Lieut. W.L. SANDERS, 2nd Lieut R.M. PERRY, 2nd Lieut R.C. MURRELL. A & S Coy go to Bathsal AGNEZ. Too wet for sports to be held in the evening.	
"	18 Tuesday		2nd Lieut N.E. LEE joined the Bn from the 6th Bn. Sports held in the evening.	
"	19 Wednesday		Fine sunny day. Sports began 11-30 am and continued until 7-0pm. The sports are being organised Captain FREWEN and Quartermaster.	
"	20 Thursday		Sports begin 10-0 am — the finals in the sunny weather. 14 Divisional Band plays from 2-30pm. MAJOR-GENERAL V. COUPER visits the sports in the afternoon, and had tea at B.H.Q.	

Army Form C. 2118.

WAR DIARY
or
INTELLIGENCE SUMMARY.
(Erase heading not required.)

Place	Date	Hour	Summary of Events and Information	Remarks and references to Appendices
DOISANS	July 20 Thursday		The Commanding Officer distributes the jumps at 7-0 p.m. Thus is attend by B in the evening. Five Compy. for Captain Parker's late Balloon Section.	WACU
"	21 Friday		Being Kit Inspection & Divisional Gas Officer instructs helmets of the B'n in the afternoon. Men divided into classes. Internal Transport competition. Captain Fraser's pony wins the military jumper prize. Moore - judge. Captain Fraser's pony wins the K2 Lewis trenches - Companies. The B'n relieves 7th B'n WRC in the K2 Lewis trenches - Companies march off at 8-30 p.m. At 7-30 p.m. a message arrived from the Division and also him to signal ordering Lt Colonel H.C.R. GREEN to report to 4th Army Head Quarters as soon as possible on special duty, - in all probability to take command of a Brigade. A Motor Car arrives from the Division shortly after 8-30 p.m. to take Colonel GREEN. Major FREWEN, who is in command of the Batt'n, Captain RIXON goes in command	M.C.U.

WAR DIARY
or
INTELLIGENCE SUMMARY.

Army Form C. 2118.

Place	Date	Hour	Summary of Events and Information	Remarks and references to Appendices
K2 Sector Trenches ROCLINCOURT			MAJOR FREWEN now in command of the Bn.	
	July 22 Saturday		The relief was carried out early last night. The wind is N.N.E. and the period of GAS ALERT is on. All troops in front and support line trenches wear their Libe helmets pinned to their shirt fastenings and waistcoat men have their helmets hanging down out of their Gas-proof Containers. At 10.30 am an enemy trench bomb on 12 S and 11 S in front here silenced by our field guns. Opposite our Left Company I wrote here "Silenced by our field guns. Opposite our Left Company the enemy has been very talkative – sings and whistles, – he has been effectively answered each time with Rifle Grenades.	M.J.C.R.
"	23 Sunday		The 60th Division are on our left 8th R.B. on our right. At 5.30 pm the 60th Div. have an artillery strafe, which drew considerable retaliation on the left of our line. Lieut. R.L. BOWEN rejoins the Bn. from hospital and is posted to B. Coy. About 9–9pm the staff on the 4.3rd Bde and the J section on our right when becomes intense. The enemy made a small raid here. Our men stand to and Liverpool Regt. who are digging the new support line in place of the cyclists, occupy the workers line. At 11.30pm troops stand down and carry on as usual.	M.J.C.R.

1577 Wt. W10791/1773 500,000 1/15 D. D. & L. A.D.S.S./Forms/C. 2118.

WAR DIARY
or
INTELLIGENCE SUMMARY.

Place	Date	Hour	Summary of Events and Information	Remarks and references to Appendices
ROCLINCOURT nr Beaton Trench	July 23	Sunday	Captain T.M. RIXON and 2nd Lt R.P.A. Cooke have been awarded Military Medals for their work at the crater when the enemy blew it up in 113 trench on July 1st. The following were awarded the Military Medal 4782 Sergeant. R. HUGHES, A/1349 Corporal G. HANNAS, 6707 L/Corpl J. BARNETT 16048 L/Cpl R. WHITEHOUSE, A/3526 Rfm. F. EDWARDS.	

WAR DIARY
or
INTELLIGENCE SUMMARY.

(Erase heading not required.)

Army Form C. 2118.

Place	Date	Hour	Summary of Events and Information	Remarks and references to Appendices
ROCLINCOURT July K2 Sector Trenches	24 Monday		At 10.0 am enemy began shelling ROCLINCOURT with 15m/5 bangs mostly near the cook house – probably going for the inevitable smoke. Between 3-20 pm and 4-30 pm an field guns – howitzers and trench mortars carried out an organised shoot on cook house in the enemy's trenches opposite what wandered shifting. The shorts was very successful – doing considerable damage to the enemy's trenches and works. The retaliation was inexpectedly small.	MW.Clk
"	25 Tuesday		At 9-0 am ROCLINCOURT was shelled with 4·2 cm's pretty heavily for half an hour. There were several direct hits on the cook house and half the chimneys of the B.Hq were shot off. The only one dixie was badly damaged. It has therefore been decided to move the cook house back to St NICHOLAS atomed, and have rations sent up cold by transport at night. The enemy got a direct hit with a whizzbang on No 5 Sniper's post in Left Cay's line and two of the Snipers were very badly wounded.	MW.Clk

WAR DIARY
or
INTELLIGENCE SUMMARY.
(Erase heading not required.)

Army Form C. 2118.

Instructions regarding War Diaries and Intelligence Summaries are contained in F. S. Regs., Part II. and the Staff Manual respectively. Title pages will be prepared in manuscript.

Place	Date	Hour	Summary of Events and Information	Remarks and references to Appendices
ROCLINCOURT Refector Trenches	July 26 Wednesday		About 9.0 am the enemy shelled ROCLINCOURT again with about 60 4.2 and our sixty pounders retaliated on THELUS VILLAGE. At 3.30pm ROCLINCOURT was again shelled and THELUS ineffectually shelled with sixty pounders. During the morning our field guns shelled the enemy rough crumps 125 - and Wednesday.	MurRll
"	27 Thursday		Patrols report the enemy very quiet at night. Between 8 and 9 am the enemy put over about 20 trans bombs towards trench 115 - most of which fell in front of our parapet. On the whole the enemy has been unusually quiet during this tour, and all efforts to draw him have been unsuccessful.	MurRll
"	28 Friday		At 10.35 am the enemy started firing a heavy trench mortar near the right company H.Q., our held guns and trench mortars retaliated and the enemy stopped, but BOGEY was flown in in several places.	MurRll

Army Form C. 2118.

WAR DIARY
or
INTELLIGENCE SUMMARY.
(Erase heading not required.)

Instructions regarding War Diaries and Intelligence Summaries are contained in F. S. Regs., Part II. and the Staff Manual respectively. Title pages will be prepared in manuscript.

Place	Date	Hour	Summary of Events and Information	Remarks and references to Appendices
ROULLECOURT K2 Posn Trenches	July 29	Saturday.	The Bn is relieved during the morning by the 1st Bt EAST YORKS. 6 & 7 Bn/Bn. The Companies begin to arrive about 10-30am - Very hot sunny day. Relief completed at 2-30pm. The Bn marches back to the SUCHERIE at LOUEZ remain here for the night.	
LOUEZ				
GRAND ROULLECOURT	30	Sunday	The Bn marches at 9-0am from LOUEZ to Starting point - to take its place in rear of the brigade marching to GRAND ROULLECOURT. Packs are carried on motor Lorries. 200/H LEE is left in charge of the Bn's packs. Very hot sunny day. The Bn is allotted an excellent place for lunch about 1-0pm on the way. Cookers have the dinners nearly cooked. The Coy's fell out about 4-30pm, about 25 men fell out, but the majority arrived in very soon after the 6th Bn. Bn. billeted here for the night. 4th Bde HQ and 8th R. B in the same village.	MyCall

1577 Wt. W10791/1773 500,000 1/15 D. D. & L. A.D.S.S./Forms/C. 2118.

Army Form C. 2118

WAR DIARY
or
INTELLIGENCE SUMMARY

(Erase heading not required.)

Instructions regarding War Diaries and Intelligence Summaries are contained in F. S. Regs., Part II. and the Staff Manual respectively. Title Pages will be prepared in manuscript.

Place	Date	Hour	Summary of Events and Information	Remarks and references to Appendices
BARLY near DOULLENS	July 31st Monday		The Bn. marches out of GRAND ROULLECOURT at 8.20 pm reaching Bde Starting point at 9.45 am. A hot day tour yesterday. Packs carried on motor lorries. The Bn. halt for dinner at 12.30 pm at LE SOUICHE and marches again at 2.0 pm. The Bn. arrived at BARLY, down in a deep valley, about 5.0 pm and is billeted there for the night. — 24 men fell out of the ranks mostly own to the heat, but all came in very shortly after the Bn.	

L. Dawson. Major

Comdg. 2/6th Kings (Royal Rifle Regt)

41st Brigade.
14th Division.

1/8th BATTALION

KING'S ROYAL RIFLE CORPS

AUGUST 1916

CONFIDENTIAL

WAR DIARY

- of -

8th (S) Bn., KING'S ROYAL RIFLE CORPS.

From: 1st August, 1916 - To: 31st August, 1916.

Volume XIII.

WAR DIARY
or
INTELLIGENCE SUMMARY

(Erase heading not required.)

Army Form C. 2118

Instructions regarding War Diaries and Intelligence Summaries are contained in F.S. Regs., Part II. and the Staff Manual respectively. Title Pages will be prepared in manuscript.

Place	Date	Hour	Summary of Events and Information	Remarks and references to Appendices
POMMIERS TRENCH	25th Aug. Friday		We arrived here between 6 am & 8 am, and stayed the whole day resting. A.M. Rhatt	
	26th Aug. Saturday		Casualties during operations on 24th afternoon later at 180. We were relieved in the evening by the 1st R. Innis & marched back to DERNANCOURT. A.M. Rhatt	
DERNAN-COURT	27th Aug. Sunday		Resting, refitting, weather bad. Brig. Gen. Green D.S.O. came over. A.M. Rhatt	
DERNAN-COURT	28th Aug. Monday		Nothing of importance. Usual routine. Capt. BARBER & Lt. MILLERY Lt. CULLINAN went down sick. 2 Lt. WOOD reported died of wounds received on 24th. A.M. Rhatt	d. Jacob Lyol B.G.T. 1/2 G 20 Dominy rt Col 1/2 G and Army
	29th Aug. Tuesday		Inspection of billets etc. nothing of importance. A.M. Rhatt	
	30th Aug. Wednesday		Received orders to left DERNANCOURT at Noon for rest area W. of AMIENS entrained at ALBERT & detrained about 3.30 pm. AIRAINES at 8.30 pm. from where we marched to HEUCOURT on arriving at Settling into billets. A.M. Rhatt	
HEUCOURT	31st Aug. Thursday		Settling into billets. A nice little village. Transport arrived in afternoon having started at the same time & coming through by road, had travelled by road. A.M. Rhatt	

Army Form C. 2118

WAR DIARY
or
INTELLIGENCE SUMMARY
(Erase heading not required.)

Instructions regarding War Diaries and Intelligence Summaries are contained in F. S. Regs., Part II. and the Staff Manual respectively. Title Pages will be prepared in manuscript.

Place	Date	Hour	Summary of Events and Information	Remarks and references to Appendices
POMMIERS TRENCH.	25th Aug Friday		We arrived here between 6 a.m. & 8 a.m. & stayed the whole day resting.	
"	26th Aug Saturday		Casualties during the action 6 & 24. approximated at 180. We were relieved in the evening by the 1st R.9nd & marched back to DERNANCOURT.	
DERNAN-COURT	27th Aug Sunday		Rest & refitting, weather bad. Brig. Genl. Green B.R.O. came over.	
"	28th Aug Monday		Nothing of note, the usual routine. Capt. BARRER & MILLER came. 9Lt. CULLINAN reported died of wounds received on 24th. WOOD	
"	29th Aug Tuesday		Inspection of billets etc. nothing of importance	
"	30th Aug Wednesday		Received orders left DERNANCOURT at noon for rest area W. of AMIENS. entrained at ALBERT & departed about 3.30 pm. arriving at AIRAINES at 8.30 pm. from where we marched to HEUCOURT.	
HEUCOURT	31st Aug Thursday		Settling into billets. A quiet, nice little place. Transport arrived in afternoon having started at the same time & coming through very bad weather by road.	

WAR DIARY or INTELLIGENCE SUMMARY

Place	Date	Hour	Summary of Events and Information	Remarks and references to Appendices
LONGUEVAL ALLEY	26th Aug. Monday cont'd		Our party made a post and took 2 prisoners. They maintained themselves in the enemy trench until withdrawn after dark. Our extreme Right bombing party progressed some way up an old trench and established a block. This also had to be withdrawn after dark. The #2 Bns. made good progress but the battns. on immediate left had $\frac{1}{2}$ temporarily to withdraw to their original line. The enemy put up an extremely effective 5.9" barrage for several hours during and after the attack. B & C Coys had to come up and reinforce the front line immediately after the attack on the line was very weak after the heavy casualties. This they did over the open with snap [?] very few casualties. We were relieved by the 7/K.R.R. during the night and went back to POMMIERS TRENCH. During the day 2Lts. HUNTINGDON, TODD-NAYLOR (killed) and 2Lts WOOD and F.C.SCOTT (wounded) were among the casualties.	

Capt. P.H.2Lt.

WAR DIARY or INTELLIGENCE SUMMARY

Place	Date	Hour	Summary of Events and Information	Remarks and references to Appendices
LONGUEVAL ALLEY	24th Aug. (Thursday)		HQrs. move up from QUARRY in morning & take over 8th RB. HQrs in LONGUEVAL ALLEY. At 4.50 pm. after 2 hrs. intensive bombardment A and D coys of 8 KRR. with the 12 brigade on our left, attack the enemy in and on the flanks of DELVILLE WOOD. Our work is to attack from HOP ALLEY, and part of BEER ALLEY which is badly "in the air" & enfiladed from the E. A. & D. Coy are accordingly in 2 waves, A on the left, D, on the Right. The preliminary bombardment has failed to cut the wire in front of A. and has not touched the enemy trench. Our Stokes guns detailed to obliterate the enemy trench on the left fail[to do so] and has one very good shooting at our own trench instead. The field gun barrage has been directed unfortunately behind the enemy trench all the time. Consequently, the enemy man their head very strongly and A. Coys attack cannot develop, its first wave falling back dead on the second. 2Lt. Todd-Naylor is killed. On the Right D. Coy. has been held up nearly as badly only about 6 R/R. and 2 sgts. reaching the enemy lines alive.	

WAR DIARY
or
INTELLIGENCE SUMMARY
(Erase heading not required.)

Army Form C. 2118

Place	Date	Hour	Summary of Events and Information	Remarks and references to Appendices
BONGBUFR.	21st Aug (cont.)		was then attempted. Coy's Casualties were, Capt. RUSSELL. B. Coy. CAPT. SHAND A Coy. CAPT. CONROY. C. Coy. and 2/Lt. MURREL.	An. Ph.2 Lt.
"	22nd Aug. Tuesday		Relieved by 51st Bn. S.L.I. and Coys to get at & from a Bn's Place. Relief completed about 2 am.	
QUARRY.			Bn went into support trenches in YORK trench. Bn H.Q is a shelter in & same trench. a 6 pm 18th letting took up its position 100 yds in rear of us. Concerning the place became unpleasant, a Bn H.Q mysed to QUARRY at N.W. of BERNAFAY WOOD	An. Ph.2 Lt.
QUARRY.	23rd Aug Wednesday		A & D Coys move up to HOP ALLEY (front line S. corner of DELVILLE WOOD) B. & C. Coys remain in support in and about YORK TRENCH 2/Lt Pearcle wounded reconnoitering front line. H.Qrs. remain for the night at QUARRY.	An. Ph.2 Lt.

WAR DIARY or INTELLIGENCE SUMMARY

Army Form C. 2118

Place	Date	Hour	Summary of Events and Information	Remarks and references to Appendices
	August 20th (Cont.)		The whole Bn. put a rest of night - some machine - and artillery - a desultory place. No C. track to the line, and a few snipers BONGUEVAL. A few rains of to this will be any approach. And C.H. 2 LT. Many patrols sent out update enemy front line troops held.	
BONGUEVAL	21st Monday		We were ordered to establish a post in the enemy's front line, this was to obviously futile from the start, but it was up to taken. Sorrowly; (recently after our last night's patrol, Zero was at 4.30 p.m. a barrage was put up along the line. In the event our Men & Lanzep. began to move on our line, & lights from our own Art. on our objective. In addition to Stokes mortars managed to put 15 shells into our own lines, killing 2 & wounding 6. The platoon which was "establishing a post" was kicked off by heavy rifle fire at 200x was emerged from a gap when to attack was to take place but of the first 8 men who emerged, 1 was killed, and 5 wounded. The futile attempt	

WAR DIARY
or
INTELLIGENCE SUMMARY

(Erase heading not required.)

Army Form C. 2118

Place	Date	Hour	Summary of Events and Information	Remarks and references to Appendices
POZIERS.	August 19th Saturday		A & D. Coys remain at POZIERES, also Bn. H.Q. Successful attack by 7th K.R.R.C. & 7th R.B. on ORCHARD TRENCH. B and C. Coys. came up for some hard work helping to carry up materials etc. Gn. Attilt	
"	20th Sunday		Major FREWEN and four Officers went at 4.30 am. to reconnoitre sector of DELVILLE WOOD and LONGUEVAL, held by 43rd Bde. as the coming to the Bn. relieving the 8th K.O.Y.L.I. in this sector. The relief was a good one & took 9 hours owing to heavy shelling. Casualties contiwary heavy. Lines of approach. Casualties were fortunately few. Bn. H.Q. is in a German dug. out is to middle of LONGUEVAL. One dug-out for all H.Q. Officers & orderlies & machine gun together.	

Army Form C. 2118

WAR DIARY
or
INTELLIGENCE SUMMARY

(Erase heading not required.)

Instructions regarding War Diaries and Intelligence Summaries are contained in F. S. Regs., Part II. and the Staff Manual respectively. Title Pages will be prepared in manuscript.

Place	Date	Hour	Summary of Events and Information	Remarks and references to Appendices
CARLTON TRENCH.	18th Aug. Friday.		Weather very bad making trenches very nasty. We were relieved at night by the 7th K.R.R. A & D Coys & H.Qrs. returning to POMMIERS TRENCH. B & C Coys occupying YORK TRENCH in reserve to the 7 K.R.R for their attack on ORCHARD TRENCH. B & C Coys under command of Lieut. RUSSELL. A.W.R.H.M.	

1875 Wt. W593/826 1,000,000 4/15 J.B.C. & A. A.D.S.S./Forms/C. 2118.

WAR DIARY
or
INTELLIGENCE SUMMARY
(Erase heading not required.)

Place	Date	Hour	Summary of Events and Information	Remarks and references to Appendices
Trenches CARLTON Trench N. of DELVILLE	August 16 Wednesday		The usual bombardment in the afternoon by our guns. Enemy working [parties] & [working] parties making communications and assembly trenches. About 8-0 p.m. the enemy shelled DELVILLE WOOD — and the valley behind Bn.H.Q. with tear shells & shrapnel. The gas from the shells became very bad from about 8-30 to 9-30 p.m. and it was necessary to put on tube helmets. Box respirators etc —	Mr Dale
"	17 Thursday		Bombardment from 1-0 a.m. 8 R.Br. relieved by 7 R.Br. 6-30 p.m. by our guns. 8 R.Br. tps R.C. Coys 8-F.B.'s. Shell fire not finished until 2-0 a.m. — returned to Pommiers Redoubt. Held began at 4-0 p.m. New Bn. in Savoy & Carlton trench as Bde reserve. Bn.H.Q. also returned to POMMIERS REDOUBT.	Mr Dale Mr W.C. 16
"	18 Friday		14th Division took part in attack on the enemy by the 4th Army. 4.1 2 6 F.Bde attack ORCHARD Trench WOOD LANE, the assaulting Battns are 7 K.R.R.C. and 7 R.B. 48 & 9 R.B. on our right attack German position in DELVILLE WOOD after [several] of its objective. B Coy of 8/66 [?] succeeded in entering and holding its objective. [?] came in for some very hard work after the attack, but were lucky regarding casualties.	Mr W.C. 16 Mr A.R. Lt.

WAR DIARY
or
INTELLIGENCE SUMMARY.
(Erase heading not required.)

Place	Date	Hour	Summary of Events and Information	Remarks and references to Appendices
Pommiers Redoubt	August 13 Sunday		Bt. moves forward into POMMIERS REDOUBT near FRICOURT, having marched from Dernancourt at 2.30 p.m. Arrived at 5.30 p.m. Attack we were to have made to be relieving a Bde of 5 or 2 of 17th Division. There was no accommodation being from Pom when we arrived.	Initialled
"	14 Monday		9th Bn. relieved 7th Bn. K.R.R.C. in front and support line trenches N.W. of DELVILLE WOOD. D Coy goes into front line, PEARS's and POTT.S's also one Platoon of A Coy, individual Lortol Taylor; another Platoon of A Coy is in support in DELVILLE WOOD an isolated trench. Rokes left behind in DELVILLE WOOD and retitioned Meto ad taken up. B & C Coy and 2 Platoons of A (Pratcoats and antinfeort) took in support trench, where BttHQ is. Relief beyond an track in Support in Savoy & Carlton trench. BERNANCOURT 8.30 am completed about 11 hours. Our Guns - Leanwieth - bombarded ORCHARD Trench, Wood Lane, and Switch trench from 3 - 6 pm 6.5 - 9 pm, a soft number of Foots of BttHQ. incessponerd. During the bombardment Germans seen to run old Orchard to Tea trench behind.	Initialled
"	15 Tuesday		Continues shelling of enemy lines being little retaliation - mostly on Piccadilly and Rear Posts. Enemy Infantry very quiet. We have taken over another 150 yards from L5 - B2 in DELVILLE WOOD. Rainy work by parties at night.	Initialled

WAR DIARY
or
INTELLIGENCE SUMMARY
(Erase heading not required.)

Place	Date	Hour	Summary of Events and Information	Remarks and references to Appendices
BERNANCOURT	August 10 Thursday		Lecture by Major FREWEN for all officers and N.C.O's in A Coy's billets at 2–3pm. Weather continues very hot.	
"	11 Friday		The Commanding Officer and four Coy officers visit trenches and POMMIERS REDOUBT. Companies exercise in the early morning and carry out night operations. Lieut Gen! HORN. C.B. in Corps Commander inspects the B'n at 11-o a.m.	
"	12 Saturday		The Commanding officer inspects billets at 11-o am	
"	13 Sunday		Very hot church day - The B'n moves forward to Pommiers redoubt. Brigadier General. H.R. GREEN D.S.O. comes to lunch	

WAR DIARY or INTELLIGENCE SUMMARY

Place	Date	Hour	Summary of Events and Information	Remarks and references to Appendices
AUTHEUX	August 6 Sunday		Transport leaves about 12-noon, under Lt BOURDILLON, Lieut TETLEY is acting Brigade Transport Officer. The Transport of the Bn. is proceeding by road to DERNANCOURT near ALBERT. Personnel of Batt. remains until tomorrow.	
"	7 Monday		Bt. marches to CANDAS for entraining - about 6-30pm. Train very late. Bt. has tea at CANDAS station - and entrains about 10-0pm	
DERNANCOURT	8 Tuesday		Bt. arrives at MERICOURT about 7.0am and detrains there, and is met by Lieut TETLEY and transport, - marches to DERNANCOURT - about 4 miles and is billeted here in very dusty crowded billets. Hammerwerfer	
"	9 Wednesday		5 officers go to 55th Div Ammunition Corps at disposal of O.C. Corps	

WAR DIARY
or
INTELLIGENCE SUMMARY

(Erase heading not required.)

Instructions regarding War Diaries and Intelligence Summaries are contained in F.S. Regs., Part II. and the Staff Manual respectively. Title Pages will be prepared in manuscript.

Place	Date	Hour	Summary of Events and Information	Remarks and references to Appendices
AUTHEUX	August 1 Tuesday		The Bn. marches about 8·a.m to AUTHEUX from BARLY a distance of about 6 miles, wearing packs. Very hot day. Two men fell out, one of whom fainted.	
"	2 Wednesday		Companies at the disposal of O.C. Companies for special Company training, with a view to operations.	
"	3 Thursday		Hot weather still continues. Coys practice wood fighting	
"	4 Friday		Major GENERAL V. COUPER comes over in the morning. Heat continues very hot.	
"	5 Saturday		Change in the weather. Cold morning. Lieut. T.L. BOURDILLON rejoins the Bn. having been have been wounded since Hooge 30th July, 1915. And is posted to "C" Company.	

CONFIDENTIAL.

WAR DIARY

-of-

8th Bn., KING'S ROYAL RIFLE CORPS.

From: 1st September, 1916.
To: 30th September, 1916.

Volume XIV.

Army Form C. 2118

Vol XIV

WAR DIARY
or
INTELLIGENCE SUMMARY

(Erase heading not required.)

Instructions regarding War Diaries and Intelligence Summaries are contained in F. S. Regs., Part II. and the Staff Manual respectively. Title Pages will be prepared in manuscript.

Place	Date	Hour	Summary of Events and Information	Remarks and references to Appendices
HEBUCOURT	Sept 1st Friday		Battalion paraded for inspection by Battalion P/Majors at 6-30 am. Details of officers present.	
"	2 Saturday		Bayonet fighting, shooting.	
"	3 Sunday		Resting	
"	4 Monday		Batt. parades under Battalion P/Major at 6-30 am. Bayonet fighting 9-11 am. Lecture by D/O Premier officer at 4-6 pm.	
"	5 Tuesday		Following Special order by G.O.C. 14th Light Division was published in the Battalion orders. "On completing our first tour of duty in the Battle of the Somme the G.O.C. wishes to express to all ranks his great appreciation of the discipline, hardihood and cheeriness shown by the Officers, N.C.O.'s and men of the 14th Light Division in the trenches. The Division was called on at short notice, and without any opportunity for general training, to take part in what will probably	

Army Form C. 2118

WAR DIARY
or
INTELLIGENCE SUMMARY

(Erase heading not required.)

Instructions regarding War Diaries and Intelligence Summaries are contained in F. S. Regs., Part II. and the Staff Manual respectively. Title Pages will be prepared in manuscript.

Place	Date	Hour	Summary of Events and Information	Remarks and references to Appendices
HEUCOURT	Sept 5 Tuesday		"In the decisive Battle of the War". The Division has carried out its task so as to earn the thanks of the Corps Commander. On all occasions when called upon to attack, the main objectives allotted to the Division have been secured, heavy casualties inflicted upon the enemy and in addition over 600 prisoners and 16 Machine Guns have been captured. To those who have fallen in the Battle a special tribute is due. The Division has to mourn the loss of many brave men and good comrades, at the same time it has the satisfaction of knowing that by its steadiness and soldierly qualities it has maintained all the advantages so far won that these brave men gave their lives. The recent exploits of the Division are to be carefully explained to all drafts	

WAR DIARY
or
INTELLIGENCE SUMMARY

Army Form C. 2118

Place	Date	Hour	Summary of Events and Information	Remarks and references to Appendices
HEUDICOURT	Sept 5 Tuesday		"So that they may know the high standard of the 14th Light Division had they up to. In all probability the Division will, after a period of rest from fighting, be called upon to take a further part in the Battle. When the call comes the G.O.C. is confident that the Division will be found ready to emulate and surpass its recent successes."	Sd/JCW
	6 Wednesday		Divisional Gas Officer inspected the helmets of the Battn. during the morning. He about him up programme cancelled.	Sd/JCW
	7 Thursday		Training.	
	8 Friday		Training and m/w operations. 4th 3rd Battn Sports. Battalion does fairly well, winning the Brigadier's prize - tug of war - Warning orders for moving head.	Sd/JCW

Army Form C. 2118

WAR DIARY
or
INTELLIGENCE SUMMARY

(Erase heading not required.)

Place	Date	Hour	Summary of Events and Information	Remarks and references to Appendices
FRICOURT	9 Saturday		Transport proceeds by road to DERNANCOURT, arriving about 3-0 pm	[initials]
"	10 Sunday		The Battalion leaves HEUCOURT by French motor transport, arriving at Dernancourt about 7-0 pm. Dusty from trip; roads - occupied the old billets in Dernancourt.	[initials]
"	11 Monday		Batt: leaves Dernancourt at 2-0 pm. In FRICOURT CAMP. Battalion bivouaced and under canvass.	[initials]
"	12 Tuesday		Batt: leaves FRICOURT CAMP at about 2-0 pm for POMMIERS REDOUBT, where Batt: has teas. Batt: moves up to DELVILLE WOOD about 8-0 pm and relieves 5th South Lancs. Relief completed about 10-0 pm. B. & C. Coys occupies [?] Rows [?]	[initials]

WAR DIARY
or
INTELLIGENCE SUMMARY

(Erase heading not required.)

Army Form C. 2118

Place	Date	Hour	Summary of Events and Information	Remarks and references to Appendices
DELVILLE WOOD	12	Tuesday	and trenches along the edge of DELVILLE WOOD. 8th R.B. in HOP ALLEY and he ched to the right. Two Coys of 6th K.O.Y.L.I. attached to 8th R.B. also in HOP ALLEY. 10th QUEEN'S West Surrey Regt W. Division on the left. Bn. H.Q. in LONGUEVAL ALLEY. S/8 C.G.S	Murdoch
"	13	Wednesday	Intermittent bombardment. Few casualties.	Murdoch
"	14	Thursday	Heavy bombardment by our artillery throughout day.	Murdoch
"	15	Friday	About 2-0am. Bn H.Q. was moved from Longueval Alley to a temporary shelter in GREEN STREET. This however took some considerable time owing to the number of troops using the communication trenches and paths in DELVILLE WOOD. GREEN St was a trench about 150 yds outside DELVILLE WOOD.	Murdoch

Army Form C. 2118

WAR DIARY
or
INTELLIGENCE SUMMARY

(Erase heading not required.)

Place	Date	Hour	Summary of Events and Information	Remarks and references to Appendices
GREEN St & SWITCH TRENCH	Sept 15	Sunday	The following account of the operations of the 9th Battalion Royal Rifle Corps on September 15th was written by Major L. Trevor, and put into H.Q. 41st Inf. Bde. front memorandum No F.B. 2 dated 22nd Sept. 1916. "The Objective was a portion of SWITCH TRENCH allotted to the Battalion, distant from our trenches some 1,200 yards. An intermediate trench, TEA SUPPORT, some 500 yds from our line, was the German advanced line, and would have to be accounted for in the advance in SWITCH TRENCH. The Battalion was drawn up for the attack on a front of two Companies, with two Companies in support constituting the second wave. The order was as follows:— B.Coy in NEW TRENCH, in front of BROWN STREET, with its	New O.O.N.

Army Form C. 2118

WAR DIARY
or
INTELLIGENCE SUMMARY
(Erase heading not required.)

Place	Date	Hour	Summary of Events and Information	Remarks and references to Appendices
GREEN St / SWITCH TRENCH	Sept 15 Friday		Our lapping COCOA LANE, and in touch with the 41st Division on its immediate left. C Coy in NEW TRENCH, on the right of B Coy, connecting up with the 8th Br. Rifle Brigade on its immediate right; A Coy in BROWN STREET, covering B Coy. D Coy " " " C Coy. Lewis Gun teams aptly disposed of by O.C. Companies. Battalion Bombing Squads as follows:— No 1 Squad attached to B Coy for the purpose of clearing COCOA LANE as the attack advanced, and for keeping touch with the 41st Division. No 2 Squad, attached to C Company for the purpose of keeping connection with the 8th Br. Rifle Brigade, and also protecting right flank on the right of SWITCH TRENCH. Nos 3 & 4 Squads. These were attached to A & D Coys respectively to be used for clearing up any part of the attack which might be held up, and were kept central during	

Army Form C. 2118

WAR DIARY
or
INTELLIGENCE SUMMARY
(Erase heading not required.)

Place	Date	Hour	Summary of Events and Information	Remarks and references to Appendices
GREEN St and SWITCH TRENCH			the attack until required. Zero hour was to be at 6-20am. By 5-30 am hot tea and rum had been issued to all the men. At 5-30 am a mina attack began, for the purpose of clearing HOT ALLEY and ALE ALLEY. 2 "Tanks" were used on this job to aid the attacking troops. As far as could be seen from my Battalion Head Quarters the enemy had evacuated the trenches. No fighting was observed, and only one round was heard to be fired from the "Tanks". At about 6-0 am our heavy artillery began a very heavy bombardment on TEA SUPPORT and SWITCH TRENCHES. The effect on SWITCH TRENCH was excellent, that on ~~the~~ TEA SUPPORT was not visible owing to that trench being in a hollow. At 5.0 am a 4·5- howitzer Battery of ours began a gas shell bombardment of my Battalion Headquarters and the surrounding country. Urgent messages	

WAR DIARY
or
INTELLIGENCE SUMMARY

(Erase heading not required.)

Army Form C. 2118

Place	Date	Hour	Summary of Events and Information	Remarks and references to Appendices
GREEN ST and SWITCH TRENCH	15 July [cont.]		Two orderlies had been asphyxiated, and the whole of Battalion Headquarters very sick from the gas. Fortunately they did not reach our troops in the front trenches). At 6.20 am the Companies got out of our trenches and formed up for the attack. The 7th Bn. K.R.R.C. at the same moment emerged from the edge of DELVILLE WOOD. Our barrage began at 6.20 am and the Companies advanced under cover of it. At a point about 150 yards from the start of the attack finale outposts of the enemy were met in shell holes; these were easily driven in or mopped up. Lieutenant DOMVILLE, commanding A Coy, was badly wounded by a bomb at this point. On reaching TEA SUPPORT considerable resistance was made, and the high line drifted over to assault the trench. Unfortunately we had some casualties here by the men going forward in to the barrage, but this was probably better	

WAR DIARY
or
INTELLIGENCE SUMMARY

Army Form C. 2118

Place	Date	Hour	Summary of Events and Information	Remarks and references to Appendices
GREEN St and SWITCH Trench.	15" Sept		than the effects of a machine gun, which was traversing the line, and fairly hot rifle fire. Judging by results afterwards, and the information of several reliable witnesses in the attack, fully 150 of the enemy were accounted for here, including two strong bombing posts, and the machine gun referred to. I, personally, saw the gun and team lying dead there as I went forward ten minutes later, and a considerable number of dead lying about. The M.O. who reached this trench late in the day for wounded cases, came upon trenches of the enemy dead, lying five and six deep in places. At about 6.30 am. the enemy awoke to the fact that we were attacked and put up a double "barrage". A heavy one on the front edge of DELVILLE WOOD, a second and lighter one on BROWN STREET. We had no difficulty in picking our way through the second one, and the	

Place	Date	Hour	Summary of Events and Information	Remarks and references to Appendices
PNITCH TRENCH	Sept 15 Friday		heavy one was fortunately behind us. The high wave continued on, which hill, from TEA SUPPORT, followed by the second wave at some 50 yards distance. After the first wave had passed a small party of the enemy which had hidden in a shell hole got up behind them and opened fire. One of our bombing squads behind them promptly rushed this party and exterminated in the second wave. No more resistance was offered until the crest of the hill was reached, there the enemy were scattered about in shell holes and offered some resistance, and our men here again caught in our barrage while counteracting this resistance. On reaching the crest, it was found that the greater part of the battalion was in the act of digging in on the rear edge of this crest, some 60 yards from	

WAR DIARY
or
INTELLIGENCE SUMMARY

(Erase heading not required.)

Army Form C. 2118

Place	Date	Hour	Summary of Events and Information	Remarks and references to Appendices
SWITCH TRENCH	Sept 15 Friday		SWITCH TRENCH. After reconnoitring and, with difficulty, discovering SWITCH TRENCH (so obliterated was it) I moved the Battalion forward and began consolidating the position. He soon got into touch with the 8/15th Rifle Brigade and he soon got into touch after that they had established touch. He informed me that they were in touch on their right. I was unable to get into touch with the GUARDS on their right. I was unable to get into touch on my left, as, although I discovered the C.O. of the battalion on my left, he informed me that his battalion had gone off into the Blue, and he could find no one. We, therefore, established a strong post, with our left flank drawn back, about 150 yards after ground to the left of our objective, in order to watch the valley South of FLERS, here taking up a Lewis Gun and two machine guns. We established a Lewis Gun at our trench.	M.O. Cox

WAR DIARY or INTELLIGENCE SUMMARY

Army Form C. 2118

Place	Date	Hour	Summary of Events and Information	Remarks and references to Appendices
SWITCH TRENCH	15 Sept Friday	7.15 am	We were fairly established and consolidated, but were much hampered by enemy snipers in from somewhere in front. A thin line of skirmishers put out a front very soon put an end to this, and judging by the amount of dead lying there, must have accounted for some 50 of the enemy in various shell holes, besides sending back a few prisoners. Hostile machine guns from opposite (Schwaben?) that part of SWITCH TRENCH occupied by the GUARDS Division) continued to give trouble and enfilade us for a further hour. In conclusion I should say that the "TANKS", except for the clearing up of HOP and ALE ALLEY were no good to us at all. Owing to the	

WAR DIARY
or
INTELLIGENCE SUMMARY

Army Form C. 2118

Place	Date	Hour	Summary of Events and Information	Remarks and references to Appendices
SWITCH TRENCH	15th Friday		"Barrage" seems trivial slow to allow the "tanks" to come up. I showed, personally, call them a hindrance. If there is an Casualties would have been less with a Quicker lifting "Barrage" as the difficulty of holding back troops keen for the assault is immense. No "tanks" crossed SWITCH TRENCH, to my knowledge, for fully 1½ hours after an assault. The "Barrage" was decidedly sketchy. I can positively state that the "Barrage" put up for us was an unpossibility to follow, owing, to the unevenly of the ground, almost some falling too short and some far too far. There was no line some falling too short and some far too far. There was no line that one could say positively that the "Barrage" was on at any time. The heavy bombardment of SWITCH TRENCH was a marvel of modern artillery, practically no part of the	

Army Form C. 2118

WAR DIARY
or
INTELLIGENCE SUMMARY
(Erase heading not required.)

Instructions regarding War Diaries and Intelligence Summaries are contained in F. S. Regs., Part II. and the Staff Manual respectively. Title Pages will be prepared in manuscript.

Place	Date	Hour	Summary of Events and Information	Remarks and references to Appendices
SWITCH TRENCH	Sept 15 Friday		trench being entrenched, and in fact being completely obliterated. The wire cutting was excellent; I did not see one bit of wire longer than a foot anywhere. The behaviour of all ranks was above beyond any praise." (Signed) L. Trower, Major. Commanding 8th Bn King's Royal Rifle Corps. Throughout the day SWITCH TRENCH has shelled with S.O.Q's and 4.2's. Captain Bower, Lieut. BOURDILLON, O.C.C.g. Lieut. SOMVILLE o.c. A Coy, 2nd Lt LISTER, 2nd Lt Cawthorn, 2nd Lt Clarke, 2nd Lt Chambers, 2nd Lt Penny, 2nd Lt Grundy, 2nd Lt Saunders were all wounded on the 15th inst., 2nd Lt Cooke Commanding D Coy	

Place	Date	Hour	Summary of Events and Information	Remarks and references to Appendices
SWITCH TRENCH	Sept 15- Friday		went through the whole Show, and did splendid work consolidating SWITCH TRENCH, also Captain J.W. Lesley who took command of B Coy. In the evening 2/Lt Pitts with No 2 = Lt MacAulay came up to SWITCH trench. 2/Lt POPE came up also and both carried on with splendid work of consolidation again. Sgt Hocken the trench beyond repeaters killed a great loss to the Batt. On casualties were 11 Officers and 320 O.R. 98 of whom were missing. Sgt LEATHER the most spl. and R/M COMER the commanding Officer's servant died splendid work throughout the day.	more
"	16 Saturday		The Battalion remained in SWITCH TRENCH until relieved in the evening by the 21st Division. The SWITCH Line and DELVILLE was heavily shelled all day. Carnoy. Except it was the 21st Division which relieved us at ROCLINCOURT. The End of July, when we started for the SOMME. M.O. Ch...	

Army Form C. 2118

WAR DIARY
or
INTELLIGENCE SUMMARY
(Erase heading not required.)

Instructions regarding War Diaries and Intelligence Summaries are contained in F. S. Regs., Part II. and the Staff Manual respectively. Title Pages will be prepared in manuscript.

Place	Date	Hour	Summary of Events and Information	Remarks and references to Appendices
FRICOURT CAMP - DERNANCOURT.	Sept 17th Sunday		That relieved by the 21st Division last night the Battalion came out to an advanced Transport camp close to MONTAUBAN and marched down on the morning of the 17th to FRICOURT CAMP - the plans it left when it went up to DELVILLE Wood on the 12th inst. The Bn. has arrived at FRICOURT CAMP and proceeds to its old billets at DERNANCOURT about 8.38 p.m.	Mulock
DERNAN- COURT	18 Monday		Battalion resting. The following orders were published in today's Battalion Orders. 4th Inf Bde letter No 3491/23. "The B.G.C. is very pleased and gratified at the very fine message which in his opinion has been able to forward the following message, which in his opinion has been very well earned. (Sgd) J.H.S. Aitken Captain for Brigade 4th Inf Bde. "Following wire from XV Corps begins aaa 14th Div. wire begins — "Following wire from Army Commander begins aaa	

Army Form C. 2118

WAR DIARY
or
INTELLIGENCE SUMMARY
(Erase heading not required.)

Place	Date	Hour	Summary of Events and Information	Remarks and references to Appendices
DERNANCOURT	18 Monday		" Please convey to 14th Division my congratulations and best thanks for their performance yesterday and the day before an after that the hard one through previously in DELVILLE WOOD, the gallantry and dash which they displayed is deserving of the highest praise and I desire to express to all ranks my admiration and gratitude etc. The Corps Commander has great pleasure in forwarding the above and desires to add his own appreciation of their good work and cols. G.O.C. directs that report hereof be communicated to all ranks on parade."	
"	19 Tuesday		The following N.C.O.s and men in this Battn. were pure. Military Medals - Divisional orders today, for good work at Pashendy on 25th August. 65-73 of C.M.R.2 (SR). 76.69 Rfn W. Smith. 9392 Pte A. Harford 2803 Lt.J.T. LAPWORTH 6554 Rfn W. Jones. 1629 " A. Bradley.	

Army Form C. 2118

WAR DIARY
or
INTELLIGENCE SUMMARY
(Erase heading not required.)

Place	Date	Hour	Summary of Events and Information	Remarks and references to Appendices
HERMAN- COURT.	Sept. 19 Tuesday		The following telegram has been received from His Majesty the King by the Commander in Chief. "I congratulate you and my brave troops on the brilliant success just achieved and have ever doubted that complete victory will ultimately crown our efforts and the splendid results of the fighting confirmed this view." GEORGE R.I.	
"	20 Wednesday		Parade of the whole Brigade at 12 noon. Brig General Officers. Mess - when Brigadier General Skinner Commanding 41st Inf. Bde. made an address to the Brigade and presented the rewards won by Officers, N.C.O's and R.p. in 41st Inf. Bde. Transport leaves at 12.30 pm to proceed by road to	
"	21 Thursday		LUCHEUX near DOULLENS	
"	22 Friday		Brigade marches to bivouac on the ALBERT-AMIENS road about 3 miles. Leaves at 6.30 am	

WAR DIARY
or
INTELLIGENCE SUMMARY
(Erase heading not required.)

Army Form C. 2118

Place	Date	Hour	Summary of Events and Information	Remarks and references to Appendices
LUCHEUX	22 Friday	11-30 a.m.	The battalion set on the train - French hosts hospitable - about ... arrived at LUCHEUX via AMIENS and DOULLENS about 4-30 p.m. Billets & bivouacs LUCHEUX - rather crowded for the troops - very comfortable for Officers.	Bullets
"	23 Saturday		The following letter was addressed to the 16th Division from the G.O.C. 4th Army was published in tonight's Battalion Orders. "It is with very sincere regret that I learn the 16th Division are leaving the 4th Army, and before they do so I desire to convey to every Officer, N.C.O. and man my gratitude and congratulations for the admirable work they have done. Both in DELVILLE WOOD and the attacks of the 15th and 16th September they showed a fighting spirit and a dash which is worthy of the best traditions of the British Army, whilst their discipline and self sacrifice has been beyond praise.	

WAR DIARY
INTELLIGENCE SUMMARY
(Erase heading not required.)

Army Form C. 2118

Place	Date	Hour	Summary of Events and Information	Remarks and references to Appendices
LUCHEUX	Sept 23	Saturday	"The artillery support has on all occasions been adequate and well directed, and is the result of careful and thorough training. I have been struck by the keenness and good comradeship which exist amongst all ranks in the 14th Division. It is a most valuable asset in war and shows that both Staff and Regimental Officers are working in harmony. At some future time, though it may be my good fortune to again find them under my command." (Sd) H. RAWLINSON, GENERAL. Commanding 4th Army. G.H.Q. 20th September. The following letter from the C.R.A. 14th Division, to B.G.C. 41st Army Reserve was published in Battalion Orders. "The C.R.A. and all the 14th Divisional Artillery send their best congratulations on hearing	

WAR DIARY
or
INTELLIGENCE SUMMARY

Army Form C. 2118

Place	Date	Hour	Summary of Events and Information	Remarks and references to Appendices
LUCHEUX	Sept 23 Saturday		of the magnificent work performed by your Brigade, and wished all of you success. Good wishes. The C.R.A. regrets to is unable to see them himself as he is not yet out of hospital. Col S W.S. Brewer 51st to CRA 51st (5yth Division)	
	24 Sunday		The Commanding Officer and 5 Coy officers go by bus to Beauvoir and do normal F.S. parades of trenches South of ARRAS. Church parade C. of E. at 11.30 a.m. a Battalion parade formed.	
	25 Monday		Bat. for plant-May take the Batt. on parade at 8.0am each day.	

Army Form C. 2118

WAR DIARY
or
INTELLIGENCE SUMMARY
(Erase heading not required.)

Place	Date	Hour	Summary of Events and Information	Remarks and references to Appendices
LOCHEA	Sept 25 Monday		The following special order was published to Brig. Genl. Ball: Acre. To Major-General V.A. COUPER, Commanding 14th Light Division. "The 14th Light Division leaves the 15th Corps today, and I wish to express to you, the Brigadiers, Commanding Officers, and indeed every Officer, N.C.O., and Soldier, the very high opinion I have formed of the efficiency, discipline, moral and fighting value of the Division. The Division cleared DELVILLE WOOD, the capture of ORCHARDS TRENCH, between Aug 12th and 27th, and the attack of the SWITCH TRENCH and the FLERS POSITION on Sept 15 were all difficult, but the fine fighting spirits of the Division carried them all to a successful conclusion. The Division has accomplished everything which it has been called upon to perform, and done its work. I hope it may be my good fortune to be associated with you again." (Sd) H.S. HORNE Lieut-General Commanding XV Corps. H.Q. XV Corps 22/9/16	

WAR DIARY
or
INTELLIGENCE SUMMARY

Place	Date	Hour	Summary of Events and Information	Remarks and references to Appendices
LOCAEUH	2/9/16 2. Tuesday		The following message from the G.O.C. 14th Light Division has been published in Battalion Orders. "On completing an record tour of duty in the battle of the SOMME, the G.O.C. congratulates all ranks of the 14th Division on the high character they have earned for dash, discipline, and hard work. The division has proved that the New Army is in fighting qualities and staying power behind the Old Army in which famous regiments represented in the Division, have, by the hardships endured and the sacrifices triumphantly made, acquired new and undying honour."	New OC H

WAR DIARY or **INTELLIGENCE SUMMARY**
(Erase heading not required.)

Army Form C. 2118

Place	Date	Hour	Summary of Events and Information	Remarks and references to Appendices
LUCHEUX		left	Transport proceeded by road to BEAUMETZ leaving LUCHEUX at 8-15am. The Bn proceeds in motor lorries leave LUCHEUX about 2-0pm and arrives at BOUY. Leave BOUY the three miles to billets in BEAUMETZ from BOUY.	
BEAUMETZ and F3 sector of trenches	27 Wednesday		The Battn relieves the 6th Bn The BUFFS in F3 subsector trenches on the left of 4th Inf Bde front 4.15 pm. S. Officers and Bucks Rifle Infantry on the left and 20 Bn KRRC on the Right at night. The relief was completed at 6-0am and completed at 10 am just CM	
F3 trench	28 Thursday		Amazingly quiet trenches, and in extremely good war, to the sounds of Enemy Saps only, visible in front. A GAS ALERT period is on.	
"	29 Friday		Lieut-Colonel FREWEN goes down to England. Major T.M. RIXON takes command of the Batt. Very quiet day.	

Army Form C. 2118

WAR DIARY
or
INTELLIGENCE SUMMARY

(Erase heading not required.)

Instructions regarding War Diaries and Intelligence Summaries are contained in F. S. Regs., Part II. and the Staff Manual respectively. Title Pages will be prepared in manuscript.

Place	Date	Hour	Summary of Events and Information	Remarks and references to Appendices
P.S. Sector Left Trench	20th Saturday		Very quiet fine snowy day. Trench held by the Bath. Strength of the Batt. in the trenches is 410.	Mun./C.H.

J. M. Inneri Major ?ol
O.C. 8th (S) ???. L. R. Fus. Corps

1875 Wt. W593/826 1,000,000 4/15 J.B.C. & A. A.D.S.S./Forms/C. 2118.

Vol 13

CONFIDENTIAL.

WAR DIARY

- of -

8th Bn., KING'S ROYAL RIFLE CORPS.

From: 1st October, 1916.
To: 31st October, 1916.

Volume XV.

WAR DIARY
or
INTELLIGENCE SUMMARY

(Erase heading not required.)

Army Form C. 2118

Place	Date	Hour	Summary of Events and Information	Remarks and references to Appendices
F3 Sub Sector	Sunday Oct 1st		8th K.R.R.C. Another quiet day. Nothing to report.	RLH
F3	Monday Oct 2nd		The battalion is relieved in the early morning by 8th R.B. and goes into billets at RIVIERE.	RLH
RIVIERE	Oct 3rd Tuesday		Being in proximity of RIVIERE to the line – about 1500 yards – little training is possible, except of reserve Bombers and Lewis Gunners.	RLH
"	Oct 4 Wednesday		Working-parties are supplied daily for building dug-outs and M.G. emplacements at various points in the F Sector.	RLH
"	Oct 5 Thursday		Weather still warm, but more rain. An occasional small HV shell drops into the village which also receives stray balls from enemy MG's. Bridge canteen opens in the village.	RLH
"	Oct 6 Friday		Brigade baths at disposal of the battalion. Usual working-parties about all available men except a few bombers & Lewis gunners.	RLH
"	Oct 7 Saturday		Considerable activity on hostile lightfield-gun battery behind the village. We're keeping cut in front of Helyton Halliery, the 46th	RLH

Army Form C. 2118

8th KRRC

WAR DIARY
or
INTELLIGENCE SUMMARY
(Erase heading not required.)

Instructions regarding War Diaries and Intelligence Summaries are contained in F.S. Regs., Part II. and the Staff Manual respectively. Title Pages will be prepared in manuscript.

Place	Date	Hour	Summary of Events and Information	Remarks and references to Appendices
RIVIÈRE	Oct 7	Saturday	Battalion down in the un-relieved right F1, to which sector we & Rifle Brigade where now belong. This new sector is the prelude to a quiet move when Monday.	RLH
	Oct 8th	Sunday	Church Parade in small Church Rut. In Villany a Scheme of getting at Sh.M the enemy expecting us attack sent an S.O.S. and heavy barrage fire opened on front, support reserve lines & turn F1 sector, 9th, 10th R.B. and Sherwood Battalion (40th Division) on front right. The 9th R.B. also sent S.O.S call. Being in Brigade reserve we were ordered to Stand to with equipment on. All was quiet by 8·45 h.m. Railway-heaps of Sherwoods at 4 a.m. Front enemy front line & sap flecked with wire.	RLH
F.1.	Oct 9th	Monday	We relieve the 8th R.B. in F1 sector. Relief completed 10·0 h.m. Trenches of right Company & FOREST Street somewhat damaged by last night's barrage. B & C in front line. A & D in support with some platoons each in PETIT MOULIN and FACTORY Rd. Day very quiet.	RLH
F.1	Oct 10th	Tuesday	Trenches in a much worse state than those in F3, especially on the right Company's front.	RLH

WAR DIARY
or
INTELLIGENCE SUMMARY

Army Form C. 2118

Place	Date	Hour	Summary of Events and Information	Remarks and references to Appendices
F1	Oct 10th	Tuesday	Having been neglected all the winter they now need renewing along almost the whole front. Trench strength is too weak to allow us to keep them in proper state under winter conditions. Everything quiet.	R.L.H
F1	Oct 11th	Wednesday	A few shells — small H.E. in Forest & two 4.2" on Foresty two 4.2" on Fine Shaft Sight retaliation right Coy. few activity over 2" mortars. Bright moonlight and alertness enemy sentries makes patrolling & approach to his lines difficult.	R.L.H
F1	Oct 12th	Thurs.	An apparent relief of divisions on the enemy sides. His Field guns & 4.2" are obviously registering along the whole front to-day. We shall have some retaliation work if being with will of the reserve division retaliation.	R.L.H
F1	Oct 13th	Friday	A great change is noticeable in the enemy lines. His rifle and M.G. fire at night has practically ceased. Some huts and huts along BLAINVILLE Wood formerly held now seem unoccupied. Probably a believed unit from the SOMME	R.L.H
F1	Oct 14th	Sat.	Enemy opened a short organised bombardment on RIVIERE & PRETENCOURT at 8 a.m. this morning, in retaliation	R.L.H

WAR DIARY
or
INTELLIGENCE SUMMARY

(Erase heading not required.)

Army Form C. 2118

Place	Date	Hour	Summary of Events and Information	Remarks and references to Appendices
F1	Oct 14th Sat.		No activity of our heavies returned close by. Some shells close to Bde. HQS.	RLH
F1	Oct 15th Sunday		Heavy rain is falling and causing the usual falls in the trenches. Enemy still abnormally quiet, especially at night. A.D. relieve B.C. Coy. going in front line.	RLH
F1	Oct 16th Monday		Our Stokes "D" mortars are registering and shooting our most of enemy traps. He retaliates only for C. Coy. where he seems to be active. An order warning us of wire cutting by 14th Bn. Artillery in connection with an operation for Red Sparrow has been cancelled. Captain Usher H. Bromilow awarded the Military Cross	RLH
F1	Oct 17th Tues.		Enemy still very inactive except as regards wire. Our heavy gunners fire every morning to strafe him. Large working party behind his line. MARTIN'S WOOD and support trench occasionally shelled occasionally.	RLH
F1	Oct 18th Wed		Heavy rain again. A few shells into RIVIERE and along Oppy Coy's front. Generally quiet. A patrol going by without reporting VSah heard nothing.	RLH
F1	Oct 19th Thurs		Getting colder, with a S. westerly wind and gas alert in near future.	RLH

WAR DIARY
or
INTELLIGENCE SUMMARY

(Erase heading not required.)

Army Form C. 2118

Instructions regarding War Diaries and Intelligence Summaries are contained in F. S. Regs., Part II. and the Staff Manual respectively. Title Pages will be prepared in manuscript.

Place	Date	Hour	Summary of Events and Information	Remarks and references to Appendices
F.1.	Oct 19th	Thurs	A few trench-mortars on our right + left front line. But as a rule our rifle-grenades and mortars draw no reply. Wind N.N.E. raid a night.	R.L.H.
F.1.	Oct 20th	Fri.	"Gas Alert" ordered but soon cancelled. Everything very quiet.	R.L.H.
F.1.	Oct 21st	Sat.	An aeroplane-pilot Lt. BELL IRVING brought down close to pumping-stn at FOREST SHEET, CHANCERY Lane during the return of a squadron from a bombing attack. The enemy shell the machine until it's intermittently all day. Carrying 4 casualties to our right-support Company. Wind due East, very cold. "Gas Alert" renewed.	R.L.H.
F.1.	Oct 22nd	Sun	Our enemy werage intercepted to the effect that there was gas ready for liberation in the German trenches N of the SCARPE. Working-parties of the R.E. busy making emplacements for gas-cylinders in our trenches. This apparently was observed and T.167 shelled, causing the first death since our relief entered this F. sector a month ago. Some gas-cylinders placed into position by night.	R.L.H.
F.1.	Oct 23rd	Mon.	Transport-lines at BEAUMETZ shelled with 5.9s this morning, the C.O.'s groom and transport-cook being badly hit. Two or three heavy minen-werfer French-mortars	R.L.H.

Army Form C. 2118

WAR DIARY
or
INTELLIGENCE SUMMARY
(Erase heading not required.)

Place	Date	Hour	Summary of Events and Information	Remarks and references to Appendices
F1.	Oct. 23rd	Monday	Fell in our front line close to PAM E Street. Fire men was buried but dug out unhurt. A German patrol was detected crawling close to the sap-head. The Lewis gat. fire men was killed and the rest scattered. He belonged to the 86th Fusilier Regiment, a normal identification.	R.L.H.
F1.	Oct. 24	Tuesday	More gas-cylinders are being installed in our line. Enemy newly-relieved to-morrow by 6th Buffs, 9th to 8th Division. The division relieved us in F.R.L. intry only a month ago. Rather more enemy H.E. artillery over to us in F.R.L. intry to-night. A well reared light rocket in our area. Their usual.	R.L.H.
SIMENCOURT	Oct. 25th	Wed.	The battalion is relieved by the 6th Buffs, less the garrison of Hughs Redoubt, goes to the 6/7 Queens. Relief completed 2.15 p.m. without incident and Batn. Hdqrs. goes into Billets at SIMENCOURT.	R.L.H.
GRAND RULLECOURT	Oct. 26th	Thurs.	Another move to-day to GRAND RULLECOURT, but luckily the time keeps being quite uncertain. In fact it is an eight-mile march at the end of a long spell of trench-work, especially one men feel it out. There seems some prospect of fortnight's stay here.	R.L.H.

WAR DIARY or INTELLIGENCE SUMMARY

Army Form C. 2118

Place	Date	Hour	Summary of Events and Information	Remarks and references to Appendices
GRAND RULLECOURT	Oct 27th	Friday	The billets are tolerably good, but the village is deficient of any of the amenities of life, such as baths, cinemas, canteens. Onen fires should be available for drying if the present conditions of weather change. The day spent in cleaning up of uniforms, kit, inspections.	R.L.H
"	Oct 28th	Saturday	Instruction of all Companies by the C.O. An 10 days' tough duty in the trenches leaves abundant traces on equipment and uniforms. U.O.R arrives a few among them old soldiers, however mostly recruits from late groups.	R.L.H
"	Oct 29th	Sunday	Heavy showers of rain. Church parade at 11 a.m. Inoculating the draft, which causes good quality.	R.L.H
"	Oct 30th	Monday	A programme of training begins to-day in spite of the difficulties of weather and depletion of the Companies by the numbers of courses in Lewis gun, bombing etc recently started.	R.L.H
"	Oct 31st	Tuesday	Rain still interferes with Company training. Two new courses in bayonet training and Vickers gun begun to-day	R.L.H

J. Bacon Lt Col

CONFIDENTIAL.

WAR DIARY

- of -

8th (S) Bn., KING'S ROYAL RIFLE CORPS.

From: 1st November, 1916.
To: 30th November, 1916.

Volume XVI.

Army Form C. 2118.

8th K.R.R.C.

WAR DIARY
or
INTELLIGENCE SUMMARY

(Erase heading not required.)

Place	Date	Hour	Summary of Events and Information	Remarks and references to Appendices
GRAND RULLECOURT	Nov 1st	Wed.	Company training continues under difficulties owing to weather.	RLH
"	2nd	Thurs	Arrival of a draft of 36 men, mostly wounded men of other Battalions. Lecture on gas Precautions by Div. Anti-gas officer. A meeting room and writing tables has been opened in one of the billets. This and a series of concerts by the Divisional Entertainments Party (FIZZESPRINGS) helps to provide amusement for the troops	RLH
"	3rd	Frid.	The VI Corps baths, near AVESNES are at our disposal all day. They can accommodate 330 men in relays.	RLH
"	4th	Sat.	Weather improving but the ground is still too waterlogged for much drill on the fields. A 4 mile cross country race between Companies in the afternoon is won by the H.Q. team.	RLH
"	5th	Sund	Church parade in a hut behind the big Chateau at 11 a.m. Ground is rapidly drying up.	RLH
"	6th	Mond	The week's scheme of work ordered by the Brigade includes fresh subjects, sanitary revetments, wiring, assaulting by waves & deployment. The companies are augmented by one for training Vickers gun Reserves. Very heavy rain towards evening.	RLH

Army Form C. 2118.

WAR DIARY
or
INTELLIGENCE SUMMARY
(Erase heading not required.)

Instructions regarding War Diaries and Intelligence Summaries are contained in F. S. Regs., Part II. and the Staff Manual respectively. Title Pages will be prepared in manuscript.

Place	Date	Hour	Summary of Events and Information	Remarks and references to Appendices
GRAND ROULECOURT	7th	Tuesday	A Brigade Route March is cancelled owing to Heavy rain. Leave, temporarily suspended owing to weather and a raid on the Channel, reopens, but only for special reasons. New draft arrived at midnight 7/8 of 67 men.	
"	8th	Wed.	C.O. expects the new draft which brings the total strength of the battalion up to 800. Mostly new recruits from home, but quite promising.	
"	9th	Thurs	The O.i.c. J.us Officers gives preliminary instruction in the use of the new small Box Respirator which will shortly replace the P.H.G Helmet. It seems a far more simple & effective device than any previous one. Weather good enough to permit of some wiring and sandbagging.	
"	10th	Fri.	Another hour wiring race v the 8th Rifle Brigade, ending in an easy win for this battalion. Weather still good.	
"	11th	Sat.	A short battalion route march to AVESNES, back in the morning. An excellent entertainment smoking concert in the Sergeant's Mess in the evening, attended by the Brigadier and all officers.	
"	12th	Sunday	Chapel parade in the morning. Inter-Company football matches in the afternoon as a preliminary to selecting the best battalion team for A Brigade Competition.	

Army Form C. 2118.

WAR DIARY
or
INTELLIGENCE SUMMARY

(Erase heading not required.)

Instructions regarding War Diaries and Intelligence Summaries are contained in F. S. Regs., Part II. and the Staff Manual respectively. Title Pages will be prepared in manuscript.

Place	Date	Hour	Summary of Events and Information	Remarks and references to Appendices
GRAND RULLECOURT	13th	Monday	The G.O.C. 3rd Bgde visited the Brigade Training area, but only inspected the work of the 2 battalions at SAMBRIN. He is much worried. It is hopeless to dig trenches for practising attacks. Another draft of 35 O.R. arrived.	
"	14	Tuesday	The Efficiency Competition arranged by the Brigade is in full swing. It includes Lewis gun, Bombing, Stretcher-bearer Competitions, as well as football running musketry. Each Contingent who takes its seat in its own company gun in each event. Weather very cold.	
"	15	Wed.	A new course in field work begins at SAMBRIN. Twenty three drafts received during the past 3 weeks are now absorbed by their Coys for training. Total strength of battalion is now raised to 844.	
"	16	Thurs.	Very hard frost & cold wind.	
"	17	Fri.	Cold again intense cross-country race in the Brigade Combination of teams. 8th R.B. getting 2nd, 3rd, and the battalion 1st & 4th places. Snow during the night. A short battalion route-march in morning to SAMBRIN.	
"	18	Sat.		

2449 Wt. W14957/M90 750,000 1/16 J.B.C. & A. Forms/C.2118/12.

WAR DIARY
or
INTELLIGENCE SUMMARY

Army Form C. 2118.

Place	Date	Hour	Summary of Events and Information	Remarks and references to Appendices
YPRND RUILECOURT	19th	Sunday	Church parade in the grounds of Brig Chateau. C.O.'s inspection of billets. A start is being made with the trenching work in the farms viso increase the accommodation. Bunks are also being put into billets as far as the limited material allows.	
"	20th	Monday	Sir Lewis-gun competition. This battalion was 3rd in the Bombing and and Transport Parade 3rd, the latter everything being won by 7th R.B. Parties of men are being turned on to retain holes in the walls of farms with good results. Captain PA-Coutre E is attacked to 42nd Inf Bde Staff. Lt-L CLAREMONT takes over D Coy.	
"	21st	Tuesday	Cold + foggy. Shooting competition postponed owing to rub conditions. Replayed match in football competition (between best Company teams) ended again in draw between our Coy and a team of 7th R.B.	
"	22nd	Wed	A battalion scheme in the morning, fld 4 hours gun teams representing the enemy holding a line of trenches in some woods N of BEUFORT which the rest of the battalion attacked. Weather bright + cold.	

2449 Wt. W14957/M90 750,000 1/16 J.B.C. & A. Forms/C.2118/12.

Army Form C. 2118.

WAR DIARY
or
INTELLIGENCE SUMMARY

(Erase heading not required.)

Instructions regarding War Diaries and Intelligence Summaries are contained in F. S. Regs., Part II. and the Staff Manual respectively. Title Pages will be prepared in manuscript.

Place	Date	Hour	Summary of Events and Information	Remarks and references to Appendices
GRAND RULLECOURT	23rd	Thurs	Postponed shooting match ends in a win for an excellent team of 7 R.B.'s own team winning by it in first round. First round of inter-Battalion football in afternoon, we beat the 9th R.B. in a fine game	R.L.H
"	24th	Frid.	Wet cold day. Bayonet-fighting and Stretcher-bearing Competition in afternoon. We were 4th in the former and 2nd in latter, a ludicrously organized test of every other faculty except Stretcher-bearing Arrival of 10 new reinforcements.	R.L.H
"	25th	Sat.	Hopelessly wet day. Battalion route-march cancelled	R.L.H
"	26th	Sun.	Another wet day. No Inspections made for Church Parade at the Chateau. Inter was held. Football match v. Brigade H.Q. Coy ended in easy win for us.	R.L.H
"	27	Mond.	Cold, frost again. Divisional cross-country meeting race at le Cauroy over heavy ground. 10 teams entered. We took third place.	R.L.H
"	28th	Tuesday	Final match of inter-battalion football v. 7th R.R.C. ends in a win for us by 1 goal to nil. Regimental parade with testing of gas-respirators "made" with testing of gas-respirators. Reports satisfactory, but some men need shewing the necessity.	R.L.H

Army Form C. 2118.

WAR DIARY
or
INTELLIGENCE SUMMARY
(Erase heading not required.)

Place	Date	Hour	Summary of Events and Information	Remarks and references to Appendices
GRAND RULLECOURT	29th Wed		Hd Qrs & Platoon practise an attack on trenches at the training ground SAMBRIN before the Brigadier. In return somewhat marred by a thick mist and the unreadiness of the trenches. The cold is very severe. Preliminary tests of training in afternoon to select winning fire Brigade competition.	R.L.H.
"	30th		Companies on the range and testing low-ret-peration in morning. Relayed match between C Coy and D Coy 7th Rifle Brigade resulted in a ludicrously easy win for us. This ends the Brigade Efficiency Competitions which has been won by this battalion with 13 points, 8th Rifle Brigade being second with 12 points.	R.L.H.

L. Brewer
Lt. Col:

CONFIDENTIAL.

WAR DIARY

- of -

8th Bn., KING'S ROYAL RIFLE CORPS.

From: 1st December, 1916.
To: 31st December, 1916.

Volume ~~XVII~~

8K KRRC

Army Form C. 2118.

WAR DIARY
or
INTELLIGENCE SUMMARY
(Erase heading not required.)

Place	Date	Hour	Summary of Events and Information	Remarks and references to Appendices
Grand Ruise Court	Dec 1st	Friday	Brigade Route March in morning through AVESNES & SOMBRIN. The weather was good, no rain falling, only the whole battalion arriving back to bed. Preliminary rounds of boxing-competition in the morning & afternoon.	RLH
"	Dec 2nd	Sat.	Cold still severe. Companies carry on with fitting of box-respirators and company training.	RLH
"	Dec 3rd	Sunday	Voluntary service in the morning owing to the unsuitability of getting accommodation for church service. Weather cold and frosty.	RLH
"	Dec 4th	Monday	Lt. Theur has set in & weather is milder. Major Rixon in command of Battalion during absence of C.O. at Conference of C.O's at 3rd Army Group Infantry School in refresher course in morning.	RLH
"	Dec 5th	Tues	Weather wet & squally. A battalion scheme for night operations cancelled in consequence.	RLH

Army Form C. 2118.

WAR DIARY
or
INTELLIGENCE SUMMARY

(Erase heading not required.)

Instructions regarding War Diaries and Intelligence Summaries are contained in F. S. Regs., Part II. and the Staff Manual respectively. Title Pages will be prepared in manuscript.

Place	Date	Hour	Summary of Events and Information	Remarks and references to Appendices
GRAND ROLLECOURT	Dec 6th	Wed.	Brigade route-March in morning through HUMBERCOURT and WARLUZEL a fairly long march in full marching order. Respective drill in afternoon.	RLH
"	Dec 7th	Thurs	Whole day devoted to paths at SOMBRIN and working party for which we have to find a heavy 250 men for work on practice-trenches on AVESNES — GRAND ROLLECOURT road.	RLH
"	Dec 8th	Friday	The Brigade scheme fixed for to-day has to be cancelled owing to the large working parties required by the Brigade and the bad state of ground and weather. The C.O. inspects a Coys in respect to drill in memory.	RLH
"	Dec 9th	Sat.	Another party of 200 men required for deep digging practice trenches. Weather has slightly improved.	RLH
"	Dec 10th	Sund.	Cold, raw day. C.O. returns from conference of C.O.'s at 3rd Army School. Voluntary service in lecture room at thirteen. No parade service.	RLH

WAR DIARY or INTELLIGENCE SUMMARY

Army Form C. 2118.

(Erase heading not required.)

Place	Date	Hour	Summary of Events and Information	Remarks and references to Appendices
GRAND RULLECOURT	Dec. 11th	Monday	Warning of intending move to trenches received and a party of officers and NCOs to reconnoitre trenches tomorrow. Cold & wet were ther.	RLH
"	Dec. 12th	Tues.	Reconnoitering trenches postponed. We shall return to the F Sector which we left in October. Parties still busy on practise trenches. Much influenza in the battalion.	RLH
"	Dec. 13th	Wed.	Reconnoitering trenches takes place. We shall relieve the 1st Buffs of 12th Division who took our place in F3 trenches on Beaumetz.	RLH
"	Dec. 14th	Thurs.	Arrival of a large draft of 145 OR brings us up to establishment. Day spent in drawing up fit kit and equipment in preparation for moving tomorrow.	RLH
"	Dec. 15th	Fri.	The battalion marches to BEAUMETZ, a long distance of 11 miles or rather trying for the new draft which had a long march to reach the battalion yesterday, but very few stragglers.	RLH
"	Dec. 17th	Sat.	The battalion relieves the 1st Buffs in morning. A, D, C Coys are in the front line with 6 Lewis guns and B Coy in reserve. 3 Lewis guns in Support. B Coy HQ also in Support. & one in reserve. Very quiet.	RLH

2449 Wt. W14957/Mgo 750,000 1/16 J.B.C. & A. Forms/C.2118/12.

WAR DIARY
or
INTELLIGENCE SUMMARY

Army Form C. 2118.

(Erase heading not required.)

Instructions regarding War Diaries and Intelligence Summaries are contained in F. S. Regs., Part II. and the Staff Manual respectively. Title Pages will be prepared in manuscript.

Place	Date	Hour	Summary of Events and Information	Remarks and references to Appendices
F¹	Dec 17	Sunday	Everything very wet in line. Trenches in bad condition owing to recent frost. The Batt. trsp't sent up to help work out train of being light wheeled, & Transport Coy for similar entrainm'nt. Gd deal of wire	RLH
F¹	Dec 18	Monday	Trsp't Coy and two Coy men in trenches have fallen in and are helping out our work. A few H.V. shells in front of their Sap. Wire reeld up nis along rest of the front.	RLH
F¹	Dec 19	Tuesday	Weather frosty again. A few rained bombs sent up on to Loy's t'd and reconnoitring to front line. A scout light in german line interfered slightly with our working parties	RLH
F¹	Dec 20	Wed.	One man wounded by a chance bomb in centre Coy. About 20 shells — 4.2" — over a Euthele Sap on right Coy. Artillery working party to have observed hits.	RLH
F¹	Dec 21	Thurs.	Gas Alert is cancelled. A few A.V. shells from a.a. guns on to front line. S.T. Fiction Street. Otherwise quiet.	RLH
F¹	Dec 22	Fri.	Battalion relieved by 7ᵗʰ R.R.C. Relief complete without incident at 2.1. M. We return	RLH

Army Form C. 2118.

WAR DIARY
or
INTELLIGENCE SUMMARY

(Erase heading not required.)

Instructions regarding War Diaries and Intelligence Summaries are contained in F. S. Regs., Part II. and the Staff Manual respectively. Title Pages will be prepared in manuscript.

Place	Date	Hour	Summary of Events and Information	Remarks and references to Appendices
BEAUMETZ			to rest billets at BEAUMETZ. Two hours after we arrived the village was shelled intermittently by 4.2" howitzers for 1½ hours. The billet of one platoon was hit, 3 men killed and 4 wounded. There were evidences too of other units and to animals. Billets had to be altered.	RLH
BEAUMETZ	Dec 23rd	Sat	Very wet and squally. Day spent in cleaning equipment. Not suitable village for a resting battalion owing to the difficulty of moving forces of troops by day and its liability to be shelled.	RLH
"	Dec 24	Sun	A German aeroplane brought down by one of our machines close to the village. Village again shelled in evening but then a rainy night and morning of this was not a few in other battalions. It up the time.	RLH
"	Dec 25	Monday	A quiet day. The village was not shelled at all, and Christmas was celebrated without disturbance.	RLH
"	26	Tue	Working party of 130 men required for front line owing to the unusually wet state. Irredescible recent liberation of front and rear village heavily shelled in afternoon. Two casualties.	RLH

2449 Wt. W14957/M90 750,000 1/16 J.B.C. & A. Forms/C.2118/12.

Army Form C. 2118.

WAR DIARY
or
INTELLIGENCE SUMMARY

(Erase heading not required.)

Instructions regarding War Diaries and Intelligence Summaries are contained in F.S. Regs., Part II. and the Staff Manual respectively. Title Pages will be prepared in manuscript.

Place	Date	Hour	Summary of Events and Information	Remarks and references to Appendices
BEAUMETZ	Dec 27th	Wed.	The C.O. goes away one month's leave. Major RIXON in command of the battalion. Bright, cold day and much aeroplane activity on both sides. Several very heavy shells fell in the village during afternoon, but no casualties. Intervening days by C.O. without difficulties.	RLH
F1	Dec 28	Thur.	We relieve the 1KRRP's again in F1 sector after a 8 days rest in not very suitable billets for a resting battalion. Conditions do not permit any real training of troops in BEAUMETZ. Our heavies bombarded enemy front line along half our front. Wochenalm front line from 2-4 p.m with good effect.	RLH
"	29th	Fri.	Fairly heavy bombardment on our front and support line between FIRST & FULLY street (between 12.30 and 3 h.m.); also 7 CHANCERY Lane and Batt H.Q. Considerable damage to trenches. Heavy rain at same time made conditions very difficult. Few men wounded.	RLH
"	30th	Sat.	Rain continues. Only one out of five communication trenches is usable. Front trenches are collecting everywhere and many posts nearly isolated. Very difficult to get meals (warm) up from Cct H.Q's to the front-line. A few men knocked out. Small Hys shell on entire Company.	RLH
"	31st	Sunday	Improvement in weather. Large parties of 4th RAMC, RE and Lineheuth's working on all communication trenches and front-line. A few 77 mm shells on right Company.	RLH

CONFIDENTIAL.

WAR DIARY

- of -

8th (S) Bn., KING'S ROYAL RIFLE CORPS.

From: 1st January, 1917.
To: 31st January, 1917.

Volume ~~XVIII~~.

Army Form C. 2118.

WAR DIARY
or
INTELLIGENCE SUMMARY

(Erase heading not required.)

Instructions regarding War Diaries and Intelligence Summaries are contained in F. S. Regs., Part II. and the Staff Manual respectively. Title Pages will be prepared in manuscript.

Place	Date	Hour	Summary of Events and Information	Remarks and references to Appendices
F.L.	Jan 1st	Friday	Weather slightly improved by high & large watering parties of 7th R.W.F. R.E. with fumes battalion. But impossible to carry beyond of from the input of dinners is being done by company cooks, & small billets are right dry and further stuff.	RLH
"	Jan 2nd	Sun	A quiet day. The artillery having been asked to fire as little as possible unit. The trenches are in the condition of a good many ?? men are billets & junction of FOREST & ?? CROSSING. A project for a given concession for some men being on & to up at funds to be stabled alarm	RLH
"	Jan 3rd	Wed	Relieved by the 14th R.W.F. and we go into billets in RIVIERE, in Brigade Reserve. D Coy in the 4 village keeps, other Coys in billets.	RLT
RIVIERE	Jan 4th	Thurs	All available men of those 3 Coys, about 300 in all, are taken for working parties by day & night in the front line. Any time available after working has to be devoted to the baths & hut-making	RLH
"	Jan 5th	Fri	Same programme of working parties. The wet hard ground for the able hands when in Reserve. Our rest was to have been one of 4 days only. But this has been extended to the usual period of 6 days.	RLT
"	Jan 6th	Sat	Considerable activity on part of artillery behind us in connection with	RLH

2449 Wt. W14957/M90 750,000 1/16 J.B.C. & A. Forms/C.2118/12.

Army Form C. 2118.

WAR DIARY
or
INTELLIGENCE SUMMARY
(Erase heading not required.)

Instructions regarding War Diaries and Intelligence Summaries are contained in F. S. Regs., Part II. and the Staff Manual respectively. Title Pages will be prepared in manuscript.

Place	Date	Hour	Summary of Events and Information	Remarks and references to Appendices
RIVIERE	Jan 6th	Sat.	a rest and instruction by 43rd Brigade 14th Division in H.T.3 & 12 w. Further North. Very little retaliation from enemy.	RLH
"	Jan 7th	Sun	Exploring parties as usual and only voluntary services in Church army Hut. Weather brighter. Getting G.S. decent in the evening.	RLH
"	Jan 8th	Mond.	A dozen 4.2 shells fell in & near Coys billets in the chateau bit the morning causing 9 casualties in this unit including 3 men who died of wounds, and one to two others in different units. Probably the intended target was an anti-aircraft gun situated behind the chateau which had been in action the day before. Very cold & wet evening. Several other 4.1" & other howitzers more only the village.	RLH
F1	Jan 9th	Tues.	We relieve the 7th R.R.C. in the line again. The trenches are in better condition and there has been less shelling of Riem lately, except for FICHEUX	RLH
"	Jan 10th	Wed.	An exceptionally quiet day. I caught for the wounded just a small H.V. shell on right Coy's support front line. Some MG activity — lightning the bright moon made work very difficult. Two men were hit in some carrying party.	RLH
"	Jan 11th	Thurs.	Some small H.V. 4.2" shells along FOREST street both live up B Coy in the afternoon. G.O.C in the evening. Quiet at night	RLH

Army Form C. 2118.

WAR DIARY
or
INTELLIGENCE SUMMARY

(Erase heading not required.)

Place	Date	Hour	Summary of Events and Information	Remarks and references to Appendices
F1.	Jan 12th	Friday	Considerable shelling of 5th K.R.R. & 4th Devons, on our right. The Devons had just relieved the 3/G.R. This Inter-Division relief was an unwired shoot on enemy strong points opposite. Several heavy trench mortars on right & by front in evening. Otherwise quiet. South light troublesome & wiring parties.	R.L.H.
"	Jan 13th	Sat.	About 10 a.m. BABY trench and trench 169 – 131 was heavily shelled by 77 mm. gun and two bays blown in. Few men wounded. Lieut. Hern. R.E. (Some waist trench on right leg in evening). Intelligence retake information. Stokes notified them.	R.L.H.
"	14th	Sun.	A fairly quiet day. A considerable number of 77 mm. fell about the RIGHT Coy.	R.H.E.M.
F1 to SIMENCOURT	15th	Mon.	The 7 K.R.R.C. relieved us in the line. The relief was a quiet one & was completed about 1.15 p.m. We went back into Divisional reserve at SIMENCOURT this time as BEAUMETZ had become too lively.	On P.M.
"	16th	Tues.	SIMENCOURT very muddy & not very comfortable. He had to find R.E. fatigue of about 270 in SIMENCOURT, BERNEVILLE, MONCHIET.	On P.M.
"	17th	Wed.	A slight frost during the night. Working parties totally about 300 had to be provided as yesterday interfering with all parades. Lt. Hardy the a/Adj. went on leave.	On P.M.

WAR DIARY
or
INTELLIGENCE SUMMARY

(Erase heading not required.)

Army Form C. 2118

Place	Date	Hour	Summary of Events and Information	Remarks and references to Appendices
SIMENCOURT	Jan 18th	Thurs.	Again a slight frost & snow during the night. Working parties as yesterday with addition of 70 men for two practice trench digging at WARLUS.	Am RH
"	19th	Fri.	Working parties as before - but Roads made very slushy with melted snow. Much snow fell on night 19th – 20th with slight frost.	Am RH
"	20th	Sat.	Same working parties only. Practice trench digging party was reduced to 10.	Am RH
"	21st	Sun.	A slight frost all day.	Am RH
SIMENCOURT to F1 section	22nd	Mon.	A very hard frost has set in. We moved up to the line & took over from the 7 K.R.R.C.	Am RH
"	23rd	Tues.	A quiet day. A certain amount of Wigg-banging on the RIGHT cay. (3 cas) completed about 2.30 pm. A quiet relief, We have now got on the battn. front 4, 9.45 T.M. & 10, 60 pdr, not to mention Stokes mortars. Night very dark. Temperature 10°–15°F. by night & 20°F. by day only. One usual amount of shelling. Some 4.2" close FICHEUX FOREST ST. Temperature about the same. RIGHT coy. received a few 90 pdr. blowing in one bay about 10 pm.	Am RH
"	24th	Wed.	FICHEUX FOREST ST. again received attention. 2 4.2" fell close to Bt. H.Q. one within 5 yds. of C.O. dug-out.	Am RH
"	25th	Thurs.	Temperature no warmer. Bt. H.Q. was more unpopular, receiving about 30 4.2" between 3 & 4 pm some very close.	Am RH

Army Form C. 2118

WAR DIARY
or
INTELLIGENCE SUMMARY
(Erase heading not required.)

Instructions regarding War Diaries and Intelligence Summaries are contained in F. S. Regs., Part II. and the Staff Manual respectively. Title Pages will be prepared in manuscript.

Place	Date	Hour	Summary of Events and Information	Remarks and references to Appendices
F1 Sector	26th	Fri.	The LEFT COY. (C. Coy.) was rather heavily French mortared with 90 pdrs. Not much trench damage was done. Usual shelling about FOREST'S, FICHEUX ST. & FINEST. Several paper balloons were sent over to us, landing behind our lines, these were filled with copies of a the German & French paper playing to the French peasants; probably a counter-stroke to our having put pamphlets in German on the enemy wire. Duke asked the enemy to give himself up.	AmRH
"	27th	Sat.	We were relieved by the 7 K.R.R.C. & went back to RIVIERE into Bde. reserve. During the relief one of our de Havilland scouts flew several times, at a height of only 500 ft., across the German lines obtaining 21 good photos. A barrage was put up by our 18 pdrs. Voluntary services at Church Army hut. The usual working parties. In spite of the intense cold very few cases of trench feet were gone no frost bite.	AmRH
RIVIERE	28th	Sun.		AmRH
"	29th	Mon.	Working parties of about 100. Temperature about 10° at night still snow on the ground.	AmRH
"	30th	Tues.	Working parties & baths & footy.	AmRH
"	31st	Wed.	Same; working parties & baths & footy. Maj. Rixon M.C. appointed temp. Lt Col.	JaRH

L W Bondillon Capt.
Critbin commd

CONFIDENTIAL.

WAR DIARY

- of -

8th (S) Bn., THE KING'S ROYAL RIFLE. CORPS.

From: 1st February, 1917.
To: 28th February, 1917.

Volume XIX.

Army Form C. 2118

8th K.R.R.C.

WAR DIARY
or
INTELLIGENCE SUMMARY
(Erase heading not required.)

Instructions regarding War Diaries and Intelligence Summaries are contained in F. S. Regs., Part II and the Staff Manual respectively. Title Pages will be prepared in manuscript.

Place	Date	Hour	Summary of Events and Information	Remarks and references to Appendices
SIMENCOURT	1st	Thurs	The 4th West Riding Regiment relieves the battalion in RIVIERE. The 4th Division is extending its front to include the whole of sector. The battalion marches by Companies to SIMENCOURT. Orders arrive for slightly large working-party to DAINVILLE tomorrow.	RLH
GRAND RULLECOURT	2nd	Fri	Capt. BARBER takes 500 men to DAINVILLE for work on light railway under RE supervision, while remainder battalion returns to the same billets in GRAND RULLECOURT occupied by us last November. We expect a fortnight's rest temporarily working-parties. Cold still intense.	RLH
"	3rd	Sat.	Major Ream in Leave. Captain Brownillon i.c. in command. Very few men available for training, except some additional reinforcements, and there's too much snow on the fields to allow any movement.	RLH
"	4th	Sund.	No church-services possible. Brigade HQ moves into the village today.	RLH
"	5th	Mond.	No signs of relaxation of the frost. Slight fall of snow. Working-Party	RLH

1875 Wt. W593/826 1,000,000 4/15 J.B.C. & A. A.D.S.S./Forms/C. 2118.

WAR DIARY
or
INTELLIGENCE SUMMARY

(Erase heading not required.)

Army Form C. 2118

Place	Date	Hour	Summary of Events and Information	Remarks and references to Appendices
GRAND RULLECOURT	Feb 6	Mond.	reports that they are in front of B.H.Q and working satisfactorily to R.H.Q R.E. A few 5.9 shells in their vicinity.	RLH
"	7	Tues.	Daainville party returns in afternoon of 1 N.C.O & 12 men. Weather & sipping roads. They thought it would be allowed before the dripping of their parties to various villages.	RLH
"	8	Wed.	The day spent in its unthusiastic cleaning up. HQC N.C.O employment in the billets. Rations have twice our efforts lim to thaw in December. Im more funds have been put in first at present there is enough room for the men.	RLH
"	9	Thurs.	Very little morning but rifle exception shoulars, 10 learns from teams for the new 4 guns being sent to us, signallers reserve stretcher bearers. The weather is too increasy cold for hardening & young, and a few horses, each by a lieutenant in the middle of the day when there is a fallow parade.	RLH
"	9	Fri.	Few work by parties, one from each Company. Reserve the return to day. 100 men to BAVINCOURT, 70 men to of for IVERGNY, LE SOUICH and LUCHEUX. They are at work mainly on hutting and bundling releiving parties to	RLH

WAR DIARY
or
INTELLIGENCE SUMMARY

Army Form C. 2118

Place	Date	Hour	Summary of Events and Information	Remarks and references to Appendices
(4th ND) ROLLENCOURT	Feb 9th	Frid	The 7th L.R.B.C. and 7th K.R.B. at the work. In the afternoon we have to evacuate billets of 7th companies to find room for 2 Coml. Coys. 9th R.B.s	RLH
" "	Feb 10th	Sat.	The accumulation in the village SOMERIN being unnoticed for the Brigade to-day behind our lines, probably attracted by the a/drome-ing, light railways and dumps in this neighbourhood.	RLH
" "	Feb 11th	Sund.	Parade remains for about 100 men. A detachment of 40 men drawn from the Brigade in the 14th Div. depot battalion. This battalion is billeted in this village. Its object is to have trained drafts available at short notice.	RLH
" "	Feb 12th	Mond.	First signs of a thaw now apparent. There seems to be considerable concentration of troops in this district. The 3rd Division now here toward billeted in neighbouring villages.	RLH
" "	Feb 13th	Tues.	An apparent thaw has set in, but still a cold wind. Our men are in comfortable quarters and not overburdened with work.	RLH

1875 Wt. W593/826 1,000,000 4/15 J.B.C. & A. A.D.S.S./Forms/C. 2118.

Army Form C. 2118

WAR DIARY
or
INTELLIGENCE SUMMARY
(Erase heading not required.)

Instructions regarding War Diaries and Intelligence Summaries are contained in F.S. Regs., Part II. and the Staff Manual respectively. Title Pages will be prepared in manuscript.

Place	Date	Hour	Summary of Events and Information	Remarks and references to Appendices
GRAND RULLECOURT	Feb 13th	Tues	The party to further & light railway on the railway bank & hut & a new mushroom hurdles for LUCHEUX Forest.	RLH
"	14	Wed	The frost has set in again & a cold wind. Activity of enemy aeroplanes continues, especially in the neighbourhood of SAULTY, BAVINCOURT.	RLH
"	15	Thurs	Daly's return to trenches being postponed. The 14th Div. is holding a frontage only 2 battalions, one of the 42nd and one of 43rd Brigade, the Coys on O/ taking & having encroached on the former Divisional line.	RLH
"	16	Fri	Major C. Seymour D.S.O. has returned to the Battalion and assumes command. A fresh working-party of 150 men Kelly went out this afternoon & very short notice to SAULTY, where they will load and ammunition under the VII Corps Siege Park.	RLH
"	17	Sat	Each Battalion furnishes a Company to practice an attack on the trenches dug near the villages. The B.G.C. himself arranges & supervising the scheme. Went to the west, the south-west of the ground and the presence in the ranks of many employed men to make up the necessary number, the operation was not successful than it might have been.	RLH

1875 Wt. W593/826 1,000,000 4/15 J.B.C. & A. A.D.S.S./Forms/C. 2118.

Army Form C. 2118

WAR DIARY
or
INTELLIGENCE SUMMARY
(Erase heading not required.)

Instructions regarding War Diaries and Intelligence Summaries are contained in F.S. Regs., Part II. and the Staff Manual respectively. Title Pages will be prepared in manuscript.

Place	Date	Hour	Summary of Events and Information	Remarks and references to Appendices
GRAND RULLECOURT	Feb 18	Sunday	Very warm & misty weather. A small church parade in YMCA tent. The detachment at SAULTY is working harder than the other parties, having to load heavy lorries for ammunition & working in shifts day and night.	RLH
"	Feb 19	Monday	A new working party of 60 or 70 will have to be found in a day or two to replace men a detachment to 8th Rifle Brigade, who are under orders to move to ARRAS for work behind the line. Weather wet & warm. At 3 a.m. this morning a fire broke out in a barn occupied by B Coy, we either from a candle that had set the straw smouldering several hours before. Some straw & oats were damaged and the rafters of the barn. After 2 hours the fire was quenched by buckets of water handed along a chain of men and by the local fire engine.	RLH
"	20	Tues.	Very wet day. The new working-party is cancelled.	RLH
"	21st	Wed.	Very wet and misty weather. Training is confined to elementary musketry and R.S.M.'s parades.	RLH

1875 Wt. W593/826 1,000,000 4/15 J.B.C. & A. A.D.S.S./Forms/C. 2118.

WAR DIARY
or
INTELLIGENCE SUMMARY

(Erase heading not required.)

Army Form C. 2118

Place	Date	Hour	Summary of Events and Information	Remarks and references to Appendices
GRAND RULLECOURT	Feb. 22nd	Thurs	All the NCO's paraded to practise artillery formations. The C.O. taking the parade. Still no signs of moving into the line to relieve the 42nd & 43rd Inf. Brigades. They have only one battalion each in the line and seem content with their present situation.	RLM
"	23rd	Frid.	A Court of Enquiry assembles at these HQ's to examine into the cause of the recent fire and responsibility for the loss. Lt Col Bury of # K.R.R.C. presiding. Weather slightly clearer and more artillery activity on the sector S. of ARRAS is noticeable.	RLM
"	24th	Sat.	Telegrams just received indicate a withdrawal by the enemy on the whole of the ANCRE to a new line. No intimation yet of any change with us in the VII Corps sector, S. of ARRAS.	RLM
"	25	Sund.	Church Parade for 80 men in YMCA tent. A conference of CO's in the Brigades discusses the question of the re-organized formation of a battalion.	RLM

Army Form C. 2118.

WAR DIARY
or
INTELLIGENCE SUMMARY

(Erase heading not required.)

Place	Date	Hour	Summary of Events and Information	Remarks and references to Appendices
GRAND RULLECOURT	Feb 26th	Monday	In connection with the scheme of reorganizing battalions attempts are being made to secure the return to duty of men extra-regimentally employed and evacuation of men unfit for duty. If these efforts meet with success, much will be done in relieving the present discrepancy between the "ration" and "fighting" strength of the battalion. The usual parades for musketry, practice in drilling from new Courtmie. The CO with 2 having NCOs and officers went the trenches in AVESNES road to compare them with those imposed on the map, in a portion of the German line S.p. ARRAS.	RLH
"	27th	Tues.	A clearer, brighter day, & more shelling & aircraft activity. Alien aerial the retirement of the enemy from SERRE has not yet affected his line between ARRAS and MONCHY.	RLH
"	28th	Wed.	This battalion and the 7th KRRC take part in a scheme this morning, the 7th ?? leading and we supporting them in an attack upon 400 yards of the ?? trenches. The scheme involved an advance in artillery formation, detailing of mopping-up parties and deployment into waves of assault.	RLH

Seymour Lt Col. 8 K.R.R.C.

C O N F I D E N T I A L.

W A R   D I A R Y

- of -

8th (S) Bn., KING'S ROYAL RIFLE CORPS.

From: 1st March, 1917.
To: 31st March, 1917.

VOLUME XX.

Army Form C. 2118.

WAR DIARY
or
INTELLIGENCE SUMMARY

8th Bn. K.R.Rif.C.

MARCH 1917

Vol. XX

Place	Date	Hour	Summary of Events and Information	Remarks and references to Appendices
GRAND RULLECOURT	March 1st Thursday		The C.O. held an interdivisional parade in artillery formation during the morning. Windy & hard frost arrival. Usual R.Sh's parade afternoon.	Ampthill
"	2nd Friday		Same parade under C.O. as yesterday only leaving out specialists being regimentally trained. Ordinary parades in afternoon.	Ampthill
"	3rd Saturday		Practice attack under the C.O. took place this morning on the ARRAS - BEAVRAINS sector. Practice trenches situated on the C.D. ROULLECOURT -	Ampthill
"	4th Sunday		AVESNES road. Lt. Pope went to the Lewis gun course at LE TOUQUET. A C of E. parade service was held by Rev. Masham, with as big a party as was available (viz. 80) because rest of the Batt. being on the permanent working parties. A case of mumps has occurred in B. Coy. necessitating segregation of the men concerned.	Ampthill
"	5th Monday		Parades as usual. 2Lt. Penly attd. to the batt. left on being seconded for duty with the R.F.C. The roads are in an extremely bad state owing to the protracted thaw. Thaw precautions are taken, ie. no traffic on roads.	Ampthill
"	6th Tuesday		R.Sh's parade in morning & afternoon. A regtl. bath house having been rigged up men can now bathe regimentally. A Coy. is now isolated for mumps.	Ampthill

WAR DIARY
INTELLIGENCE SUMMARY

Army Form C. 2118.

Place	Date	Hour	Summary of Events and Information	Remarks and references to Appendices
Gd.-RULLECOURT	July 7th	Wed.	Parades as usual under R.S.M.; specialists attack in afternoon but not in morning.	
"	8th	Thurs.	Usual parades under R.S.M. The working parties from LUCHEUX, SUS-ST.-LEGER and IVERGNY returned this afternoon (about 250 all told). This still leaves parties at RAVENCOURT (100 odd) SAVITY (100) & MONDICOURT (20) with regard to these parties taken from the Baths of this Bde. It is believed that some of the higher authorities think that the battn. are doing tactical training, not realising that about 85% - 90% of the efficient fighting strength are doing fatigue work in different villages	
"	9th	Friday	Coys. at disposal of O.C. Coys. in the morning & under R.S.M. in the afternoon. The parties of A+B Coys. who are guaranties for months drill are hard to instil.	
"	10th	Sat.	C.O.'s full marching order inspection in the morning. All N.C.O.s & men in future are going to have 15 min. practice daily, at rapid loading. 2 LT. Tagg went to the VII Corps Lewis gun school. 2 LT. Cook takes over the duties of bombing officer.	

WAR DIARY
or
INTELLIGENCE SUMMARY

Army Form C. 2118.

Place	Date	Hour	Summary of Events and Information	Remarks and references to Appendices
GRAND RULLECOURT	11th Sunday		A C. of E. parade service was held by the Rev. Meacham. Its Y.M.C.A. tent. 80 men on parade. Also R.C. & Non-conformists services. One party of 40 men & 2/Lt. Lyle returned from the Depot Battn. today. No more men are being sent, it having been decided to send drafts direct from BASE to the Depot Battn. One party of 100 under 2/Lt. Mackinlay returned from working at BAINCOURT this afternoon. The weather has changed & is quite pleasant & Spring-like.	Am Ritchy
"	12th Monday		A Battn. parade under the C.O. in the morning. R&M's parade in the afternoon. It has been decided to have 1 each Coy. for active operations - 4 regular S.B.s. (including 1 N.C.O) & 9 reserve making up 3 squads of 4 & 1 N.C.O.	Am Ritchy
"	13th Tuesday		The same parades as yesterday.	Am Ritchy
"	14th Wed.		Battn. parade in morning under the C.O. in artillery formation working.	Am Ritchy Am Ritchy
"	15th Thur.		Same parades as yesterday. The party of 20 men from MONDICOURT returned today. All the parties have now come back.	Am Ritchy

Army Form C. 2118.

WAR DIARY
or
INTELLIGENCE SUMMARY

(Erase heading not required.)

Instructions regarding War Diaries and Intelligence Summaries are contained in F.S. Regs, Part II. and the Staff Manual respectively. Title Pages will be prepared in manuscript.

Place	Date	Hour	Summary of Events and Information	Remarks and references to Appendices
GRAND RULLECOURT	15th Continued.		Lt. Col. Seymour. D.S.O. takes up the temporary command of the brigade while the B.G.C. is on sick leave. Maj. Rixon.M.C. & Capt. Bordiller.M.C. are acting as commanding officer & second in command respectively. Lt Clermont takes over the command of D. Coy.	Ap.Pkh
FOSSEUX -	16th Friday		The battn. moved to huts in FOSSEUX a distance of 5 miles towards the line. FOSSEUX is the HdQrs. of the VII Corps. Our hut camp is in a very small area & rather crowded. As the enemy is in rapid retreat towards the HINDENBORG LINE, and has been driven out of BAPAUME, a further move up of the brigade is expected.	Ap.Pkh
"	17th Sat.		The day was spent with kit inspections & cleaning up. A good deal of difficulty was found in procuring any trenching grenads. Working parties totalling about 200 men have to be found for unloading ammunition at railhead in FOSSEUX.	Ap.Pkh
"	18th Sun.		A parade service 280 strong (Capt Lesley.M.C. in command) was held.	Ap.Pkh
"	19th Mon.		There was a C.O's parade in the morning for a extended order work, on the limited ground available.	Ap.Pkh

Army Form C. 2118.

WAR DIARY
or
INTELLIGENCE SUMMARY

(Erase heading not required.)

Place	Date	Hour	Summary of Events and Information	Remarks and references to Appendices
FOSSEUX	20th	Tues.	Coys. at the disposal of O.C. Coys. in the morning. Rapid fire practice is carried on at short range nearby. It has been a wet and windy day. The French & British are following up the enemy retreat as quickly as is possible in unfavourable weather.	An. Rfh
"	21st	Wed.	Same parades as yesterday. The batt. had to stand-by all day in readiness to move at 2 hours notice to DAINVILLE.	An. Rfh
"	22nd	Thurs.	At 2 p.m. today we received orders to march up to ARRAS at 3 p.m. The march was very unpleasant owing to driving sleet for most of the 9-10 miles march. We eventually reached our billets at about 8.30 p.m.	An. Rfh
ARRAS	23	Fri.	The day was spent reconnoitring the line, by parties from each coy. and H.Qrs. Fortunately it was a quiet day. The trenches we were preparatory to taking over were the old German trenches in front of H. sector, which the 42nd & 43rd Bdes. had occupied on the enucleation front by the enemy. The line roughly runs 700yds. E. of BEAVRAINS in a N.N.E. direction. The line is front is on old front line in Q.36. sheet 51B.	An. Rfh

WAR DIARY
or
INTELLIGENCE SUMMARY

Army Form C. 2118.

(Erase heading not required.)

Place	Date	Hour	Summary of Events and Information	Remarks and references to Appendices
ARRAS.	24th	Sat.	We relieved the 6th Bt. Somerset L.I. (43rd Inf. Bde.) in the front line.* One relief was quiet & was completed about 7 p.m. During the night the enemy intermittently shelled Bn. H.Q. and the back trenches with 105 mm. & 77 mm. shells.	*Vide 23rd. Alm. R. Kelly
Trenches in front of BEAURAINS.	25th	Sun.	Our artillery shelled the enemy about the HARP and TILLOY fairly heavily. During the day the enemy were fairly quiet except for occasional shelling with los mm. shells about our L. Coy. H.Q.	Alm R Kelly
Do.	26th	Mon.	Our artillery was fair active owing to poor observation, but some wire cutting on the HARP (TELEGRAPH HILL) was carried out. Our enemy shelled our front line Coy's H.Q. & Back trenches during the day; this increased during the night rather harassing working & carrying parties at the enemy were searching rather than trying on any very definite positions. We had a few casualties.	Alm R Kelly
Do.	27th	Tue.	A very similar day to yesterday. Our artillery was rather aggressive. The enemy fire was rather troublesome again at night.	Alm R Kelly

WAR DIARY
or
INTELLIGENCE SUMMARY

(Erase heading not required.)

Army Form C. 2118.

Place	Date	Hour	Summary of Events and Information	Remarks and references to Appendices
Old enemy trenches in front of BEAURAINS.	28th	Mon	We were relieved in the line by the 7th K.R.Rif.C. One relief was pretty quiet except for some shelling of one L.&R. front coys' H.Q.s. During this tour considerable work was done each night on digging assembly & C.T.s in front of our line (PREUSSENWEG.) 20 wires were put out in front of our line. Gas. O. strong evening party was always found to cover our parties & sappers. About 12 casualties occurred during the tour.	(Mr. R.A.H?)
RONVILLE CELLARS & CAVES.	29th	Tues.	We are now in Bde. reserve in RONVILLE with H.Q. & A.Coy in the RONVILLE CAVES. Lt.Col. Seymour D.S.O. returned to the Battn. from Bde. & Major Rixon left for the Aldershot Co's. Course starting on 9.IV.17. Capt Haley went on leave. Several working parties have to be found at night for digging in the line.	(Mr. R.A.H?)
Do.	30th	Wed	Working parties have to be found again tonight. The men are able to have baths here. Our artillery shelled the enemy heavily.	(Mr. R.A.H?)
Do.	31st	Thur	All same parties again tonight. During the day and evening RONVILLE was shelled with a good many 4.2" & 5.9's shells.	(Mr. R.A.H?)

Seymour Lt. Col.

CONFIDENTIAL.

WAR DIARY

- of -

8th (S) Bn., THE KING'S ROYAL RIFLE CORPS.

From: 1st April, 1917.
To: 30th April, 1917.

Volume XXI.

Army Form C. 2118.

WAR DIARY
INTELLIGENCE SUMMARY
(Erase heading not required.)

8TH K.R.R.C.
APRIL 1917.
Vol XXI (L)

Place	Date April	Hour	Summary of Events and Information	Remarks and references to Appendices
Trenches E. of BEAURAIN.	1st.	Sunday.	We left the RONVILLE CAVES and relieved the 7 K.R.R.C. in the line. The relief was fairly quiet. We took over a lot of work to be done on the new assembly trenches in front of the HARP (TELEGRAPH HILL) Usual shelling by 4.2" hours. & 77 m.m. on our front & rearward trenches.	Am. A till.
Do.	2nd	Mon.	The usual amount of shelling. Our artillery continue to bombard the enemy & to cut wire. Much work was done on the assembly trenches.	Am. A till.
Do.	3rd	Tues.	A similar day to yesterday. Very large parties were working on the night of the 3rd/4th. under the personal command of Lt.Col. Seymour D.S.O.	Am. A till.
Do.	4th	Wed.	During the night of the 4th/5th. we were relieved by a battn. (D.C.L.I.) of the 43rd I.B. and went into billets in ARRAS. The relief was quiet. Our own artillery was very active during the day.	Am. A till.
ARRAS.	5th	Thur.	We spent the day in ARRAS in the neighborhood of the PLACE VICTOR HUGO. ARRAS, especially around the station was intermittently shelled with 4.2" and 8".	Am. A till.
Do.	6th	Fri.	Another day in ARRAS with intermittent shelling of batteries in the Town; one going Am A till being very active & sleep being nearly impossible	

Army Form C. 2118.

8TH. K.R.R.C.

APRIL 1917.

WAR DIARY
INTELLIGENCE SUMMARY

(Erase heading not required.)

Place	Date April	Hour	Summary of Events and Information	Remarks and references to Appendices
DAINVILLE	7th.	Sat.	During the night of the 6th-7th. an artillery cordite dump was set on fire near our billets, fortunately there was no explosion. The enemy shelled the vicinity a little. In the afternoon the battn. moved back to DAINVILLE to some very good billets. Being the best billets we had had for some time, we of only slept the one night in them.	[signature]
RONVILLE CAVES.	8th.	Sun.	In the afternoon the battn. moved up into the RONVILLE CAVES (WELLINGTON CAVE.) Two of our large shell dumps "went up" in the afternoon, one at the CITADEL (ARRAS) & the other at ACHICOURT, the latter being so bad that we had to march into ARRAS by a different route.	[signature]
Old nos. Trench in RONVILLE	9th.	Mon.	The opening day of the battle of ARRAS. The 41.S.T.B. were in divl. reserve the 8.K.R.R.C. being in Bde. reserve, The 42nd & 43rd.Bde. had to take the RED, BLUE and BROWN objectives. The RED being the front line of the HARP, the BLUE being the support line, and the BROWN, the WANCOURT-FEUCHY line. The battn. emerged from the CAVES and went into one old res. line in RONVILLE at Zero + 2 h.o. 40 min. A few shells came over wounding 2 newly joined officers.	[signature]

Army Form C. 2118.

8th K.R.R.C.

APRIL 1917.

(IV.)

WAR DIARY
or
INTELLIGENCE SUMMARY
(Erase heading not required.)

Place	Date	Hour	Summary of Events and Information	Remarks and references to Appendices
	9th Contd.		We spent the whole day in it's position. The other 2 Bdes. got to the midway between the BLUE and BROWN lines & dug in. We reconnoitred the line in the evening.	Am.R.Mibye
BLUE LINE.	10th Tues.		In the morning we moved up to the BLUE line, extending into artillery formation on the S. slope of TELEGRAPH HILL. The 8th K.R.R.C. has still in Bde reserve. The night 10th/11th was spent in the BLUE line, the 7th R.B. & the 7 K.R.R.C. relieving the other Bdes. in front of the BROWN line, as yet uncaptured. We had practically no casualties.	Am.R.Mibye
BROWN LINE.	11th Wed.		During the night 10th/11th & early morning, the BROWN line was occupied by small detachments of the other batts. The 7 K.R.R.C. sustaining heavy casualties from M.G. fire from HILL 90 (S. of WANCOURT) which had not been taken by the 56th Div. on our Right. The 7 R.B. finally cleared the BROWN line so that we could take it over in the evening. The 8th K.R.R.C. relieved the 7 K.R.R.C. in the BROWN line front trench in the evening, it not being certain whether	Am.R.Mibye

2449 Wt. W14957/M90 750,000 1/16 J.B.C. & A. Forms/C.2118/12.

WAR DIARY
INTELLIGENCE SUMMARY

8th K.R.R.C.
APRIL 1917.

Place	Date	Hour	Summary of Events and Information	Remarks and references to Appendices
	11th contd.		The enemy occupied the BROWN line enfront trench or not.	Amplify.
WANCOURT	12th	Dawn.	Dispositions of coys.— A & C. Coys in front in BROWN LINE (Front trench of FEUCHY-WANCOURT LINE) W. of WANCOURT; and B & D. in support behind them. HILL 90 was reported captured by the 56th DIV. on the RIGHT and the enemy was reported to be in retreat from WANCOURT. Accordingly at about 8.30 a.m. the 8 K.R.R.C. sent out a patrol to see if WANCOURT was clear. This was proved to be the case, with the exception of a few of the enemy who gave themselves up. On patrol got in touch with the 56th DIV. S.E. of WANCOURT, and 8th R.B. towards GUEMAPPE, which to the LEFT. WANCOURT was occupied at about 11 a.m. WANCOURT was occupied by A Coy. In the afternoon we received orders to cross to the E. side of the COJEUL and attack the WANCOURT TOWER RIDGE (GUEMAPPE was reported occupied by us, by CORPS H.Q.)	Amplify.

WAR DIARY
INTELLIGENCE SUMMARY

8th K.R.R.C.
APRIL 1917.
V.

Place	Date	Hour	Summary of Events and Information	Remarks and references to Appendices
	12th contd.		The attack was ordered for about 7 p.m. and a creeping barrage was arranged, but the orders came so late that the troops had not got time to get into position properly. The enemy put down a very heavy barrage on the COJEUL VALLEY and much m.g. from GUEMAPPE (which was untaken afterall), was encountered. The 8th R.B. was to attack on our LEFT, we were attacking with A & C. Coys. in front. However at the last minute the attack was cancelled, C. Coy. received the cancelling order in time but A. Coy. did not. They therefore went over by themselves under LT. N.E. LEE directly our barrage lifted. They established themselves without much loss on the ridge N.E. of WANCOURT TOWER. The Coy. however had to be withdrawn at dusk as they were quite "in the air" on both flanks. Our total casualties for the day did not exceed 70 O.Rs. We were relieved in the evening by battns. of the 50th DIV. and went back to the BLUE LINE.	

WAR DIARY or INTELLIGENCE SUMMARY

Army Form C. 2118.

8th K.R.R.C.　APRIL 1917.

Place	Date April	Hour	Summary of Events and Information	Remarks and references to Appendices
Ht. ARRAS.	13th Fri.		Having had a short rest in the BLUE LINE, the batln. marched back very tired, into ARRAS and billeted there early in the morning. The weather during the operations was bad, snow and very cold winds prevailing, which did not add to our comfort. However we were all in good spirits at the success of the operations & the fewness of our casualties.	Appendix A
MONCHIET 14th Sat.			In the afternoon we left ARRAS and marched to MONCHIET for the night, on the way to GRAND RULLECOURT.	Appendix A
GRAND RULLECOURT	15th Sun.		The whole brigade marched to rest billets in GRAND RULLECOURT, the batln. taking up its old quarters which we had come back to, on and off ever since we first went down to the SOMME in AUG. 1916.	Appendix A
DO.	16th Mon.		A day of general cleaning up and kit inspections.	Appendix A
DO.	17th Tues.		Rain set in. Coys were at the disposal of O.C. Coys all day for drill.	Appendix A

Army Form C. 2118.

8th K.R.R.C.

APRIL 1917.

VII.

WAR DIARY
INTELLIGENCE SUMMARY
(Erase heading not required.)

Instructions regarding War Diaries and Intelligence Summaries are contained in F. S. Regs., Part II. and the Staff Manual respectively. Title Pages will be prepared in manuscript.

Place	Date April	Hour	Summary of Events and Information	Remarks and references to Appendices
GRAND ROLLECOURT	18th	Wed.	Rain again. The day was spent in smartening up drill during the fine intervals.	An.Ph.I
Do.	19th Thurs. 20th Fri. 21st Sat.		There was an R.S.M's. parade in the early morning and a long C.O's parade in open formation and the attack.	An.Ph.I
Do.	20th Fri.		no service for today	
D.O.	22nd Sun.		Parade service by Capt. T.W.A. JONES C.of E. in morning.	An.Ph.II
LA CAUCHIE	23rd Thur.		The Bde. left GRAND ROLLECOURT and marched (units at 500" interval) to the POMMIER area S.E. of SAULTY on the ARRAS - DOULENS road. The 8 K.R.R.C. went into billets at LA CAUCHIE.	An.Ph.II
RANSART	26th Thur.		In the early morning we received orders to march at once to the RANSART - BLAIREVILLE area. We started for RANSART at about 8:30 a.m. and bivouaced in the ruined village, staying there the night of the 24th/25th.	An.Ph.I

Army Form C. 2118.

WAR DIARY
INTELLIGENCE SUMMARY

8th K.R.R.C.

APRIL 1917.

(VIII)

(Erase heading not required.)

Place	Date	Hour	Summary of Events and Information	Remarks and references to Appendices
FICHEUX	25th Wed.		We left RANSART about 6PM and marched to FICHEUX (here we stayed the night in tents) E. of the remains of the village.	Ph/Bh/R.C.
COJEUL SWITCH	26th Thurs.		An early start from FICHEUX marching as a Brigade to take over trenches from the 151st Brigade in the COJEUL SWITCH, S. of the HARP. The weather was left behind at FICHEUX. The battalion marched via HERCATEL and NEUVILLE VITASSE reaching (the area allotted to us i.e. the maze of crump holes and battered trenches which had once been the COJEUL SWITCH & there were no dug outs in the area but luckily the weather was fine so the men were quite happy in the shelters they rigged up.	Ph/Bh/R.C.
"	27th Friday		A very fine day. The battalion found working parties of 150 during the day to work on a track running South through the HARP. Also small parties from the Coys did some salvage work.	Ph/Bh/R.C. Ph/Bh/R.C.
"	28th Sat.		Still fine & warm. Same working parties as yesterday.	
NIGER TRENCH.	29th Sun.		We relieved the 5th Ox & Bucks in NIGER & NEPAL trenches just S of the FRUCHY – WANCOURT LINE. Trenches in much the same state as the ones we left. We found a working party of 200 at night to dig assembly trenches in front of the present front line. No casualties.	Ph/Bh/R.C.
"	30th Mon.		A quiet day. Spent in issuing to the equipment to the men. The weather still fine & good.	Ph/Bh/R.C.

R.L. Henry
Lt & Adjt.
for Lt. Col. Cmg. 8th K.R.R.C.

CONFIDENTIAL.

WAR DIARY

- of -

8th Bn., KING'S ROYAL RIFLE CORPS.

From 1st May, 1917.
To 31st May, 1917.

Volume XXII.

Army Form C. 2118.

WAR DIARY
or
INTELLIGENCE SUMMARY
(Erase heading not required.)

S K R R C
MAY 1917
(1)

Place	Date	Hour	Summary of Events and Information	Remarks and references to Appendices
NIGER & NEPAL TRENCH	1	TUES	The Battalion moved up at night into trenches on the ridge E. of WANCOURT on the left of the sector from the Y.K.R.R.C., the 8th R.B. taking over the right. The Battalion was disposed in depth in about 8 trenches. The relief was carried out with few casualties considering the amount of hostile shelling.	(A)(B)(C)
TRENCHES E. of WANCOURT	2nd	WED.	A slight hostile shelling during the day. The battalion moved up widened in advance of our front line, HERON TRENCH, & occupied 1B15 JACKDAW in front of HERON with the leading Coys on a tape line in front of JACKDAW preparatory to the assault.	(A)(B)(C)
"	3rd	THURS.	The Battalion attacked at zero hour in accordance with the plan of attack for the 1st, 3rd & 5th Armies. The 42nd Brigade was on our left with the 4th Ox & Bucks next to us. The 56th Division was on the left of the 42nd Brigade. On our right was the 8th R.B. being the right battalion of the Division with a battalion of the 18th Division on their right. The battalion was disposed as follows. A & C Coys in the front line, A Coy on the left. C on the right. D Coy was in support. B was held in reserve in 1B15 TRENCH. The objective allotted to the battalion were two. The first was a track running from TRIANGLE WOOD to CHERISY called ST MICHAELS ROAD & known as the BLUE LINE. No. 2nd, the RED LINE, was about 800 yds further on & roughly parallel to OPHIR TRENCH and about 50 yds short of it. Zero hour was 3.45 AM at which time it was quite dark. We were given 48 minutes to reach the BLUE LINE about 1500 yds distant, NARROW TRENCH a shallow untraversed trench being taken on the way. The 18 Pdrs put up an excellent	(A)(B)(C)

(cont)

Army Form C. 2118.

Instructions regarding War Diaries and Intelligence Summaries are contained in F. S. Regs., Part II. and the Staff Manual respectively. Title Pages will be prepared in manuscript.

WAR DIARY or INTELLIGENCE SUMMARY

(Erase heading not required.)

8. K. R. R. C.   MAY 1917.   II

Place	Date	Hour	Summary of Events and Information	Remarks and references to Appendices
TRENCHES E. of WANCOURT	3	THURS (contd)	excellent barrage which could easily be followed by the front line companies. The BLUE LINE was reached at 4.43 A.M. by A + C Companies, who had accounted for a good many Bosch on the way. Our casualties up to that time were very slight. Consolidation of this line was then begun with D Company filling up some 200 yds in rear. Touch had been lost with the 4th Brigade on our left and A + D Coys both sent patrols out to try and regain it without success as the 42nd had been met with overwhelming M.G. fire and had never got further than a couple of bushes just in front of their trenches suffering very severe casualties. Our left was swung back a bit towards TRIANGLE WOOD + HILL TOP WORK and Lewis Guns sent to this flank as an additional protection. Our right was now in touch with the 8th R.B. who had also reached the BLUE LINE without difficulty. For the first half hour after reaching the first objective very little interference was met with from the Bosch but about 5.0 am small parties of the enemy were seen entering TRIANGLE WOOD along a shallow trench coming from the direction of VIS-EN-ARTOIS. Our Lewis guns and riflemen caused a good many casualties on them and inflicted some of them inevitable machine guns unfortunately a few Bosch will some of their machine guns managed to reach the far side of the wood, either by crawling along the bottom of the said trench or by another route, and having a commanding	
		5.0 A.M		

Army Form C. 2118.

WAR DIARY
or
INTELLIGENCE SUMMARY

(Erase heading not required.)

8th K.R.R.C.   MAY 1917   III

Place	Date	Hour	Summary of Events and Information	Remarks and references to Appendices
TRENCHES E. of MONCHY	3 Thurs (cont)		field of fire towards CHERISY, sweeping straight down the BLUE LINE causing the Brigade many casualties during the reassemble of the Coys. Bear in mind a Bosch aeroplane suddenly appearing from nowhere flew low over our line dropping lights at about intervals. This was immediately followed by the a rain of 150 m.m. shells. The situation was now changed somewhat. A + C Companies could not dig anywhere as the troops had to be quite flat to avoid the attention's of the M.G in TRIANGLE WOOD. D Company was fortunate & a little better off in this respect and continued digging, almost unharmed by the M.G. fire.	
		5.00am	Captain Leslie M.C., who was in command of the front line, realised that it was out of the question to move forward after to the RED LINE as long as out left was in the air. His advance should have taken place at 5.45 AM at which time the 8 R.B. advanced and reached its RED LINE with a battalion of the 18th Division on their right. By this time it had become obvious that the attack had failed somewhere on the right of the 18th Division and that there was no chance of the 42nd Brigade on our left taking their final objective without considerable further assistance information. A Company of the 8th R.B. was sent up to fill in the gap caused by that battalion's further advance. Our Coy of A Company D was helping to form a defensive flank towards TRIANGLE WOOD in conjunction with A Coy.	

WAR DIARY / INTELLIGENCE SUMMARY

Army Form C. 2118

8. K.R.R.C.

IV MAY 1917

Place	Date	Hour	Summary of Events and Information	Remarks and references to Appendices
TRENCHES E of WANCOURT	3	Thurs (cont)	**Night** During this time the enemy had been shelling the whole country with H.E., the barrage of 150 & 210 mm being particularly heavy between our Battalion H.Q. and the BLUE LINE and between B. H.Q. and Advanced Brigade H.Q., thus rendering any communication very difficult. The wire to Battalion H.Q. was finally cut about 2.30 AM after which the two attacking Battalions of Brigade received no message from Brigade until 11.0 p.m. that night, although runners got through several times from the Battalions to Brigade. About 9.0 AM the hostile shelling began to increase in violence and reports began to reach Batt. H.Q. which was situated in HERON TRENCH the old front line, that parties of men of now supporting troops from the front line were trying to retire through CHERISY and further to the right. Large forces of the enemy were rumoured to be massing for a counter-attack against our new positions. No positive news in regard of CHERISY was untenable as the troops there were much in advance and the right and Thus a retirement started from the right through CHERISY or running in the air. The 19th Div were seen falling back towards Battalions of the 19th Div front line trenches. The retirement then extended to the D/L front line trenches and Company in turn found its right flank the left as each battalion and Company in turn found its right flank in the air. The 41st In. Bde, which had sent 4 guns up to the BLUE LINE,	(illegible initials) ok

Army Form C. 2118.

8.KRRC

MAY 1917

WAR DIARY
INTELLIGENCE SUMMARY
(Erase heading not required.)

Place	Date	Hour	Summary of Events and Information	Remarks and references to Appendices
E of HANDCOURT	3	THURS (cont)	Did great execution amongst the Boche ably assisted by the Lewis guns of the front & support companies. The retirement was completed by about 10.30 a.m. When the survivors of all three companies were back in JACKDAW, 12/1st, HERON TRENCHES. The M.Gs in TRIANGLE WOOD and one south of CHERISY did great damage to my brigade during the retirement from The Boche sent a line of skirmishers over the ridge in front of JACKDAW about an hour later but met with such heavy fire from the French that no further attack was attempted by him during the day. Later on a few snipers got into some shell holes and caused a few casualties amongst the snipers (2/Lt. J.G. LYNDALL at B.Hq. Our snipers got close to them & unfortunately killed) 2/Lt. J.G. LYNDALL at B.Hq. Our snipers got close to them & have hauled out 5 of the enemy that evening. Another attack was made by the 18 th DIV on ANDRON TRENCH about 7.0 P.M but failed. Our battalion was relieved at 11.30 P.M. by the 1/KRR who also Evacuated the 6th R.B. The casualties in the battalion were heavy chiefly in A.C. & neither R. in D. C. Coy. came out only 37 O.Rs & 2 officers. Casualties Officers 10. O.Rs 270. The Officer casualties were. Capt. J.W. Daly M.C.; 2/Lts. T.W. Dyke, C.F. Butcher, H.M. Cook, H.W. Little; wounded & missing; 2/Lts S.G. Lyndall killed; 2/Lt J. Wenham died of wounds (G.S.W.); 2/Lts A.H. Hele, S.R.C. Shaft, J Fence, wounded.	(Ap. 99, pp. p6)

Army Form C. 2118.

WAR DIARY
or
INTELLIGENCE SUMMARY

(Erase heading not required.)

9ᵗʰ K.R.R.C.

VI

MAY 1917

Place	Date	Hour	Summary of Events and Information	Remarks and references to Appendices
ALBATROSS TRENCH	4	FRIDAY	After orders to the 1/16 the battalion stayed the rest of the night and left Y.T.2 at 4.45 in BUZZARD (B+D) NETAL (A+C) and H.Q. in ALBATROSS. We were relieved in the evening by a unit of the 63ʳᵈ Brigade and returned to our old trenches in the COSCUL SWITCH.	Pa. PP. 1t-1t
COSCUL SWITCH	5	SAT	Day spent in inspecting equipment etc. Red Party informed in the evening.	Pa. PP. 1t
"	6	SUND	Kit inspections etc.	Pm. PP. 1t / Pa. PP. 1t
"	7	MOND	Large drafts expected. 1 officer and 7 men arrived. 6/Lt Todd (RAMC) relieving Lt -	Pm. PP. 1t
"	8	TUES	The fine weather broke for one day and a wet night ensued.	Pa. PP. 1t
"	9	WED	No training is possible here except a little bombing and lewis gunning. Drill takes place in camp. Holes A. Co's fired musketry. Reorganisation of the R.S.M. Transport officers billet etc. by Pioneers.	Pa. PP. 1t
"	10	THURS	Recd. segments went away for a few days rest. Major Bourdillon took over command of the battalion meanwhile. R.S.M. Holmes A.C. to Ply. wood 7-9 by splinter of H.E. Whilst returning A.Co's duties at R.S.M. C.S.M. Powell@Blakes over duties of R.S.M.	Pa. PP. 1t
"	11	FRID	Going into the BIRD TRENCHES again in a few days time. Lt/Col de Cestry & 2 killed.	Pm. PP. 1t / Y. PP. 1t
"	12	SAT	C.O., Adj., + 2 P.O. recommie trenches, we shall take over and by him S.D.C.L.I.	Pa. PP. 1t
"	13	SUND	Quiet & very hot day. Voluntary services in the morning.	Pa. PP. 1t / Pm. PP. 1t

Army Form C. 2118.

WAR DIARY
or
INTELLIGENCE SUMMARY

(Erase heading not required.)

Instructions regarding War Diaries and Intelligence Summaries are contained in F. S. Regs., Part II. and the Staff Manual respectively. Title Pages will be prepared in manuscript.

Place	Date	Hour	Summary of Events and Information	Remarks and references to Appendices
COJEUL SWITCH.	14.5.17	Mond.	Very hot day. Major Bouillon went up again to reconnoitre new position for Bn. Hd Qrs in Bird Trenches. Batt. paraded at 11.30 p.m. and marched up to the Trenches. We had a quiet relief with no casualties relieving The D.C.L.I. of the 43rd Bde. The trek carts were heavily loaded & soon after relief was over.	J.H.Bouillon Major
Tunnels E. QUANCOURT.	15.5.17	Tues.	The Batt. was disposed in support to the 7th/Som. L.I. with an O.P. Hd Qrs. was in a deep German M.G. dug-out giving an excellent view W & N. Movement had to be restricted, as we were overlooked from the high ground about BOIS DU VERT. A & B Coys. were together close by Bn. Hd. Qrs. in a tangle of trenches known as the NEST. C & D Coys. were formed into a joint double company and occupied DUCK and EGRET trenches, with their left on SHIKAR LANE.	J.H.Bouillon Major
"	16.5.17	Wed	Quiet day. Large working parties found to work on tram, bivouacs & new support line. C & D left a garrison of 50 men for work in their own trenches only.	J.H.Bouillon Major
"	17.5.17	Th.	Occasional shells near C & D Coys. No casualties. Rain. The trenches became waterlogged. Wire work was in progress, and about midnight working parties were stopped.	J.H.Bouillon Major
"	18.5.17	Fri.	Quiet. Weather improved. Working parties as before.	J.H.Bouillon Major
"	19.5.17	Sat.	The second anniversary of our arrival in France. At 9 p.m. a division on our left made an attack on enemy trenches near BOIS DU VERT, which was unsuccessful. In the night we relieved 7/10th in the front line.	J.H.Bouillon Lt.Col.
"	20.5.17	Sun.	Disposition in front line as follows:- B Coy. on right with A in support: C & D on the left with JACKDAW and BULLFINCH TRENCH	J.H.Bouillon Major

Army Form C. 2118.

WAR DIARY or INTELLIGENCE SUMMARY

(Erase heading not required.)

Place	Date	Hour	Summary of Events and Information	Remarks and references to Appendices
			a) 181's trenches. Sd Ops here in a deep Boche dugout. Flanks as before. In the early morning the 33rd Div. made an attack on the Hindenburg Line N. of RULLECOURT. Our Div. and the 18th Div. made a "Chinese attack" and put over an 18 pdr. barrage. The enemy reply was unusually let up being and no casualties were only two or three slightly wounded. As a heavy retal. after had been anticipated the two 7" Bns had withdrawn on a relief (?) the NIGER TRENCH area, and C.I.D. togr left a garrison behind in DUCK trench. That night the two 7" Bns came up to the support positions and the garrison NCO came up to the front line.	J.H.Bond Allen Major
	21.5.17 Mon.		Fairly quiet. Contact fire maintained in enemy sap at STOKES(?) rifle grenades. A German N.C.O. who had lost his way was taken by C. Coy, he belongs to the 86th Regt. 181 Div. Run Sir Sir he had replied in the front line -87th and 86th. They rec'd MARROW which with several paro in shell holes in front. Rain fell at night. I made the bivouac very damp. Bn. M. Bn. Pontecheil with 5.9" gun about half an hour in the middle of the Bay. M.O's dresser killed. German patrols 2 shell hole posts caught by L.M.G. fire from B Coy.	J.H.Bond Allen Major
	22.5.17 Tues.		Some shelling on 181's trench and trench mortar activity along front line. They were twice silenced by our guns. B Coy sent a fighting patrol to the German sap. turn it had been evacuated. Our patrols had enlarged several shell h/15 & the sap was made two tones shell holes. Six Stokes bombs were carried into the sap and exploded. C Coy took another prisoner wounded by their L.M.G. on patrol.	J.H.Bond Allen Major
	23.5.17 Wed.			

Army Form C. 2118.

WAR DIARY
or
INTELLIGENCE SUMMARY

(Erase heading not required.)

Place	Date	Hour	Summary of Events and Information	Remarks and references to Appendices
Trenches E FLAMICOURT	25.07.17	Thurs.	Enemy T.M activity increased. Also some previous by shelling. From 9 p.m - 11 p.m. a fairly heavy B.T.M & rifle was opened on TRENCHES & 1833 but activity was fair, & indeed the stuff went well over. The Posts were relieved at night by the K.S.L.I. (42nd Bde.) Relief kept to time about 1 a.m. We had expected a raid but during the two days, but the Boche was faintly quiet, no infantry certainly had a bad time and our L.M.Gs, snipers and rifle grenades gave him a good warm time & all. Our own casualties were 2 killed and about 12 wounded.	[signature]
COMBLES SWITCH	25.5.17	Fri.	The Bn. quitted GR back into an old place in the COMBLES SWITCH a little before dawn. Or rather 3:30 A.M. Gas Curtains which had been in position on our right for some days, were up, apparently with very little effect beyond gassing some of the K.S.L.I. 1 Prisoner stated that tunnel had been carried by it. On relief the day previous, and in the evening were relieved by 2 Bn. of the 63rd Bde. and marched back to a rest camp just S.W. of BEAUREGARD. 2/Lts. REYNOLDS & CONNOR (London Scottish) joined the Bn.	[signature]
BEAURAINS	26.07	Sat.	A Quiet Day - spent in cleaning up, kit inspection ate. Some small aeroplane bombs were dropped by the Transport Camp, but did no damage.	[signature]

Army Form C. 2118.

WAR DIARY
or
INTELLIGENCE SUMMARY
(Erase heading not required.)

Instructions regarding War Diaries and Intelligence Summaries are contained in F. S. Regs., Part II. and the Staff Manual respectively. Title Pages will be prepared in manuscript.

Place	Date	Hour	Summary of Events and Information	Remarks and references to Appendices
Beaurains	27.5.17	Sun.	Quiet day. Services in the open air.	Shandille
do	28.5.17	Mon.	Special training and Coy. or- dis-trast of Coy Commanders. C.O. starts riding class for junior Officers before breakfast.	Shandille
do	29.5.17	Tues.	As above. Hottest in the evening. Mr. A.E. BARRETT, Mr. E. THACKERAY-TURNER and 180 O.R. reinforcements	H. Shandille
do	30.5.17	Wed.	As above. Very heavy thunderstorm in the evening. Camp flooded, but water soon drained away.	
			In the evening we held the anniversary dinner, postponed from the 19th. All the Officers dined together, and were honored by the a rest-[?] Gen. General Skinner & his staff. The Sergeants gave a smoking concert, lasting ¾ the "Fuzes Spring 15" before. The Officers went in after dinner. On the second half of the programme. Things ended soon after midnight.	H. Shandille
do	31.5.17	Thurs	On the Range all day. This is a 25 yard range built in the new-[?] Caves E. SAGNY.	H. Shandille

[signature] Lt. Lt. Col. 8 KRRC
for Comdr.

Army Form C. 2118.

WAR DIARY
INTELLIGENCE SUMMARY
(Erase heading not required.)

8.K.R.R.C.
JUNE. 1917. Vol 2.

Place	Date	Hour	Summary of Events and Information	Remarks and references to Appendices
BEAURAINS REST CAMP	JUNE 1st	FRIDAY	Battalion on the Field Firing Range until 11.0 A.M. Rest of day spent in Coy Parades etc. Football match v. Y/60 in evening won by the Battalion 3-1.	Ph/Ph/L.
"	2nd	SAT.	Battalion on miniature range. Working parties of 150 on Corps Dumps required. Lt. S.F.Toms? Camp shelled by long range gun in the evening. No damage done.	Ph/Ph/L. Ph/Ph/L.
"	3rd	SUNDAY	Church Parade in morning under Captain Mackenzie.	Ph/Ph/L. Ph/Ph/L.
"	4th	MONDAY	Move up to one of old quarters in COJEUL SWITCH in the evening.	Ph/Ph/L. Ph/Ph/L.
COJEUL SWITCH	5th	TUESDAY	Very hot day with some thunder showers. Parties working on Corps Dumps return.	
"	6th	WED.	Parties found for working on roads near WANCOURT. Remainder of battalion shortage miniature Range. NEUVILLE VITASSE. CAPT. E.V. TETLEY awarded the MILITARY CROSS and C.S.M. BULL (B Coy) the D.C.M.	Ph/Ph/L. Ph/Ph/L.
"	7th	THURS	Practically the whole battalion working until the 43rd Brigade in the front line system. in the General Harness List.	Ph/Ph/L.
"	8th	Friday	Working parties as on the 7th	Ph/Ph/L.
"	9th	Sat	Relieved by a unit of the 50th Division and return to BEAURAINS Rest Camp. a few shells sprung in camp in the evening. 411th M.G.C. had a few men wounded etc	Ph/Ph/L.
BEAURAINS REST CAMP	10th	SUNDAY	Day spent in preparing for 3 days of week, washing parts, boots etc.	Ph/Ph/L.

Army Form C. 2118.

WAR DIARY
INTELLIGENCE SUMMARY

(Erase heading not required.)

8th K.R.R.C.

JUNE 1917.

Place	Date	Hour	Summary of Events and Information	Remarks and references to Appendices
BEAURAINS	11th	MONDAY	41st BRIGADE moved to MONCHIET en route to BERTRANCOURT. Battalion moved off at 1.30 A.M. Very heavy rain during march. Very hot sun after arrival in MONCHIET. Battn. enabled battalion to dry itself.	Pa. Off. lt.
MONCHIET	12th	TUESDAY	Battalion moved at 8.0 AM to GAUDIEMPRÉ. A very hot march.	Pa. Off. lt.
GAUDIEMPRÉ	13th	WED.	Battalion moved about 8.0 AM to BERTRANCOURT. Battalion is in huts. The camp (long time) in a very filthy condition. Sgt LEATHER & Rfm WHITEHEAD awarded the D.C.M. for exceptionally good work on MAY 3rd.	Pa. Off. lt.
BERTRANCOURT	14th	Thurs	Day spent in cleaning the camp, looking for parade grounds, etc.	Pa. Off. lt.
"	15th	FRIDAY	Day spent in cleaning the camp, inspections etc. Camp has by now become quite clean.	Pa. Off. lt.
"	16th	SAT.	Company parades, Musketry, skill at arms. A battalion parade ground available here which makes training for shots and skill at arms equally difficult.	Pa. Off. lt.
"	17th	SUN.	Church Parade with 8th Rifle Brigade.	Pa. Off. lt.
"	18th	Monday	Company on the range in morning. Two firms in afternoon harrassed by battalion being Drill, Bombing & skill at arms. A battalion rest has been started in a large Russian Hospital Hut. Such makes an excellent ante-room and mess room.	Pa. Off. lt.

Army Form C. 2118.

WAR DIARY
or
INTELLIGENCE SUMMARY

(Erase heading not required.)

8 K R R C
June 1917.

Instructions regarding War Diaries and Intelligence Summaries are contained in F. S. Regs., Part II. and the Staff Manual respectively. Title Pages will be prepared in manuscript.

Place	Date	Hour	Summary of Events and Information	Remarks and references to Appendices
BERTRANCOURT	19th	Tuesday	Parades as on Monday. The weather still continues fine & hot	Ph/Appdx
"	20th	Wed.	Parades as on Tuesday. The Colonel SEYMOUR D.S.O returns from leave	Ph/Appdx
"	21st	Thurs	Company training with C & D Coys in morning on ground behind old front line trenches near MAILLY-MAILLET. Night operations with A & B Coys.	Ph/Appdx
"	22nd	Friday	Company training. A & B Coys in morning. Rain interfered with training somewhat so night operations were postponed. Funks & battalion boxing competition in evening.	Ph/Appdx
"	23rd	Sat	Battalion training. Battalion in the attack.	Ph/Appdx
"	24th	Sunday	Battalion sports all day. 10AM - 9.30PM. A very nice day. E Coy (Transport) won the championship. Barrel of beer.	Ph/Appdx
"	25th	Monday	Inter-Coy events in battalion sports (ld) in morning. Night operations cancelled on account of wet weather. The 9th R.B. won most of the events.	Ph/Appdx
"	26th	Tuesday	Divisional Horse Show. A great success.	Ph/Appdx
"	27th	Wed.	Battalion training in morning. Inter-Coy events completed in the Brigade sports in the afternoon. The battalion went 2nd in the Bombing Competition.	Ph/Appdx

WAR DIARY

INTELLIGENCE SUMMARY 8. K.R.R.C.

(Erase heading not required.)

JUNE 1917

Army Form C. 2118.

(4)

Place	Date JUNE	Hour	Summary of Events and Information	Remarks and references to Appendices
BERTRANCOURT	28th Thurs.		A Brigade attack scheme arranged for the day had to be cancelled owing to the weather. Infantry training took its place.	Ph Pope Lt
"	29th Friday		The first day of the Brigade sports. No parades today.	Ph Pope Lt
"	30th Sat.		Brigade scheme with Y/60, 6-0 A.M — 12 noon. Spoilt by wet. About 200 reinforcements arrived at the battalion during the month including C.S.M. Jagger who arrived on the 27th from a reformation of returned wounded. Four officers also joined the 6th Battalion to take over the duties of R.S.M. Four officers also joined the battalion, 2/Lieuts. SPILLING, MARTIN, RAYNER and RALPH all from the 5th & 6th battalions.	Ph Pope Lt

Ph Pope Lt. I.O.
for O.C. 8. K.R.R.C.

Army Form C. 2118.

8/4/ K.R.R.L

JULY 1917

WAR DIARY
or
INTELLIGENCE SUMMARY
(Erase heading not required.)

Place	Date	Hour	Summary of Events and Information	Remarks and references to Appendices
BEAURAINCOURT	July 1st	Sunday	Church Parade under Colton S.O. LEE with the 8th Rifle Brigade on the parade ground.	Ph/8/R.e C/L
"	2nd	Monday	C + D Coys on the range in the morning. Military events in Brigade sports took place in the afternoon. The battalion were 2nd in the bombing and 3rd in the stretcher bearing. Signalling + Rifle shooting.	Ph/8/R.e C/L
"	3rd	Tuesday	Brigade Sports Day. A beautiful day for the meeting. The Battalion won the relay race and did well in most of the other events. The success of the day was contributed to by the attendance of Charley's Boys from Amiens, which did excellent business throughout the day.	Ph/8/R.e C/L
"	4th	Wed.	Brigade Field Day. An attack through the ruins of Auchonvillers to a French infant at BEAUMONT HAMEL, well carried out considering the difficult nature of the ground.	Ph/8/R.e C/L
"	5th	Thurs.	A wet day Coys did some training in camp between the showers.	Ph/8/R.e C/L
"	6th	Friday	A combined attack with the 8th R.B. in the morning. Practice for R.Cos in taking charge of mixed sections. The battalion Rifle Meeting began in the afternoon.	Ph/8/R.e C/L
"	7th	Sat	Battalion Rifle Meeting. U/R.S.M. Jagger battalion shot. U.O's + Sergts. beat the Brigade Staff in the final of the battle competition. Officers beat the Sergeants at Rifle shooting, but the Sergeants turned the tables in the knotted shoot. A very successful meeting. In the evening the new battalion concert party gave a very successful first concert which was much appreciated by a large audience.	Ph/8/R.e C/L

Army Form C. 2118.

8/K.R.R.C.

WAR DIARY
INTELLIGENCE SUMMARY
(Erase heading not required.)

JULY. 1917.

II

Place	Date	Hour	Summary of Events and Information	Remarks and references to Appendices
BERTRANCOURT	8th	Sunday	Church parade cancelled owing to the weather. A day of rest.	Ph.Offr.C/t.
"	9th	Monday	Finish of Rifle meeting + Lewis gun, range Competition. Preparations for the move.	Ph.Offr.C/t.
"	10th	Tuesday	Battalion marched to TERAMESNIL. Preparatory to entraining the next day at DOULLENS.	Ph.Offr.C/t.
TERAMESNIL	11th	Wed.	A quiet day before proceeding to DOULLENS.	Ph.Offr.C/t.
In the Train	12th	Thurs.	Battalion entrained with transport + staff DOULLENS at 4.30 am arrived at CAUDESWERVELDE at 10 P.M. where it detrained and marched to its billets, read BERTHEN, about 5 miles away. A very nice part of the country + very good billets in 3 Farms with a certain number of the troops in tents. 2 Co.ys in each of 2 Farms + HQ + Transport in the 3rd.	Ph.Offr.C/t.
BERTHEN.	13th	Friday	We are now in the IX Corps with the 19th, 37th + 41st Divisions. The Corps HQ's the line East of the MESSINES Ridge. Company ranges.	Ph.Offr.C/t.
"	14th	Sat.	Inter company cricket starts. Each Farm has an excellent (for the country) cricket field.	
"	15th	Sunday	Church Parade in field at H.Q. not a very large attendance as 2 companies are to tking.	Ph.Offr.C/t.

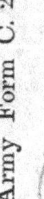

Army Form C. 2118.

WAR DIARY
INTELLIGENCE SUMMARY
(Erase heading not required.)

8/K.R.R.C.

JULY 1917

Place	Date	Hour	Summary of Events and Information	Remarks and references to Appendices
BERTHEN	16th	Monday	Company parades. Some Officers went to reconnoitre the ridge defences of WYTSCHAETE.	Ph/Pfe C/Lt
"	17th	Tuesday	A working party of 100 to work under the R.E. on the ridge defences. Also to be found by this battalion. "B" Coy finds these.	Ph/Pfe C/Lt
"	18th	Wed.	Company parades & cricket matches.	Ph/Pfe C/Lt
"	19th	Thurs.	Battalion route march in the morning. Officers v Sergeants cricket match in the evening. Won by the Sergeants by 1/2 runs to 32.	Ph/Pfe C/Lt
"	20th	Friday	Range (150yds) allotted to the battalion & used till all day.	Ph/Pfe C/Lt
"	21st	Sat.	Company parades started at 7am. 8am, 9am & 13th Battalions. The 18th & 21st battalions also took part on the relay race. The 1st team in hounds, & the 9th team close behind. We won the relay Race.	Ph/Pfe C/Lt
"	22nd	Sunday	The wrestling on horse back. LT.GEN. MORLAND was present. Some of the Church Parade, held Capt. Lee. Lt H.E. Houson returned to the battalion & took over the 2. E.O. of Lithgow officer.	P. & Ph/Pfe C/Lt
"	23rd	Monday	Battalion sent parties out on the morning. "C" Coy went out to relieve "B" Coy on the "ridge" defences to WYTSCHAETE.	Mt. Robertson
"	24th	Tuesday	Company parades in the morning. Rain in the afternoon made it impossible to do anything.	Mt. Robertson
"	25th	Wednesday	Battalion sent parties in "Battle Order" in the morning. Cricket matches in the afternoon.	Mt. Robertson

Army Form C. 2118.

WAR DIARY
INTELLIGENCE SUMMARY
8th K.R.R.C.
July 1917.

IV

(Erase heading not required.)

Place	Date	Hour	Summary of Events and Information	Remarks and references to Appendices
BERTHEN	26th Thursday		The Army Commander, 2nd Army, General Sir Hubert Plumer, inspected the 14th Division today. The Battalion was inspected at 11 A.M. The Army Commander spent a considerable time inspecting the Battalion, speaking to many of the Officers, N.C.Os and men personally. Ten of the Officers of the Battalion went up in the afternoon to reconnoitre the support and reserve line east of St. Eloi.	2/Lt. Ihorton killed
"	27th Friday		The 150 yard range on Mt KOKEREELE was allotted to the Battalion today, and was used all day.	2/Lt. Ihorton killed
"	28th Saturday		Company Parade and cricket practice.	
"	29th Sunday		Church Parade under Captn Chaiseront. Rain all day.	2/Lt. Rosenheint 2/Lt. Ihorton Lieut
"	30th Monday		Lis Oiddis had our received to be ready to move at short notice. The day was spent in getting ready. Their kit etc handed in.	2/Lt. Ihorton Lieut
"	31st Tuesday		Company Parades. As the Battalion was under orders to be ready to move at one hour's notice, none was allowed to leave billets. A cricket match was played in the afternoon 8th 60th Officers v 7th 60th Officers, which after a very good game resulted in a win for the 7th 60th Officers by one run.	2/Lt. Ihorton Lieut

J. M. Vincent
Major
for Lt Col
8th KRRC

WAR DIARY

Army Form C. 2118.

4/ 8th K.R.R.C. 14 August 1917.

INTELLIGENCE SUMMARY
(Erase heading not required.)

Place	Date	Hour	Summary of Events and Information	Remarks and references to Appendices
BERTHEN	August 1st		The Battalion was still under orders to be ready to move at an hour's notice. Very heavy rain fell all day - Orders to be ready to move at an hour's notice cancelled in the afternoon. Still raining all day.	F.B. Retreat
"	August 2nd		Short Company route marches in the morning. Continued rain. The 4th Division were transferred to G.H.Q. Reserve. At present however they are to remain where they are. Rain.	F. Retreat
"	August 3rd		Companies at the disposal of Company commanders. Weather slightly improved. The Battalion received orders to move to the next army rail. Day was spent in preparation.	F. Retreat
"	August 4th			F. Retreat
"	August 5th			F. Retreat
KORTON LOOP	August 6th		The Battalion moved from its billets near BERTHEN to KORTON LOOP about three miles N.E. of HAZEBROUCK. The Battalion went into billets. The billets were scattered, and many of the men had to bivouac, but the weather was fine and there were plenty of fields. The Battalion arrived in one coll in the morning. Various just before dinner, without any stragglers.	F. Retreat
"	August 7th		Coys at the disposal of Coy Commanders	F. Retreat
"	August 8th		Training was carried out. Duties of the day. The Tribes making a gradual training. Coys and	F. Retreat
"	August 9th		Rats-aid in the morning. Archer training in the afternoon.	F. Retreat
"	August 10th		Coys at the disposal of Coy Commanders. Archer training.	F. Retreat

Army Form C. 2118.

WAR DIARY
or
INTELLIGENCE SUMMARY

(Erase heading not required.)

8th KRRC. August 1917

Place	Date	Hour	Summary of Events and Information	Remarks and references to Appendices
Kasrai Loop	August 12th		In training for S.R. attack and to bed early. There was a lot of rain. Church Parade in the morning. General ordered march 8th K.R.R.C. Officers & 7th K.R.R.C. Officers in the afternoon. The 7th K.R.R.C. Officers won after a close game.	Lt Robin Lt
"	August 13th		Bn. Route marched in the morning. Lecture by the C.O. in the afternoon.	Lt Shelton Lt
"	August 14th		Divl'l Horse Show. Bn. could when the aeroplane some scouted, advance guard, etc. Day spent in preparation.	Lt Shelton Lt Lt Jackson Lt
"	August 15th		The Bn moved in the evening to CAESTRE station where they were entrained to enterain. The Hour being 7.0 p.m. and 9.10. p.m. armd. until the arrival of trgt 8.8. Entrained at CAESTRE and then left CAESTRE at 2AM.	Lt Jackson Lt
DICKEBUSCH Hts	2AM	Bn. detrained at ODDERDOM, for than to march to DICKEBUSCH HUTS arr. arriving	
	6AM	about 7.20 AM.	
	9.10 PM	Bn. Rendezvous, and Bde XXX Moved to CHATEAU SEGARD Area where they built in a field.	Lt Macdonald
Chateau Segard	Aug 17th	Bn. left CHATEAU SEGARD at 5PM, and went into Support on Observatory Ridge. The 8th K.R.R.C., and with the 7th K.R.R.C. The 7th K.R.R.C. was on the line. The 8th K.R.R.C. was not at a trench called CRAB CRAWL. The machine gun CRAB CRAWL was an old gun shaft. The machine gun CRAB CRAWL could not accommodate all. Had by their known except to the headgunner's shelter.	Lt Shelton Lt
"	Aug 18th	Bn. still in CRAB CRAWL under Observatory Ridge. The only part of the shelter was the front line the Kennetocks rifle from shellfire.	Lt Morton Lt

WAR DIARY
INTELLIGENCE SUMMARY

Army Form C. 2118.

8th KRRC

August 1917

Place	Date	Hour	Summary of Events and Information	Remarks and references to Appendices
Glencorse Ridge	August 19th		The Bn. still remained in CRAB CRAWL. Officers went out in the evening to reconnoitre the front line. All entrances to the H. found wire blocked and dug outs given in and all our wounded and our dead all buried.	Att. Matter H
Glencorse Ridge	August 20th		The Bn. Hold Camp. owing to the Bn having been taught it was on the relief the Bn decided to wait until the morning.	Att. Matter H
Chateau Begard	August 21st		The Bn. lift CRAB CRAWL at the evening of 6am and would had been in the assembly trenches by 6am and the following night. Owing to the way they had a great deal of severe and little rest was observed. Orders were received at midday to deliver a dawn of K support line 43rd Bn Rd. who had suffered very bad success. August 2 PM the Bn. aware by 5 platoon head. The assembly getting up and informed a considerable number of casualties. The Bn. sheltered in a bank in Sanctuary Wood assisting after dawn the set in Sanctuary Wood the ammunition broken down to the wood having about to 60 casualties at 10.30 PM the Bn. moved up to take over K CLAPHAM JUNCTION	Att. Matter H
Clapham Junction	August 22nd		STIRLING CASTLE line (K. side) for which the 133rd Bde had stated her morning) from reinforced route of the 43rd Bde. the day passed quietly considerable casualties caused by his shelling. The Bn. was relieved by the 9th R.B. at night when night came the shelling increased. The 9th RB came up and the Bn. began	Att. Matter H
	August 23rd			

Army Form C. 2118.

WAR DIARY
or
INTELLIGENCE SUMMARY 8th K.R.R.C.

(Erase heading not required.)

August 1917
IV

Instructions regarding War Diaries and Intelligence Summaries are contained in F.S. Regs., Part II. and the Staff Manual respectively. Title Pages will be prepared in manuscript.

Place	Date	Hour	Summary of Events and Information	Remarks and references to Appendices
CLAPHAM JUNCTION	August 24th		B11 B. Coy, 3 D Coy and 2 Platoons of A Coy had been detailed and trained to Zillebeke Bund, then SOS signal went up from the Bde to know who had occupied the Camp Front attacked by the Boches. The remainder of the 8th KRRC at the time were as follows:- H.Q and Communication Section in CLAPHAM JUNCTION tunnel under the MENIN ROAD. 2 Platoons of A Co, in JAM RESERVE had just taken STIRLING CASTLE. C Co. forming a defensive flank from South to INVERNESS COPSE & STIRLING CASTLE. The counter-attack was a failure, proof on the left between GLENCORSE WOOD and INVINEER COPSE where patrols of ours were pushed forward. They did not get far. It appears to be to still to withdraw to INVERNESS COPSE, and till the hours for the fight. The suffered badly for their shell fire during the stay, and but 6 Officers killed and 3 Officers wounded. 2nd Lt BOURDILLON, 2nd Lt Field (R.E. Capts) & Lt Lee, 2nd Lt Shipman, 2nd Lt BARRETT, L. Spilling MM wd W.d. ORs — amongst ORs this was about 100 casualties. The casualties were partly caused by shell fire, & owing to the breaking of the sides for the carrying parties of the Bn who recalled for ZILLEBEKE BUND. Shift on him after they arrived the W.d. The Bn was relieved and reached about 230 OR	Mr. Jackson Lt
CHATEAU SEGARD	August 25th		The Bn. moved to the camp for ZILLEBEKE BUND to CHATEAU SEGARD arr. there shortly after 9. J. Ck.	Mr. Jackson Lt
HALFWAY HOUSE	August 26th		At 2.45 PM the Bn left the CHATEAU SEGARD also for DICKEBUSCH ROT. arr. the curved the about 5 PM. Orders were immediately received that the Bn was to relieve that right to Suffolk Reg. Bn. the lie of the HALFWAY HOUSE at the R. at DICKEBUSCH Cross Roads on the ECOLE MENIN ROAD. This lie the Bn. moved to day out and reached at HALFWAY HOUSE	Mr. Jackson Lt

Army Form C. 2118.

August 1917
8th KRRC
V

WAR DIARY or INTELLIGENCE SUMMARY

(Erase heading not required.)

Place	Date	Hour	Summary of Events and Information	Remarks and references to Appendices
HALFWAY HOUSE	August 28th		The Bn. remained at HALFWAY HOUSE during the day. At night the Bn moved up to the Trench line at 8.15 pm. Two Coys (A & D) for the front line, with remainder of the Bde relief not completed till 2 am. The remainder of the Bn on the B. [?] line [?] [?] about 1.30 am accn. We received the back of the ASYLUM at YPRES with Bn [?] [?] the B to be [?] Coy A & B Coy 1 & 2 & the toe had been caught out to the C in C at [?] [?] Rely. We intercepted on the way back to the trenches over Zillebeke [?]	Attached
DICKEBUSCH	August 29th		DICKEBUSCH Road [?] [?] Bn [?] camp. Raining all day. Rest battle next morning difficult	Attached
PRINC BOOM	August 29th		Bn moved to PRINC BOOM (near WESTEREN) & rested here. Fine [?] battle[?]	Attached
"	August 30th		Day spent in refitting, reorganisation etc.	Attached
"	August 31st		Rain all day, [?] [?] of [?] [?] the rest of the Bn is also [?]	Attached

[signature]
Lt. Col.
Comdg 8/KRRC

CONFIDENTIAL.

WAR   DIARY

- of -

8th.(S) Bn. KING'S ROYAL RIFLE CORPS.

From 1st. September. 1917.
To: 30th. September. 1917.

Volume XXVI

Army Form C. 2118.

WAR DIARY
INTELLIGENCE SUMMARY

September 1917.
8/N.R.N.C. (1)

(Erase heading not required.)

Place	Date	Hour	Summary of Events and Information	Remarks and references to Appendices
METEREN	1st	SAT.	Companies at disposal of Company Commanders. Rugby match took place B Coy v. The Rest & was won by the Rest by 8 points to 3.	Pte Pfc C/Lt
"	2nd	Sunday	The Battalion marched to Aldershot Camp about 3 miles from BAILLEUL. The 41st Brigade is now in support, the 42nd being in the line East of MESSINES. The 14th (EIGHT) DIVISION being on a one brigade front. A little aerial activity at night, bombs being frequently dropped in the neighbourhood.	(Pte Pfc C/Lt)
Aldershot Camp	3rd	Monday	Day spent in cleaning up the camp.	Pte Pfc C/Lt Pte Pfc C/Lt
"	4th	Tuesday	The Commanding Officer inspected A & B Coys in the morning. C & D Coys had the use of the range.	Pte Pfc C/Lt
"	5th	Wed.	The Commanding Officer inspected C & D Coys. A & B Coys were on the range.	Pte Pfc C/Lt
"	6th	Thurs.	A party of officers went up to reconnoitre the line we take over from the 42nd Bttn.	Pte Pfc C/Lt
"	7th	Friday	10 Military Medals have been awarded to this battalion for its actions in Inverness Copse. See Appendix (6) attached. V.M.	Pte Pfc C/Lt
"	8th	Sat	A party of officers went up to inspect the trenches in the evening. A Rugby Match V. 41st & 249th M.G. Cs was lost	Pte Pfc C/Lt

Army Form C. 2118.

WAR DIARY
INTELLIGENCE SUMMARY

(Erase heading not required.)

September 1917 8th/K.R.R.C.

Place	Date	Hour	Summary of Events and Information	Remarks and references to Appendices
ALDERSHOT CAMP.	9th	Sunday	Parade Service in Camp at 11.0 A.M. Rest of day spent in getting ready for trenches.	Ph.Offe.C/lt
BRISTOL CASTLE	10th	Monday	LT. COL. C.H.N. SEYMOUR. D.S.O went to Field Ambulance, MAJOR J. MAXWELL M.C. 7th Rifle Brigade given temporary command of the battalion. The battalion moved up to Bristol Castle in the morning and stayed there for the day, relieving the 9th R.B.s in the line in the evening. A & D Companies in front line (A on right) C Coy in support. B in reserve.	Ph.Offe.C/lt
In the line East of MESSINES	11th	Tuesday	Relief over by 2.30 A.M. A quiet night. The front line is a series of detached posts, the exact whereabouts of which are at present uncertain. A lot of work to be done in taking them up. No communication by day to front line.	Ph.Offe.C/lt
"	12th	Wed	A quiet day. Some M.G. fire at night.	Ph.Offe.C/lt
"	13th	Thurs	One Company of the 7th R.B.s relieved the centre of our line for some 24 hours, as it was going to do a raid on that front in a few days. Our guns more active than recently, especially at night.	Po.Offe.Capt.
"	14th	Friday	We ought to have been relieved on night of 14/15 but this was postponed owing to following operation, so that the Brigade should be in the line as the relieving brigade has not been in the sector before. Enemy guns more active especially about midnight, around Batt. H.Q. which was hit by a shell but no damage done. Rifle wounded See Appendix (7) A. attended J.M.	Ph.Offe.C/lt

Army Form C. 2118.

WAR DIARY
INTELLIGENCE SUMMARY
(Erase heading not required.)

8/KRRC

September 1917.

III

Place	Date	Hour	Summary of Events and Information	Remarks and references to Appendices
In the line	15th	SAT.	The night of 15/16 was much quieter than previous nights especially in the front line. There were a marked absence of M.G. & Rifle Fire & firing of Very Lights on part of the Boche, which was very suspicious.	Pr R. Offr Capt.
"	16th	Sund.	In the early morning the Boche raided one of our posts near the MILL on the HIRON DELLE ROAD. His real objective was apparently the hill which we did not hold. The party that attacked the right post of D Coy was probably a flank guard. Four of our post were wounded & 1 (the 2/Cpl) captured. The Boche had 4 or 5 casualties which he took away with him. The light was very bad & other posts took some time identifying other raiders as Boche at first believing them to be one of our working parties returning. For casualties see Appendix (D) B attached. J.M.	Pr R. Offr Capt.
"	17th	Mond.	The battalion was relieved by the 9th R.B. on the night of 16/17. The relief was much more quickly carried out than the one on the 10/11 owing to the amount of work done by the battalion in theirline marking out tracks, linking up posts, digging new trenches & restoring old ones, + in having had are written maps made out. He had to leave 2 companies of wher the 9.R.B, as they ing the Company training for the raid left out. The remainder of the battalion went into Brigade Reserve at BRISTOL CASTLE.	Pr R. Offr Capt.
"	18th	Tuesday	The battalion & companies at BRISTOL CASTLE find working parties at night. There is no movement allowed by day.	Pr R. Offr Capt.

Army Form C. 2118.

WAR DIARY
INTELLIGENCE SUMMARY
(Erase heading not required.)

8/KRRC. September 1917. IV

Place	Date	Hour	Summary of Events and Information	Remarks and references to Appendices
In the trenches	19th	Wed.	Working parties as usual at night	Ph Pfe Cpt
BRISTOL CASTLE.	20th	Thurs.	A big attack by the 5th & 2nd Armies. Zero at 5.40 A.M. An artillery demonstration on our Corps (VIII) Front including a raid by the 7th R.B. which was quite successful, 6 Prisoners being taken & about 20 enemy killed. We were relieved by the 6th K.O.Y.L.I. in the afternoon, & came back to Aldershot Camp halting for a few hours at SHANKILL Camp on the way. One casualty See Appendix (1) D	Ph Pfe Cpt
Aldershot Camp	21st	Friday	Day spent in cleaning up equipment etc. also 2 working parties during the day. The two Companies from the line joined us here in the early morning.	Ph Pfe Cpt
"	22nd	Sat	Cleaning up & smartening up parades. Capt. C.L. DOMVILLE & 2/Lt T. MARTIN awarded Military Crosses for their work in operations round Inverness COPSE.	Ph Pfe Cpt
"	23rd	Sund	Church Parade in Concert Hut under Capt F.G. Scott. The Battalion had a bit of working parties to find during the day + night.	Ph Pfe Cpt
"	24th	Mond	Companies doing Company Drill, March Discipline, Wiring etc. Concert in the evening by the Fusee Springs.	Ph Pfe Cpt

Army Form C. 2118.

WAR DIARY or INTELLIGENCE SUMMARY

Sept. 1917 8th K.R.R.C.

Place	Date	Hour	Summary of Events and Information	Remarks and references to Appendices
ALDERSHOT camp	25		Bn. cleaning equipment and training	J.M.
	26		Bn. found 1 Offr. and 150 O.R.s for washing and sweeping in the forward area. Remainder cleaning and training in musketry and Lewis guns.	J.M.
	27		Bn. found 8 Offrs. and 370 O.R.s for working and carrying in the forward area. Rest of Bn. on musketry.	J.M.
	28		Bn. cleaning and training, musketry, Lewis gun, Bombing instructing.	J.M.
	29		Bn. found working parties for forward area. 7 Offr. + 270 O.R.s casualties. Killed No. R/31792 Rfn. Dean F. } Buried in Military Cemetery by R.A. " A/20,361 " Fisher T. } a party of D.Coy. on 30/9/17 at 28T106 80.75 " R/31754 " Cook G. Wounded: R/10695 " C. Cotter " A/301388 " English C. " A/27211 L/Cpl. Marshall A " R/12080 Rfn. Smith J " R/28644 " Osborne J. All the above by shell fire at Public Horse Dump. Total Strength with Bn. on Sept 30th 1917 Officers 22 O.R.'s 608 ——— 630 J. Marwood Major (7th Rifle Brigade) comdg. 8th K.R.R.C. 30/9/17	J.M. J.M.

Army Form C. 2118.

WAR DIARY
INTELLIGENCE SUMMARY

(Erase heading not required.)

September 1917
APPENDIX
8th K.R.R.C.

(6)

Place	Date	Hour	Summary of Events and Information	Remarks and references to Appendices
			Awards referred to in sheet ①	
			Military Medal.	
			No. A/7730 Sgt. Pinnany. H.	
			" 1532 Cpl. Johns. W.H.C	
			" R/10244 " Weir. J	
			" R/4418 L/C Hoolam. W	
			" R/18461 " Townsend. J	
			" R/3372 Rfn. Trinder. E	
			" R/22156 " Hunn. R	
			" A/201403 " Luxford. F	
			" R/23224 " Midgeley. P.	
			" 27765 " Buchanan. G	

Army Form C. 2118.

WAR DIARY
—or—
INTELLIGENCE SUMMARY

Appendix (7)

(Erase heading not required.) 8th Bn. K.R.R.C.

Place	Date	Hour	Summary of Events and Information	Remarks and references to Appendices
			CASUALTIES	
	14/9/17	A	No. R/32060 Rfn. Crispin. J. wounded shell	
	15/9/17	B	" R/14244 Cpl. Ward J. " " MISSING	
			" R/20319 Rfn. Cooke J. " gout	
			" R/21148 " Fluton, H " "	
			" R/37782 " Pigon, E " "	
			" R/37698 " Madows, G " "	
			" R/11846 L/Cpl. Stanley. H. prisoner	
			" R/37017 Rfn. Swindells. H wounded shell	
	15/9/17	C	" R/8342 Cpl. Lindsay. A wounded shell	
	20/9/17	D	" 9814 Rfn. Braggs W. wounded shell	

J. Maxwell
(7th Rfn Bgde) K.R.R.C.
anog 8/9/17
8/9/17

Army Form C. 2118.

WAR DIARY
or
INTELLIGENCE SUMMARY

(Erase heading not required.)

Oct. 1917

8th Bn. K.R.R.C.

Place	Date	Hour	Summary of Events and Information	Remarks and references to Appendices
ALDERSHOT CAMP	Oct. 1		Bn. found working parties for forward area. "A" Coy. inspected by C.O. Training g. 1-6 on range wiring and musketry for remainder.	J.M.
	2		Bn. found working parties. Bn. training in wiring, bayonet fighting and L-g. Bde. 8 o/c N.C.O. tested all trajectors and reported favourably.	J.M.
	3		Bn. Parade. Major J.H. Bolto, D.S.O. of the Army Gymnastic Staff lectured the Bn. on Sword fighting. Bn. concert partly gave a concert in the evening. Capt. C.L. Donin(?) the rejoined	J.M.
	4		Coy Training continued. Boxing Competition in the afternoon and evening	J.M.
	5		Coy. Training continued. Warning order for a move towards received about 4 pm.	J.M.
	6		Bn. marched out of ALDERSHOT CAMP at 1 pm and proceeded via DRANOUTRE and LOCRE to bivouacs near ZEVECOTEN (28 M.5.d.55.2.). The following officers joined the Bn. from the A.S.C. Capt. D.A. Brownsword, Lt. A.J. Bell, Lt. G.A. Burnett, 2/Lt. L.C. Butler	J.M.
ZEVECOTEN	7		Weather very bad, obtained tents from corps which did not however arrive till dark, when camp was pitched on drier ground. The following 2 officers joined the Bn. from the A.S.C. 2/Lt. R. Robertson, 2/Lt. H.C.R. Seaber. At 1 am the clock went back to midnight (6th/7th)	J.M.
	8		Bn. Parade at 11.30 am up to which time corps were refitching(?) kits. Afternoon very wet.	J.M.
	9		Bn. moved by corps to 28.H.31.d.5.5.	J.M.

H.31.d.N.W.

WAR DIARY or INTELLIGENCE SUMMARY

(Erase heading not required.)

Army Form C. 2118.

Oct. 1917

8th Bn. K.R.R.C.

(9)

Place	Date	Hour	Summary of Events and Information	Remarks and references to Appendices
31d.d.5.5.	10		Bn. moved by Coys to RIDGEWOOD at 2 8 N 5 & 3.14 and again at 11.20 p.m. to BEDFORD HOUSE at 28 I 26 a 9.4. At 1 p.m. the Bn marched out to go into shelters in support to 7th K.R.R.C. on right 7th R.B. on left. The Scouts lost their way and the Bn eventually dug in at dawn about 600 yds. E of Inverness Copse. D Coy on the right with its flank on the Menin Road A & B Coys. in left of B protecting the Brigade left flank on the Menin Road A & B Coys. in left of B protecting the Brigade left flank on the REUTEL BEEK R. Casualties 7 killed and 8 wounded. see Appendix 12	V.M.
POLDERHOEK	11		Army Barrage at 5 a.m. to 5.10 p.m. The enemy replied with a heavy barrage on 12th measures. Casualties 11 killed + 14 wounded.	V.M.
	12		Army Barrage at 5.25 a.m. "A" Coy moved two platoons N. of Menin Road and two platoons N. of Inverness copse about 100 E of FITZCLARENCE Farm. Casualties 5 killed and 19 wounded	V.M.
	13		continual shelling accounted for 8 killed 11 wounded	V.M.
	14		Slightly quieter. has increased amongst the Bn and was shelling consequently. Casualties 1 killed 4 wounded	V.M.
	15		Enemy put over gas shells. Casualties 1 killed 4 wounded 1 gassed.	V.M.

Army Form C. 2118.

WAR DIARY or INTELLIGENCE SUMMARY

Oct. 1917

8th Bn. K.R.R.C.

(10)

(Erase heading not required.)

Instructions regarding War Diaries and Intelligence Summaries are contained in F. S. Regs., Part II. and the Staff Manual respectively. Title Pages will be prepared in manuscript.

Place	Date	Hour	Summary of Events and Information	Remarks and references to Appendices
POLDERHOEK	16		Bn relieved about 9.30 p.m. by 8th K.S.L.I. and proceeded to RIDGE WOOD.	J.M.
RIDGEWOOD	17		Casualties No. A/4418 Rfn. Hadaun. W. B Coy.	J.M.
	18		Bn cleaning and re-equipping. Enemy aircraft dropped about 12 bombs in the vicinity of camp.	J.M.
	19		Bn reorganising into 3 platoons of 3 sections. Musketry training. E.A. again bombed us.	J.M.
	20		Bn bathed. Weather continues favourable for training. E.A. again bombed us.	J.M.
	21		Bn bathed. Working parties of 100 found by the Bn. E.A. again bombed us. Casualty 1 O.R.	J.M.
			Church Parade 10.30 am. E.A. bombs again near the camp.	J.M.
CHIPPEWA CAMP	22		The Bn. marched to CHIPPEWA CAMP at 28 M.b.6.4.	J.M.
METEREN	23		The Bn marched to METEREN at 27 X 9 c and d. A & B Coys at X 3 d. 6.6. H. & T. Coy	J.M.
			X 9.d.3.6. D Coy at X 14 & 9.4. The weather was bad for the forward	
	24		Day spent in settling in and cleaning. Draft of 5 officers arrived.	J.M.
			37 O.R. arrived.	J.M.
	25		Coy and Specialist training. Weather very wet. Draft of 7 O.R. joined.	J.M.
	26		Coy and Specialist training	
	27		Coy and Specialist training	J.M.
	28		Coy and Specialist training. A & B Coys on Range Lewis gunners on range in afternoon.	J.M.

2449 Wt. W14957/M90 750,000 1/16 J.B.C. & A. Forms/C.2118/12.

Army Form C. 2118.

WAR DIARY
or
INTELLIGENCE SUMMARY

(Erase heading not required.) 8th Bn. K.R.R.C.

Oct. 1917

(11)

Instructions regarding War Diaries and Intelligence Summaries are contained in F. S. Regs., Part II and the Staff Manual respectively. Title Pages will be prepared in manuscript.

Place	Date	Hour	Summary of Events and Information	Remarks and references to Appendices
METEREN	29		Coy and specialist training. "C" coy. inspected. Draft of 4 officers and 63 O.R's joined.	J.M.
	30		Coy and specialist training. "D" coy. and Sig. section inspected.	J.M.
	31		Coy. and specialist training. "A" & "B" coys. inspected. Draft of 18 O.R's joined.	J.M.
			Strength as 31/10/17 Officers 31 O.R. 652 ___ 683	
			J. Maxwell Lt. Col. Comdg. 8th Bn. K.R.R.C. 31/10/17	

WAR DIARY or INTELLIGENCE SUMMARY

Army Form C. 2118.

Appendix 6 Oct
8th Bn. K.R.R.C.

Place	Date	Hour	Summary of Events and Information	Remarks and references to Appendices
Killed	10.10.17		4436 Cpl. W. McCarthy R/12149 L/Cpl. F. Cardy 2877 L/Cpl. J. Eagling A/201333 Rfn. C. Bain R/13795 Rfn. M. Hodson R/11148 Rfn. H. Funnell 3110 Rfn. F. Doylay	
Wounded	10.10.17		R/8964 L/Cpl. J. Rancarte R/33645 L/Cpl. C. Hoult 1263 L/Cpl. G. Grand 2668 L/Cpl. W. Stoker 79 Rfn. W. Newton C 11626 Rfn. G. Train A10886 Rfn. A. Knight R/33615 Rfn. H. Lane	
Killed	11.10.17		R/12118 Rfn. G. Burgess A/1023 Rfn. H. Stowers 18002 Rfn. G. Chappell 36921 Rfn. A. Berry 6663 Rfn. A. Skelton R/10123 Rfn. F. Vidler R/30446 Rfn. J. Gerard. 5827 Rfn. E. Fieldhouse R/37896 Rfn. J. Donald A/200457 Rfn. W. Russell 12980 Rfn. A. Clost.	
Wounded	11.10.17		38169 Rfn. W. Greenwood R/34313 Rfn. T. Greenhalgh A/201113 Rfn. E. Newman A/201410 Rfn. W. Oakins R/33312 Rfn. W. Grounds R/34907 Rfn. W. Nove. A/201091 Rfn. W. Edwards R/32304 Rfn. N. Daniels A/144190 Rfn. P. Poult R/38011 Rfn. R. Parker A/201353 Arcs J.M. Rfn. F. Ewing R/35465 Rfn. H. Hower S/4293 Rfn. M. Bentham 31555 Rfn. G. Apps 20169 L/Cpl. P. Johnson A/201093 Rfn. T. Eastham 8898 Rfn. J. Hawley 31359 Rfn. B/Sickling 31777 Rfn. C. Winsford	
Killed	12.10.17		4420 Cpl. W. Moore 15056 L/Cpl. E. Hiatch C/6776 L/Cpl. C. Holstead R/6729 Rfn. A. Lather R/23337 Rfn. L. Kings(?) A/201433 Rfn. F. Winterford 32261 Rfn. F. Rozelay R/34198 Rfn. A. Underwood 36900 Rfn. G. Dodd 166856 Rfn. W. Dyer 323334 Rfn. F. Gore 323143 Rfn. H. Noyes 15770 Rfn. C. Church 37739 Rfn. J. Hudson 9709 Rfn. W. Lawton 13168 Rfn. S. Loker 20116 Rfn. W. Mallan 16151 Rfn. W. Sanders 30403 Rfn. F. Nelson	

J.M.

Army Form C. 2118.

Appendix 6 Oct 1917 (13)

WAR DIARY
or
INTELLIGENCE SUMMARY

(Erase heading not required.) 8th Bn. K.R.R.C.

Instructions regarding War Diaries and Intelligence Summaries are contained in F. S. Regs., Part II. and the Staff Manual respectively. Title Pages will be prepared in manuscript.

Place	Date	Hour	Summary of Events and Information	Remarks and references to Appendices
Killed	13/10/17		R/32075 Rfn. G. Ashdown R/13525 Rfn. A. Hants A/201396 Rfn. H. Joy R/32432 Rfn. V. Lloyd A/201405 Rfn. W. Rowland A/201341 Rfn. W. Reid 37695 Rfn. R. Vennings 201416 Rfn. J. Shepherd.	
Wounded	13/10/17		11532 Sgt. W. Johns (since died of wounds) R/34134 Cpl. H. Portwy A/201087 L/Cpl. A Ayant S34995 L/Cpl. V. Fargwhar S35050 L/Cpl. C. Haw. R/37763 Rfn. A. Bah R/30094 Rfn. F. Robinson A/201326 Rfn. A. Barber R/30083 Rfn. L. Hancton 26169 Rfn. W. Hants 45734 Rfn. A. Partridge 3374 Rfn. A. Shortman	
Killed	14/10/17			
Wounded	14/10/17		A/201099 Rfn. F. Green R/13640 Rfn. C. Staples R/37964 Rfn. A. Luck R/30057 Rfn. T. Hunt	
Killed	15/10/17		A/201430 Rfn. H. Whitley	
Wounded	16/10/17		31595 Rfn. H. Cooper A/201658 Rfn. J. Ammis 10744 Rfn. J. Russell 201434 Rfn. W. Wood 10868 Sgt. W. Day gassed.	

Vol 26

Confidential

War Diary

of

8th (S) Bn. K.R.R.C.

From 1st November 1917
to
30th November 1917

Volume XXVIII

Army Form C. 2118.

WAR DIARY
or
INTELLIGENCE SUMMARY

(Erase heading not required.)

Nov. 1917

8th Bn. K.R.R.C.

Instructions regarding War Diaries and Intelligence Summaries are contained in F. S. Regs., Part II. and the Staff Manual respectively. Title Pages will be prepared in manuscript.

Place	Date	Hour	Summary of Events and Information	Remarks and references to Appendices
METEREN	Nov. 1		Coy. and specialist training	J.M.
	2		Platoon Tournament and drill competition won by No. 14 Platoon. Vintage. Brig. Genl. Smythe 41st Bde.	J.M.
	3		Coy. bathed. Coy. and platoon training	J.M.
	4		Church Parade 12 noon.	J.M.
	5		Bn. Route March	J.M.
	6		Coy. and platoon training	J.M.
	7		Coy. and platoon training. Weather unfavourable	J.M.
	8		Coy. and platoon training. 15th Platoon football league commenced	J.M.
	9		Coy. and platoon training. Draft of 12 O.R. joined for duty.	J.M.
	10		Coy. and platoon training	J.M.
TATTINGHEM	11		Battalion moved by train to (illeg) in TATTINGHEM. Transport (limbers) moved by road	J.M.
	12		Day spent in cleaning up and settling down	
	13		Battalion on Range.	J.M.
	14		Coy. training. Draft 3 O.R. rejoined	J.M.
	15		Coy. training. Bn. Am. Range	J.M.
	16		Bn. Route March. 1 off. joined for duty	J.M.

Army Form C. 2118.

WAR DIARY
INTELLIGENCE SUMMARY

Nov. 1917

8th Bn. K.R.R.C.

(Erase heading not required.)

Instructions regarding War Diaries and Intelligence Summaries are contained in F.S. Regs., Part II. and the Staff Manual respectively. Title Pages will be prepared in manuscript.

Place	Date	Hour	Summary of Events and Information	Remarks and references to Appendices
TATTINGHEM	Nov. 17		C + B coys on Range. A + D coys on a tactical scheme.	J.M.
	18		Sunday – no church parade – football morning + afternoon.	J.M.
	19		Combined training with 7/60th	J.M.
	20		Range. Draft of 4 – O.R. joined.	J.M.
	21		Brigade training	J.M.
	22		A + B coy on Range. C + D coys in attack	J.M.
	23		Brigade cross country Run.	J.M.
	24		Coy. training	J.M.
	25		Church Parade	J.M.
	26		Range. A + B Coys. C + D. Coy training	J.M.
	27		Coy training. 7 – O.R's rejoined for duty	J.M.
	28		Visit by Corps Commander.	J.M.
"B" Camp	29		Bn moved by train to "B" camp at 2.8 to 6.64 4.4	J.M.
	30		Bn preparing to go into the line	J.M.

Fighting Strength
32 offrs.
662 O.R.
——
694

J. Marwick
Lt. Col.
Comdg. 8/60th.

CONFIDENTIAL.

WAR DIARY

of

8th. (S) Bn. KING'S ROYAL RIFLE CORPS.

From. 1st. Dec. 1917.
To. 31st. Dec. 1917.

VOLUME XXIX.

WAR DIARY
or
INTELLIGENCE SUMMARY

Army Form C. 2118.

8 K R R C /.
Dec 1917

Place	Date	Hour	Summary of Events and Information	Remarks and references to Appendices
"B" Camp. BRANDHOEK	1/12/17		Battalion preparing to go into line.	Elliott Capt.
CALIFORNIA CAMP. WIELTJE.	2/12/17		The Bn entrained at BRANDHOEK at 10 AM. detrained at WIELTJE about 12.30 (noon), marched to CALIFORNIA CAMP, the picking up battle stores preparatory to going into line. Moved up to PASSCHENDAELE via GRAVENSTAFEL was meeting guides at WATERLOO. A quiet relief. The chief feature of which was the absence of the hope to be relieved in the 9th. Division, 2 RIR + 1st Royal Irish Bn HQ at BELLEVUE about 2000 yards behind the line. Some shelling of BELLEVUE spun front line Friday guest. COL. MAXWELL M.C. left H.Q to reconnoitre.	Elliott Capt.
R the line. 3.				

WAR DIARY
or
INTELLIGENCE SUMMARY

Army Form C. 2118.

J/C.K.R.R.C.

Dec 2

Place	Date	Hour	Summary of Events and Information	Remarks and references to Appendices
	3 (con)		The front line accompanied by 2/LT R.H. WOODS together g.P.M. There was discovered by BRIG. GEN. SKINNER 80 yards beyond METCHELE, both LT. COL. MAXWELL & 2/LT. WOODS had been badly hit by the same shell. They were taken to WATERLOO. 2/LT. WOODS died on arrival. LT. COL. MAXWELL died the following day. BRIG. GEN. SKINNER came to BELLEVUE & sent for CAPT. E. DOMVILLE to command the Bn. pending the arrival of MAJOR BOWEN. MAJOR BOWEN arrived at H.Q. at 10 A.M. & took over command. A very heavy bombardment shelling Kept 3 of the commanders officers & their adjutants in the trenches over two hours.	2/Left Bays
	4			

WAR DIARY or INTELLIGENCE SUMMARY

Army Form C. 2118.

8th K.R.R.C. Dec 3

Place	Date	Hour	Summary of Events and Information	Remarks and references to Appendices
	4 (cont)		MAJOR BOWEN, CAPT DOTHVILLE reconnoitred wire & front line, position proved to be in advance of some maps.	Abbott Capt.
	5		At greatest dry, "B" Coy was relieved by 7/60 + came back to CALIFORNIA CROSSROADS. The men had on the march out Relief was attempted but was had on the march out. "B" Company being relieved by enemy barrage, "B" Company being relieved by Coy H.Q. Casualties during tour officers Lt.Col MAXWELL H.Q. 2Lt. WOODS. J Skelas Lt. REYNOLDS. Wounded. O.R. 6 K. 65 Killed & Wounded	

Lt. Col. MAXWELL buried at PRISON, YPRES with full military honours.

Abbott Capt.

WAR DIARY or INTELLIGENCE SUMMARY

Army Form C. 2118.

8th R.R.R.C.
Dec.

Place	Date	Hour	Summary of Events and Information	Remarks and references to Appendices
WIELTJE.	6.		Scheme of trench feet, no complaints of trench feet has been received in the line. B. funning carrying parties to 7/60.	Abcott Capt
	7.		Carrying parties to 7/60.	
BRANDHOEK	8.		B. left CALIFORNIA CAMP. entrained at WIELTJE detrained BRANDHOEK proceeded to BRAKE CAMP.	Abcott Capt
	9 to 18.		Training & working parties for Light Railway Coys.	Abcott Capt
	18.		Regt. BRAKE CAMP. at 3 P.M. marched to WIELTJE B. H.Q. & B.C. Coys to CALIFORNIA CAMP. A & D Coys to JUNCTION CAMP. ST JEAN.	Abcott Capt
	19.		Working parties for Light Railway construction.	Abcott Capt

WAR DIARY or INTELLIGENCE SUMMARY

Army Form C. 2118.

F. KERR Dec S

Place	Date	Hour	Summary of Events and Information	Remarks and references to Appendices
	20th & 22nd		Intelligent at Pt CALIFORNIA & JUNCTION CAHRS	Sh. off Rpt
	22nd		Bn moved up to take up line N of GOUDBERG COPSE. Hoarputz Farm row on account of 50s on left & fault. Quiet relief. Wireleria 9/60. Bn H.Q. at VIRILE FARM. 70 yards of front. Bn. strength 270 O.R.	
tobi	23rd		Heavy hostile barrage before dawn, enemy reconnoitering, first inspected activity on both sides, dispersed parties of enemy advancing & retiring from shell hole position met L.G. fire. Our front line positions worried by hostile M.G., these were taken on by L-Guns.	Sh. off Rpt
	24th		Heavy barrage again before dawn causing no casualties Capt CHAMBERS killed by M.G. fire while visiting the	

WAR DIARY or INTELLIGENCE SUMMARY

Army Form C. 2118.

8 (S) K.R.R.C.

Dec 6

Place	Date	Hour	Summary of Events and Information	Remarks and references to Appendices
	24 (cont)		posts. The enemy allows our stretcher parties to collect wounded under Red Cross flag, we extend similar privilege to him.	Shoff — Capt
	25.		CAPT. BROWNSWORD hit by M.G. fire while proceeding at 1. A.M. carried down at daybreak under red-cross flag, he died before reaching dressing station while carried in B Coy HQrs to relieve the sentry recovering 2LT SIMPSON. to be sent down with BROWNSWORD. CAPT CHAMBERS buried just behind front line.	Elliott Capt
	26.		Bn. relieved by 2nd Northamptons. 8 Cas. Owing to the lightness of moon & clearness of snow, the	

WAR DIARY
or
INTELLIGENCE SUMMARY

(Erase heading not required.)

Army Form C. 2118.

5th K.R.R.C.
DEC (2)

Place	Date	Hour	Summary of Events and Information	Remarks and references to Appendices
	26 (contd)		enemy spotted the relief, and up lights for distress(?) fire, which called down a heavy barrage. The Batln our left + right put up S.O.S. under cover of our fire we relieved our right company without difficulty but left company however not showing getting thereof through owing to activity of enemy M Guns.	Elliott Capt
WIELTJE.	27—		The battalion entrained at WIELTJE at 12 noon & proceeded to WIZERNES station whence by lorry motorbus to QUELMES. Owing to the snow most of the busses stuck on a steep hill + had to be helped up by the troops. The details rejoined Bat. in the evening. The transport which went to road) leaving its camp on the 26th arrived about 4.30 PM just before the battalion after a very difficult march owing to the condition of the roads.	[signature]
QUELMES	28th		A day of rest.	[signature]

Army Form C. 2118.

WAR DIARY
INTELLIGENCE SUMMARY

8/K.R.R.C.
December 1917

(Erase heading not required.)

Place	Date	Hour	Summary of Events and Information	Remarks and references to Appendices
QUELMES	29th		Day spent in cleaning up & settling into billets.	P/29/2/c C/Atts
"	30th Sunday		No parade service possible owing to lack of accommodation.	P/30/2/c C/Atts
"	31st		Cleaning up still. Great Christmas Dinner in the evening to all ranks. Thoroughly enjoyed themselves & were in great form to usher in the new year.	P/31/2/c C/Atts

Casualties during December.

Officers.
Killed & Died of wounds. LT. COL. J. MAXWELL M.C.
C/R D.A. BROWNSFORD
C/R R.S.B. CHAMBERS
2/LT R.H. WOODS.

Wounded.
2/LT J. RALPH
2/LT D.J. SIMPSON
LT W.S. REYNOLDS
2/LT J. GOW. (at duty)

O.R.s:
Total Casualties.
Killed. 18   Missing. 7.
Wounded. 68

O.R.s
6th 65
41

Strength of Battalion 31st December.   Forms/C.2118/12.

[signature] MAJOR
Comdg 8/KRRC.

CONFIDENTIAL.

WAR DIARY

- of -

8th. (S) Bn. KING'S ROYAL RIFLE CORPS.

From :- 1st. January. 1918.
To :- 31st. January. 1918.

VOLUME XXX

Army Form C. 2118.

WAR DIARY
INTELLIGENCE SUMMARY
(Erase heading not required.)

8/K.R.R.C.
January 1918. (1)

Place	Date	Hour	Summary of Events and Information	Remarks and references to Appendices
QUELMES	1st		Holiday. New Years Day, spent in recovering from New Years Eve Dinner.	Ph/Pfe C/ft. PaPfe C/ft.
"	2nd		Marched to ST OMER in the evening, preparatory to entraining for the south	
"	3rd		Battalion entrained at ST OMER at 3.0 A.M., arrived EDGEHILL near DERNANCOURT at 11.0 A.M. Marched to SAILLY LAURETTE through thick snow.	PaPfe C/ft.
SAILLY LAURETTE				
"	4th		Battalion settling in. Billets pretty good.	Ph/Pfe C/ft.
"	5th		Thaw followed by frost made all training impossible.	PaPfe C/ft.
"	6th		Church Parade under Capt F.G. Scott at church at VII Corps Convalescent Camp.	PaPfe C/ft.
"	7th		Training, including a good deal of range work.	Ph/Pfe C/ft.
"	8th 9th 10th 11th		Commander of 5th Army, General Sir H de la P. Gough, N.C.O's etc inspected a draft of 93 O.R's. The test draft we have yet had.	PaPfe C/ft. Ph.Pfe C/ft. Ph/Pfe C/ft.
"	12th		Training. Church Parade at VII Corps Convalescent Camp.	
"	13th		1st round of Brigade Football Tournament to decide which Battalion should represent Brigade in Divisional Competition. Beat 7th K.R.B. 3-2.	PaPfe C/ft.

Army Form C. 2118.

WAR DIARY
or
INTELLIGENCE SUMMARY

(Erase heading not required.)

9th K.R.R.C.

January, 1918.

(2)

Place	Date	Hour	Summary of Events and Information	Remarks and references to Appendices
SAILLY LAURETTE	14th	—	Training. Played 7th K.R.R.C. in final & beat them 4-2.	Ph.Pfe Goft.
"	15th		Training. 1st Round of Div. Football Competition. We played 43rd F.A. on pouring rain & got beaten 1-2.	Ph.Pfe Goft.
"	16th		Training. Inter platoon Rifle Competition for medals given by the A.R.A. No 14 Platoon represented the battalion, having won the battalion competition. The 7th K.R.R.C were 1st, beating us by 17 points. The 9th R.B. 3rd & 8th R.B. 4th. The 1/60 won the Divisional Competition with great ease from the Durhams.	Ph.Pfe Goft.
"	17th		Training. R.S.M's Parades & Musketry.	Ph.Pfe Goft.
"	18th	}		Ph.Pfe Goft.
"	19th			
"	20th		The Army Commander attended Church Parade & saw the battalion march past afterwards.	Ph.Pfe Goft.
"	21st		Preparing for move.	Ph.Pfe Goft. Ph.Pfe Goft.
MEZIERES	22nd		Marched to MEZIERES about 10 miles. 1 R/n fell out.	Ph.Pfe Goft.
ROYE	23rd		" to ROYE about 12 " 2 " "	
BERLANCOURT	24th		" to BERLANCOURT " 12 " 4 " "	
CLASTRES	25th		" HQ + A+C Coys to CLASTRES; B + D Coys to Essigny Station. Great reception by the French Troops all along the line of march & especially on marching into CLASTRES.	Ph.Pfe Goft.

WAR DIARY
INTELLIGENCE SUMMARY
(Erase heading not required.)

Army Form C. 2118.

8/K.R.R.C.

January 1918

(3)

Place	Date	Hour	Summary of Events and Information	Remarks and references to Appendices
In the line S. of ST QUENTIN	26th		The battalion relieved the 3rd Battalion of the 416th Inf. Regiment 154th French DIVISION in the line S. of ST QUENTIN. The 36th (ULSTER) DIVISION on our left. The 8th Rifle Brigade on the right. We are the left battalion of the Division. The relief was effected easily & without incident. 2 Frenchmen stay at each Coy HQ in the front line & at Bn HQ to fire S.O.S. Rockets till noon 1st Feb. B Company went in on the left, D Coy on right, C in support & A in reserve.	Ph. Op. left
"	27th		Very quiet day. A good deal of wiring to be done & amongst the trenches want a lot of work done on them. There is a great lack of firesteps in the main line of defence. All round. Cookshops & all Coys are in the line. Transport comes up to Batt "MAES TRENCH". Dugouts are good. No wag done at a central Cookhouse. Cooking except for HQ S.a been done at a central Cookhouse. A limber also goes of the BRUILLERS - IVANCOURT Rd. as far as MAES TRENCH. 8th R.E. Materials. In front of MAES, there was originally HQ & also to central Cookhouse. To its front line which originally suffered the want a series of isolated posts of Grenade trenches. We hold these posts as outpost line connecting these posts having been obliterated by the French. by days, night. a daily day so everyone can walk about on left, but nothing can be seen of the Boscht on the general line of the ground. Bosch exceptionally quiet. This is so far the quietest sector we have been in & being open quicker than the "Sectes" S. of AVRAS which the Bngde held last winter.	Ph. Op. left
"	28th		A Coy which has previously been of B's HQ at ESSIGNY Rlw stations brought up forward and the occupied positions between Batt HQ & support Coy. Quiet day.	Ph. Op. left

Army Form C. 2118

WAR DIARY
INTELLIGENCE SUMMARY
8/K.R.R.C.
January 1918

(Erase heading not required.)

Place	Date	Hour	Summary of Events and Information	Remarks and references to Appendices
In the line S. of ST QUENTIN	30th	—	A quiet day. LT. COL. B.J. CURLING. D.S.O. arrived to take over command of the battalion from H.Q. 42nd Division. C Cy relieved B + A relieved D. B Cy into support + D into reserve.	Pp. Off. C.A.H.
"	31st	—	A considerable improvement has been made in the defences of the sector since taking over but a lot more remains to be done. Map References of places in the line now held by us are as under. Ref. France. 66.d. N.W. Batt. H.Q. B. 27. b. 9. 7. Line held from B. 17a. 5. 2. to B. 23. d. 5. 1. Left Coy H.Q. B. 23. a. 2. 6. Right B. 23. a. 5. 2. Support B. 22. d. 7. 7. Reserve B. 28. a. 8. 3. Casualties. Nil. Reinforcements joined during the month 1 Officer. 2/LT. BUTTIFANT 213. O.Rs Strength of battalion at 31st January. 43. Off. 812. O.Rs.	To Offe. C.A.H.

B.J. Curling
LT. COL.
Comdg. 8/K.R.R.C.

8th Bn K.R.R.C.

War Diary

From February 1st 1918
to
To February 28th 1918

Volume XXXI

Army Form C. 2118.

WAR DIARY
or
INTELLIGENCE SUMMARY
(Erase heading not required.)

8th K.R.R.C.

February 1918

Place	Date	Hour	Summary of Events and Information	Remarks and references to Appendices
URVILLERS N. Sector	13th/8th		Very quiet time in trenches in front of URVILLERS. Bn holding four posts in advance line extending 1500 x. Bomboys very busy wiring in posts & trenches leading out to them. No patrol encounters. No casualties.	Elliott Capt.
	9th		Bn relieved by 8th R.B. Onrelief HQ & C Coy to CLASTRES. D. Coy to LA CASIERE (HSa)	Byrtt Capt. 6 Lt. C. NW Jones 2nd Lt Elliott 2nd Lt Abbott 2nd Lt Little Rice
CLASTRES	10th		A & B to railway embankment (G.12.c.0.5). Day of Kit inspections, settling in & cleaning. Bn working on defences in "Battle Zone".	
	11th/14th			
URVILLERS S. Sector	15th		Bn relieved 7th R.B. in line, & as the relief was taking place R.B. sentries heard sounds of wire cutting in front of SOMME POST. They put up a Lewis gun Burst, they then dropped shouting in one of them, shot through the head, he was too bad to give information. Otherwise relief was without incident. Dispositions 2 companies in front line "Don" with "B" on left. "A" Coy in support "C" Coy in reserve round Bn HQ at H.H.6. Whole Bn wiring & strengthening trench generally. Patrols were sent out every night of 1 officer + 11 O.R. They did not encounter any enemy patrols but kept enemy line under observation.	Zl. Maps
	16th/21st		A wire Company relief "A" Coy relieved "D" & "C" relieved "B". D & B went into support & reserve.	
	21st/22nd		A patrol discovered a BANGALORE TORPEDO 15 feet long & two boxes in a valley in the land between the lines about halfway across. They did not bring	Elliott Capt.

2449 Wt. W14957/M90 750,000 1/16 J.B.C. & A. Forms/C.2118/12.

WAR DIARY or INTELLIGENCE SUMMARY

Army Form C. 2118.

8th K.R.R.C.

February 1918.

Place	Date	Hour	Summary of Events and Information	Remarks and references to Appendices
URVILLERS S. Secte.	22nd (cont)		(cont) Relieved us as they did not know the nature of them.	Eslott Capt.
	23rd		A quiet day. Our Patrols went out with an R.E. Corporal to examine the boxes, they found them in the same place but they expressed did not like the look of them as one was	Adcott Capt
	24th		Patrol bought in the trench & the box there which were found to be boxes of explosives with wires attached fixed in centre. They were evidently intended the trench being cut ([illegible]) while the trips so was of the ordinary variety used for wire cutting.	
	25/28th		Patrols examined where of enemy wire in front but found nothing of interest They saw enemy wiring & also enemy patrols. The latter however did not often come outside their own wire.	Eslott Capt

Effective Strength on 28th. 42 Officers 950 O.Rs.
Drafts joined during month 191. O.Rs.
Casualties " " " 8. O.Rs. Wounded.

Honours. Croix de Guerre (Belgium) awarded to
6490 Sgt. E. Carter
9362 R/t. E. Smith.

R.B.[signature] Major
Comdg
8/KRRC

41st Brigade
14th Division.

8th BATTALION

KING'S ROYAL RIFLE CORPS

MARCH 1918

CONFIDENTIAL.

WAR　　　　　　　DIARY

of

8th. (S) Bn.　King's Royal Rifle Corps

From.　1st. March. 1918

To.　31st. March. 1918.

VOLUME No. XXXVI

INTELLIGENCE SUMMARY

Army Form C. 2118.

Place: J. Eagle
Date: March 18 (continued)

Summary of Events and Information

It is remarkable how we conceal and collect information of the doings of the Bosch. For this month we have had 15 officers come out of the line 2nd Battn. From letters that have since been received from Germany it appears that the Bosch was quite surprised that the Bosch who had attacked when the weather was bad did not until the Armistice [illegible] capture one prisoner.

Major Baker commanding "A" Coy went to a listening post for purpose of showing roommates the way that his party had to force a way back. He and people who were out were deceased by men of his company who have never for[illegible] the incident in the conversation then occurred.

All ph 18 7 men are worried. Common P[illegible] the sergeant they were captured. All the stuff we lost [illegible] or [illegible] can be pure.

2449 Wt. W14957/M90 750,000 1/16 J.B.C. & A. Forms/C.2118/12.

WAR DIARY or INTELLIGENCE SUMMARY

(Erase heading not required.)

Instructions regarding War Diaries and Intelligence Summaries are contained in F.S. Regs., Part II. and the Staff Manual respectively. Title Pages will be prepared in manuscript.

March 15

Place	Date	Hour	Summary of Events and Information	Remarks and references to Appendices
Satelieu around URVILLERS	20/3/18		The Bn. was in the first line & potion. A & C Companies holding the actual front line "B" in support along the Route Nationale. 1st & "D" in various strong points around URVILLERS. Asked about whether the Bn. After the enemy were about to attack the following morning, the outposts however were of frequent occurrence. Nothing unusual happened during the night. (However continue)	Should be Ex st
	21/3/18		The morning was very misty, when our gunners put down a barrage at 4.45 AM on the enemy's [?] of assembly points. At 5 AM the enemy opened up a fire, shelling right away from the front line to Divisional Hqrs which were at CHASTRES. Also large quantities of gas shell. Off the entire Bn. in the line, only two reached the transport camp. Their story is that owing to the thick mist the Boche was able to get past our position, through a gap to [?] made in Rs 363 Div on our left, without being seen. They say that the enemy were at Bn. H.Q. & finding ourselves on our front line. We have since heard from another officer who was taken prisoner (Major Borden emg. Adj.) that the company was completely surrounded & fought to [?] town & were under the ammunition was exhausted. (1) There was no force on our own the front line, officers & men at the	

Army Form C. 2118

WAR DIARY
or
INTELLIGENCE SUMMARY

(Erase heading not required.)

Instructions regarding War Diaries and Intelligence Summaries are contained in F. S. Regs., Part II. and the Staff Manual respectively. Title Pages will be prepared in manuscript.

March 18 (2)

Place	Date	Hour	Summary of Events and Information	Remarks and references to Appendices
	27th (cont)		transport carts were organised into a body under CAPT TETLEY for the defence of the canal crossing at JUSSY, where they engaged the enemy and fought a rearguard action to FLAVY where they held the enemy for about 1 hour. During the fighting Capt Tetley's horse was shot under him. From this time until the next afternoon 27th, I received detailed information and no orders can be given for the fighting during this period.	Blakett Capt
	28th		The Division was relieved in Helene attack by 2 + CAPT TETLEY brought back what remains of Btttalion was, Chadd + Remains of the HQ TMB (in all about 90 men) to GRANDVILLERS	Cheviot Col
GRANDVILLERS	29th		In the morning, alarm was given. WB took up defensive position to the N.N.E. of GRANDVILLERS. At 1 P.M. the Bn was ordered to march to CINQUEUX	
	29th		Marched from CINQUEUX to NOGENT. The next day came to HERBECOURT	Blackett Col
	30th		Marched to VERS	
	31st		Marched to BACOUEL	

8th. Battn. King's Royal Rifles.   Sheet 1.

Nominal Roll of Officers & other ranks proceeding with Unit vide
D.R.O.1029 d/18/12/15.

OFFICERS

RANK	NAME	REMARKS
Lieutenant-Colonel	Green, H.C.R.	
Major	Crum, F.M.	
Major	Seymour, C.H.N.	
Captain	Frewin, L.	
Captain	Barber, N.E.	
Lieutenant	Tetley, E.W.	Transport Officer
,,	Loudoun-Shand, E.G.	
,,	Warry, R.A.	
,,	Bowen, R.L.	
,,	Cullinan, M.W.F.	Adjutant.
2nd. Lieutenant	Wood, C.H.	
,,	Rodway, R.A.	
,,	Hill, A.M.F.	
,,	Sidney, L.P.	
,,	Tyler, J.H.	Hospital
,,	Scott, F.G.	
,,	Hardy, R.L.	
,,	Ingman, J.E.	
,,	Rogers, R.M.	
,,	Scott, C.E.	Hospital
,,	Mackinlay, R.M.	
,,	Inigo-Jones, C.R.	
,,	Cooke, P.A.	
,,	Roddick, S.D.	
,,	Nesling, P.E.	
,,	Conroy, S.	
,,	Chambers, W.F.A.	Hospital
Lieutenant & Qr.Master	Moulsher, H.	
Lieutenant	O'Loghlen, J.E. (R.A.M.C.)	Medical Officer

OTHER RANKS

Regl.No.	Rank.	Name	Remarks.
7483	Regl.Sergt.Major	Archer, W.	
1143	Coy.Sergt.Major	Mc.Intyre, W.L.	
3188	,,	Powell, W.	
1587	,,	Webb, A.	
8270	,,	Hunter, R.	
2444	Coy.Qr.Mr.Sgt.	Linfoot, C.R.	
2543	,,	Hardisty, E.	
729	,,	Hindle, E.	
546	,,	Wallis, H.	
3291	Sergeant	Swanwick, B.	Orderly R.Clerk.
1015	,,	Parry, V.	Pioneer Sergt.
343	,,	Reekie, A.	Signalling Sgt.
2473	,,	Nelson, J.	Transport
654	,,	Pearce, F.G.	Master Shoemaker
1290	,,	Mc.Coll, A.	Machine Gun.
1515	,,	Patrick, J.	do
1469	,,	Fillingham, S.	Sergt.Bugler
11690	,,	Brooks, R.	Cook Sergt.
4048	Regl.Qr.Mr.Sgt.	King, A.H.	

Sheet 2.

Regl. No.	Rank	Name	Remarks
6083	Sergeant	Aitken, A.	
7784	,,	Bennett, P.	
773	,,	Bull, J.	
1200	,,	Beddingfield, E.	
1729	,,	Barber, T.	
4	,,	Clarke, W.	
1272	,,	Evans, P.	
2809	,,	Friday, H.	
2816	,,	Gaiger, T.	
10153	,,	Hitch, C.	
3109	,,	Jennings, T.	
6573	,,	Kidd, R.	
432	,,	Knight, J.	
7225	,,	Law, F.	
1692	,,	Leather, L.	
119	,,	Lord, H.	
9542	,,	Morris, C.	
527	,,	Manning, H.	
3186	,,	Orchard, J.	
730	,,	Pinney, G.	
130	,,	Remington, H.	
789	,,	Rowney, C.	
3698	,,	Richardson, T.	
9702	,,	Strand, J.	
1719	,,	Stevens, E	
425	,,	Simpkins, W.	
543	,,	Taee, F.	
3289	,,	West, A.	
9695	,,	Wesley, H.	
~~1429~~			
1743	Corporal	Law, J.	Machine Gun
157	,,	Crewe, W.	Signalling Cpl.
10589	,,	Brownrigg, D.	
288	,,	Brotherton, J.	
10502	,,	Burridge, S.	
1395	,,	Cant, A.	
2963	,,	Davis, C.	
5996	,,	Dunn, G.	
209	,,	Edwards, F.	
6431	,,	Fry, G.H.	
~~7577~~ 156	,,	Grieg, W.	Lance Sergt.
11612	,,	Grey, A.	
728	,,	Hughes, G.	Lance Sergt.
6026	,,	Hickford, A.	
1089	,,	Handley, R.	
357	,,	Kirk, F.	
1031	,,	Leaver, A.	
3287	,,	Millard, J.	
1151	,,	Mc.Gill, P.	
6109	,,	Metchette, J.H.	Lance Sergt.
5994	,,	Otterwell, F.	
11567	,,	Pretty, W.	
6749	,,	Podmore, S.	Lance Sergt
6330	,,	Pickering, W.	
1236	,,	Quick, C.	
1069	,,	Rowley, T.	Lance Sergt.
3694	,,	Riley, T.	
8244	,,	Rooke, W.	
8088	,,	Riches, J.E.	
3396	,,	Swindell, F.	
1300	,,	Snow, H.	
1439	,,	Stone, A.	
6110	,,	Saunders, F.	
1676	,,	Saysell, C.	
320	,,	Wright, A.	
1279	,,	Woolf, C.	
780	,,	Weston, C.	
644	,,	Wainwright, W.	Lance Sergt.
1850	,,	Wagstaffe, T.	

Sheet 3

Regl. No.	Rank	Name	Remarks
10711	Lance Corpl.	Adams, J.	
6005	,,	Arrowsmith, F.	
3280	,,	Burns, C.	
3458	,,	Bradshaw, W.	
12159	,,	Boddy, A.	
3677	,,	Beer, J.R.	
8379	,,	Bryan, J.	
7098	,,	Barton, J.	
134	,,	Busby, F.	
542	,,	Beal, H.	
2821	,,	Brownlow, J.	
640	,,	Collier, A.	
3184	,,	Dobson, E.	~~Hospital~~
5985	,,	Downes, F.	Hospital
6925	,,	Frazer, J.	
7635	,,	Fields, W.	
2891	,,	Gardner, H.	
3327	,,	Gale, J.	
2811	,,	Hodge, T.H.	
1648	,,	Harvey, H.	
6008	,,	Hill, G.	
1560	,,	Hooper, W.	
8233	,,	Hewitt, D.	
604	,,	Heath, F.	
4325	,,	Hudson, J.	
8099	,,	Johnson, P.	
9337	,,	Lewis, F.	
3455	,,	Maloney, F.	
434	,,	Martin, A.	
8841	,,	Nott, J.	
9698	,,	Rouse, R.	
3107	,,	Stephenson, J.	
39	,,	Sheehan, R.	
423	,,	Shepherd, E.	
6021	,,	Simmonds, D.	
9688	,,	Turner, W.	
6000	,,	Tucker, R.	
463	,,	Taylor, G.	
7144	,,	Tilbrook, C.	
4040	,,	Vivian, C.	
6004	,,	Wheatley, L.	
8312	,,	Wilson, R.	
943	,,	White, H.	
3618	,,	Wood, B.S.	
1859	,,	Walters, G.	
10684	,,	White, T.	
8101	,,	Yates, J.T.	
3392	,,	Faulkner, H.	
1349	,,	Hannas, J.	
5995	,,	Metcalfe, G.	
198	Rifleman	Addis, M.	
438	,,	Andrews, C.	
3525	,,	Atkins, F.	
8371	,,	Allsopp, E.	
11569	,,	Astley, T.	
12509	,,	Allen, F.	
13463	,,	Anning, W.	
3606	,,	Andrews, J.	Hospital.
1236	,,	Alcock, E.	
6007	,,	Aldhouse, J.	
14452	,,	Anstey, J.	
11112	,,	Arkinstall, J.	Hospital.
10574	,,	Arnold, J.	do
357	,,	Andley, W.	
11274	,, (L/C)	Aldridge, W.	
1547	,,	Allden, E.T.	
3235	,,	Allsop, H.	
13635	,,	Archbold, W.	
2972	,,	Aspin, R.	
8089	,,	Allen, G.E.	
8055	,,	Annable, H.	
6762	,,	Allen, W.J.	

Sheet 4.

Regl.No.	Rank	Name	Remarks.
2810	Rifleman	Ayres, R.J.	
8219	,,	Appleton, E.	
14085	,,	Archer, J.	
1332	,, (L/S)	Arnold, J.	
3032	,,	Abbott, E.H.	
8053	,,	Abbott, L.	
10802	,,	Adams, G.H.	
12048	,,	Ackrill, J.	
12704	,,	Allen, W.E.	
4886	,,	Andrews, A.	
10596	,,	Allock, J.	
7011	,,	Apted, J.	
13516	,,	Allen, H.E.	
3104	,,	Brown, R.	
2975	,,	Barnard, H.	
349	,,	Baker, F.	
3767	,,	Burford, J.	
447	,,	Bartlett, C.	
1702	,,	Brown, G.	
123	,,	Berwick, G.	
525	,,	Blackett, R.	
129	,,	Bone, H.	
71	,,	Brockman, H.	
312	,,	Brown, J.	101 Divl.Train.
7908	,,	Barrett, J.	
11420	,, (L/C)	Berridge, A.	
9828	,,	Burroughs, C.	
11920	,,	Best, W.	
11439	,,	Boswell, B.	
1128	,,	Beech, J.	
6445	,,	Bath, F.	
12338	,,	Bowen, R.	
7176	,,	Bradshaw, A.	
1881	,,	Box, J.	
12034	,,	Boyall, W.	
12846	,,	Betts, F.	
12139	,,	Bradley, J.	
12138	,,	Bradley, H.	
12492	,,	Brandon, H.	
13458	,,	Bachelor, A.	
612	,,	Baker, C.	Hospl.
10893	,,	Bettley, L.	
1310	,,	Barley, C.	Hospl.
13478	,,	Balderstone, A.	
4530	,,	Baxter, A.	
13795	,,	Baker, H.	
319	,,	Beavington, A.	
1250	,,	Barry, M.	
969	,,	Barratt, W.	Brigade Orderly.
10811	,,	Barrowcliffe, A.	
6670	,,	Bann, A.	
3677	,,	Beer, J.	
6108	,, (L/C)	Bentley, F.	
11953	,,	Bergin, E.	
6009	,, (L/C)	Beale, A.	
1401	,,	Biggs, R.	
650	,,	Booker, H.	
681	,,	Bourne, H.	
970	,,	Brades, J.	
8066	,,	Brooks, W.	
7009	,,	Brooks, A.	
3607	,,	Broughton, A.	
1012	,,	Brown, E.	
720	,,	Brown, G.	
8312	,,	Buckley, E.	
12150	,,	Bullas, A.	
12155	,,	Bulmer, J.	
12469	,,	Bunce, J.	
14258	,,	Burgess, G.	
3752	,,	Butler, C.	
990	,,	Butler, J.	

Sheet 5.

Regl.No.	Rank		Name	Remarks
8216	Rifleman	(L/C)	Brewer, R.	
834	,,		Bates, C.H.	
7348	,,		Bayliss, A.	
8092	,,		Bayliss, C.	
3540	,,		Bell, G.H.	
2552	,,		Binks, W.	
1396	,,		Bannister, C.	
1029	,,		Bradley, H.	
980	,,		Bidanville, E.	
317	,,		Burbank, H.	
3531	,,		Bostock, W.	
1130	,,		Burton, W.E.	
6960	,,		Butler, R.	
7167	,,		Beadle, J.	
8997	,,		Burn, W.P.	
11255	,,		Brown, L.	
11198	,,		Ball, J.	
12393	,,		Brookes, W.	
10151	,,		Beer, J.	
14049	,,		Bagnall, H.G.	
6707	,,		Barrett, J.	
1855	,,		Brooks, H.	
13636	,,	(L/C)	Brown, A.V.	
10018	,,	(L/C)	Bramble, M.	
2560	,,		Bagnall, J.	
2974	,,		Bainton, L.A.	
3240	,,		Baggott, C.B.	
11542	,,		Brand, W.	
12879	,,		Badder, R.	
2958	,,		Barr, H.	
11239	,,		Back, C.	
12005	,,		Bonser, H.	
13585	,,		Bowyer, R.J.	
2603	,,		Bassett, J.	
13455	,,		Brown, E.	
13637	,,		Boys, T.H.	
3377	,,		Braes, R.	
3115	,,		Brown, H.V.	
1451	,,		Burdett, J.	
8221	,,		Brown, O.	
6703	,,		Brearley, F.	
10781	,,		Bates, A.	
3041	,,		Bendall, W.	
731	,,		Calbreath, J.	
287	,,		Claydon, G.	41st.Bd.Provost.Estb.
124	,,		Clayton, C.	
1239	,,		Cooper, F.	
1224	,,		Craythorne, G.	Ypres Police.
6727	,,		Carter, F.	
4675	,,		Clifton, E.	
1101	,,		Crowhurst, P.	
10344	,,		Cornwall, G.E.	
1150	,,		Covington, A.	
4510	,,		Chapman, F.	
10821	,,		Cottee, J.C.	
12473	,,	(L/C)	Carter, G.	
12476	,,		Cowhig, M.	
11280	,,		Coleman, G.	
12258	,,		Cairns, H.	
9555	,,		Cornwall, A.	
12513	,,		Chilton, W.	
11739	,,		Carter, W.	
13148	,,		Cardy, V.	
1240	,,		Chilliner, F.	
572	,,		Chilvers, V.	
470	,,		Clark, H.	
1836	,,		Clench, A.	Hospl.
718	,,	(L/C)	Coggins, B.	
371	,,		Coles, A.	Hospl.
639	,,		Coles, H.	
13416	,,		Coles, A.E.	

Regl.No.	Rank.		Name.	Sheet 6. Remarks.
106	Rifleman		Collins, G.	Hospl.
12619	,,		Collins, J.	
653	,,		Compton, G.	
770	,,		Comer, C.	
1849	,,		Coleman, C.E.	
1182	,,		Copper, A.	
12588	,,		Corns, J.	
13746	,,		Craze, J.	
112	,,		Creswick, B.	
460	,,		Crumplin, F.	
123	,,	(L/C)	Crosby, F.	
5055	,,	(L/C)	Crouch, L.	
8008	,,	(L/C)	Chilton, T.	
892	,,		Cotton, A.	
9879	,,		Cook, B.	
3766	,,		Crowdy, F.E.	
7088	,,		Cross, C.	
12470	,,		Cooper, C.W.	
13053	,,		Charles, W.W.	
12149	,,		Cardy, F.	
6697	,,		~~Croppy~~ Crossley, A.	
13294	,,		Cooksey, H.	
6460	,,	(L/C)	Carter, G.	
2201	,,	(L/C)	Cox, T.D.	
1958	,,		Caine, E.	
11889	,,		Cast, H.	
12239	,,		Cox, J.	
3050	,,		Chester, A.	
2886	,,		Coley, S.	
7097	,,		Clarke, F.	
7232	,,		Collins, E.	
2808	,,		Conniff, J.	
3108	,,		Cook, H.	
2807	,,		Cox, H.	
2889	,,		Cross, H.	
10698	,,		Cottee, S.	
12026	,,		Cox, E.	
10798	,,	(L/C)	Cottee, T.	
12925	,,		Champion, G.	
14086	,,		Carter, W.	
12580	,,		Cox, G.	
12002	,,		Chappell, G.	
155	,,		Davenport, F.	
286	,,		Davis, A.	
533	,,		Downes, G.	
2681	,,		Denyer, A.	
3034	,,		Doidge, W.	
6020	,,		Dexter, R.	
6002	,,		Davis, H.	
7766	,,		Dodd, J.	
9916	,,		Dawson, H.	
958	,,		Dean, G.	
11318	,,		Deffee, H.	
14004	,,		Draycott, J.	
26	,,		Dickson, M.	
1776	,,		Dawson, C.	
10888	,,		Day, W.	
7879	,,		Day, W.	
9289	,,		Davison, E.	
7967	,,		Dean, S.	
9842	,,		Delaney, L.	
6019	,,		Diggory, G.	
12366	,,		Dowley, J.	
10500	,,		Dudley, H.	
9420	,,	(L/C)	Duce, A.E.	
2897	,,	(L/C)	Draper, F.	
3757	,,		Dutton, A.	
1038	,,		Durrant, T.	
12612	,,		Durst, T.	

Sheet 7.

Regl.No.	Rank		Name	Remarks
1895	Rifleman		Davies, R.	
12611	,,		Deamer, E.	
12816	,,		Dunnington, H.	
1639	,,		Dyer, T.E.	
3375	,,		Dodd, H.J.	
8358	,,		Dale, H.	
12383	,,		Degg, J.	
11426	,,		Dumbleton, F.	
12253	,,	(L/C)	Dyke, J.	
2604	,,		Diggins, G.	
3110	,,		Doyley, F.	
6102	,,		Dobson, G.	
13817	,,		Doyle, J.	
11754	,,		Dulson, E.	
12532	,,		Davis, G.	
7952	,,		Enderby, T.	
11882	,,		Easter, J.	
305	,,		Edmunds, J.	
637	,,		Ellis, G.	
239	,,		Elsom, J.	
8266	,,		Everley, A.	
1610	,,	(L/C)	Earl, W.	
3528	,,		Edwards, F.	
7091	,,		Edwards, A.	
7176	,,		Evans, H.J.	
6437	,,		Edwards, J.	
2877	,,		Eagling, T.	
7237	,,		Eddyshaw, A.	
3123	,,		Ellis, J.	
3376	,,		Ellis, H.J.	
3287	,,		Evans, J.	
7172	,,		Everett, W.	
1843	,,		Emery, W.T.	
6542	,,		Edwards, A.	
13414	,,		Emery, G.	
43	,,		Fisher, H.	
202	,,		Francis, C.	14th Div.Cyclist Coy.
864	,,		French, T.	
6243	,,		Fletcher, J.	
107	,,		Fox, A.	
1515	,,		Finch, J.	
6034	,,		Flynn, M.	
5996	,,		Farnsworth, G.	
1087	,,		Farrington, W.	
2694	,,		Fitter, G.	
216	,,		Findon, A.	
13045	,,		Franklin, G.	
1564	,,		Fynn, W.	
560	,,		Freeman, A.	Hospl.
1128	,,		Floyd, A.	do
12598	,,		Fenn, S.	
1073	,,		Fitzgerald, J.	
10858	,,		Fowler, G.	
5108	,,		Froment, W.W.	
1024	,,		Freeman, A.T.	
8806	,,		Freeman, C.F.	
12481	,,		Frusher, F.T.	
11148	,,		Furnell, H.	
15796	,,		Farr, C.	
12523	,,		Floy, W.	
8406	,,	(L/C)	Fitton, E.	
1591	,,		Fallshaw, G.	
11655	,,		Finding, W.	
12085	,,		Farmer, R.	
1961	,,		Farmer, W.	
2882	,,		Feeney, H.	Ypres Police.
3398	,,		Fennemore, C.	
365	,,		Gray, A.	
741	,,		Gambrill, S.	
12258	,,		Green, H.	

Sheet 8.

Regl. No.	Rank	Name	Remarks
11484	Rifleman	Gray, J.D.	
4162	,,	Griggs, H.	
9510	,,	Gunnell, F.G.	
6276	,,	Gilbey, H.	
4839	,,	Gregory, F.	
7233	,,	Green, W.E.	
1081	,,	Gibbs, A.	
6362	,,	Glass, A.	
12040	,,	Gooden, G.	
974	,,	Goodrick, W.	
331	,,	Gibson, A.	
6404	,,	Gregory, W.	
11847	,,	Green, H.D.	
648804	,,	Grace, G.	
648670	,,	Griffiths, J.A.	
11262	,,	Greenhalgh, W.	
1333	,,	Griffiths, J.	
7230	,,	Griffiths, A.	
12945	,,	Griffiths, G.	
1025	,,	Greenhill, F.	
10845	,,	Green, F.	
10862	,,	Gilling, B.	
12046	,,	Gent, T.	
12364	,, (L/C)	Garbett, W.	
3077	,, (L/C)	Gill, G.W.	
3199	,,	Green, J.H.	
3380	,,	Griffin, H.	
3600	,,	Griffiths, H.W.	
1014	,,	Gussin, G.	
281	,,	Gaydon, E.	
9923	,,	Gratton, J.	
13453	,,	Gomm, A.	
10419	,,	Gowlett, C.	
3051	,,	Harrison, H.	Hospl.
619	,,	Harrison, E.	3299 Rfn.Goldsmith, E.
42	,,	Heath, A.	
140	,,	Hefford, R.	
739	,,	Higginbotham, H.	Hospl.
5988	,,	Humphreys, J.	
5990	,,	Hall, J.	
8043	,,	Hayward, G.	
9348	,,	Hill, J.	
11430	,,	Harris, H.	
516	,,	Harris, W.	
1450	,,	Holland, E.	
4648	,,	Handley, S.	
11744	,,	Hooper, G.	
9392	,,	Hanford, A.	
12497	,,	Higginbotham, F.	
12616	,,	Humphreys, F.A.	
7541	,, (L/C)	Havenhand, H.	
8098	,,	Hawley, J.	
331	,,	Holloway, A.	
876	,,	Harris, F.	
13525	,,	Harris, A.	
10789	,,	Harrison, J.	
559	,,	Harrison, F.	101 Divl.Train.
8276	,,	Heaton, H.	
1256	,,	Hoskins, B.	
11491	,,	Hopewell, J.	Hospl.
10299	,,	Hogan, M.	
9402	,,	Howard, W.	
7002	,,	Howell, H.	
5976	,,	Hutchins, H.	Hospl.
1130	,,	Hawkes, J.	
1607	,, (L/C)	Hicks, P.A.	

Sheet 9.

Regl.No.	Rank	Name		Remarks.
11757	Rifleman	Higgins, J.		
948	,,	Howell, W.	11132 Rfn.	Harpham, W.
7179	,,	Hickman, L.	1615 ,,	Hart, A.J.
7082	,,	Holmes, H.	8051 ,,	Howes, C.
12212	,,	Howard, W.	7850 ,,	Hallett, A.
11776	,,	Hall, H.	1336 ,,	Hallick, W.T
5072	,,	Horwood, W.	1386 ,,	Hewston, F.
11518	,,	Harling, R.	1393 ,,	Hesom, J.
11566	,,	Hinsley, A.C.	1398 ,,	Holliday, L.C.
6885	,,	Harman, W.	878 ,,	Hornsey, W.
13798	,,	Hodson, M.	8354 ,,	Hutton, L.N.
11635	,,	Highton, A.	1498 ,,	Hertzberg, N.
5362	,,	Holmes, H.	3253 ,,	Hurst, W.
11930	,,	Hutton, R.T.		
3119	,, (L/C)	Hillier, A.		
12932	,,	Hawkins, L.		
1654	,,	Holt, H.		
13042	,,	Harrington, F.		
6962	,,	Howard, T.		
1592	,,	Hutchins, B.		
8098	,,	Hassell, D.		
2893	,,	Hands, S.		
6736	,,	Hammersley, G.		
8096	,,	Havers, R.		
3246	,,	Hannen, C.		
8433	,,	Howarth, J.		
8405	,,	Hill, J.W.		
1497	,,	Harris, J.C.		
3200	,,	Harrison, J.		
2612	,,	Hartery, R.W.		
3183	,,	Hawkins, A.		
3111	,,	Hayes, A.		
3035	,,	Hubball, H.A.		
3248	,,	Illingsworth, C.T.		
10769	,,	Iliffe, H.		
381	,,	Jenkins, D.		
2957	,,	Jarvis, H.		
6035	,,	Johnson, J.		
6554	,,	Jones, W.		
10455	,,	Jeal, F.		
434	,,	Jones, R.		
1181	,,	Judd, W.		
3671	,,	Jones, T.		
12460	,,	Jolleys, G.		
1677	,,	Judges, A.		
10018	,,	Jones, A.		
1392	,,	Jackson, A.		
1248	,,	Jackson, R.		
9578	,,	Jenkyn, B.H.		
1079	,,	Jones, G.C.		
10540	,,	Johnson, F.		
1442	,,	Jones, B.H.		
2128	,,	Joyce, W.G.		
2804	,,	Johnson, P.		
3051	,,	Jones, F.A.		
3118	,,	Joyce, J.		
12591	,,	Jamison, J.		
12417	,,	Jones, W.		
12519	,,	Jones, T.		
2605	,,	Kane, G.		
367	,,	Kiddle, C.		
6720	,,	Key, C.		
3380	,,	Kedward, J.		
1223	,,	Keeling, G.		
1808	,,	Kenny, J.		
13399	,,	Kidd, J.		
740	,,	Keasey, A.	(Hospital)	
2228	,,	King, J.		
3543	,,	King, A.		
6730	,,	Kimberley, H.		

Sheet 10

Regl.N.	Rank.	Name	Remarks.
1288	Rifleman	Kenyon, T.A.	
~~14373~~	,,	~~Kilby,~~ ~~H.~~	
578	,,	Knott, T.H.	
1545	,,	Kelly, W.	
2894	,,	Kemp, T.	
7298	,,	Landill, A.	
2805	,,	Lapworth, J"C.	
3244	,,	Lawless, P.	
1960	,,	Lester, A.W.	
13418	,,	Laundy, B.	
11840	,,	Lacey, W.	
6748	,,	Lockett, T.F.	
2968	,,	Lloyd, G.	
7239	,,	Lloyd, W.	
3028	,,	Lodge, H.	
1706	,,	Lucas, E.	
8651	,,	Lawrence, J.W.	
12419	,,	Lane, E.	
439	,,	Lewington, W.	
237	,,	Lewis, H.	
358	,,	Levi, J.	
6018	,, (L/C)	Liddiard, J.	
6031	,,	Lynam, E.	
6032	,,	Lang, J.	
11639	,,	Lovatt, W.	
738	,,	Lawrence, T.	14th.Div.Cycle Coy.
6408	,,	Lund, R.	
13696	,, (L/C)	Little, B.	
14047	,,	Lycett, W.	
8068	,, (L/C)	Laughna, J.	
981	,,	Lawson, A.	
1254	,,	Lee, G.	
6729	,,	Leather, A.	Hospl.
1019	,,	Lock, A.S.	
457	,,	Lockwood, R.	
12242	,, (L/C)	Leach, E.	
4305	,, (L/C)	Littlewood, A.S.	
1604	,,	Lambert, G.	
10687	,,	Lambert, A.	
1092	,,	Ledain, R.H.	
1326	,,	Lavender, W.	
1342	,,	Lees, G.	
1511	,,	Lloyd, B.	
7089	,,	Lowe, A.	
11526	,,	Lane, T.H.	
12381	,,	Lowe, W.H.	
12454	,,	Lomas, W.H.	
1750	,,	Leach, G.	
268	,,	Marney, T.	
382	,,	Mowl, H.	
616	,,	Mutch, A.	
3177	,,	Matthews, A.	
3043	,,	Martin, E.	
1683	,,	Martin, W.	
10214	,,	Mason, E.	
12093	,, (L/C)	Murcott, A.	
7346	,,	Moule, P.	
8744	,,	Madin, G.H.	
6700	,,	Manning, R.	Hospl.
7229	,,	Marshall, A.	
12828	,,	Mc.Auliffe, J.	
11227	,,	Mc.Carthy, F.	Hospl.
536	,,	Melvin, W.	
8198	,,	Millgate, W.	
7644	,,	Moloney, E.	
7010	,,	Moore, R.	
12668	,,	Moreton, H.	
8064	,,	Mc.Cann, J.	
1180	,,	Martin, A.	
8069	,,	Maher, J.	

Regl.No.	Rank		Name	Sheet 11	Remarks
636	Rifleman		Mc.Carthy, H.		
842	,,		Mather, A.		
837	,,		Mazey, F.N.		
7479	,,		Mekin, W.		
1541	,,		Myhatt, H.		
11170	,,		Mc.Gee, W.		
152	,,		Mc.Gregor, E.G.		
11121	,,		Moulder, J.		
12926	,,		Mayhew, W.G.		
3387	,,		Mortimer, H.J.		
2805	,,	(L/C)	Maskell, O.H.		
12418	,,	(L/C)	Massey, H.		
1641	,,		Mc.Cormick, J.		
2814	,,		Marshall, F.		
1562	,,		Marson, R.		
3049	,,		Matthews, F.		
290	,,		Mead, T.		
13520	,,		Mills, H.		
1563	,,		Mitchell, F.A.		
3192	,,		Melia, L.		
8082	,,		Malone, J.		
8374	,,		Milton, E.		
8373	,,		Milton, W.		
826	,,		Messer, G.H.		
12407	,,		Morley, R.		
12519	,,		Maisey, C.		
12245	,,		Mason, W.		
1607	,,		Moore, H.		
13893	,,		Millington, W.		
12253	,,		Maybury, P.		
3042	,,		Nash, E.		
9403	,,		Noakes, H.W.		
11339	,,		Newman, C.		
10924	,,		Noakes, C.A.		
11069	,,		Nuttall, F.		Hospl.
942	,,		Nash, J.		Bde.Orderly.
554	,,		Nicholls, R.		
949	,,		Nicholls, A.		
7486	,,		Nicholson, R.		
7466	,,		Noyce, J.		
1141	,,	(L/C)	Neighbour, J.C.		
7082	,,		Nixon, A.		
1102	,,		Nicholls, S.N.		
11028	,,		Newman, W.R.		
341	,,		Osborne, H.		
13596	,,		Oakes, W.		
8067	,,		Oldfield, W.		
1230	,,		Owen, W.L.		
831	,,		O'Brien, J.		
10173	,,		O'Connor, W.		
2811	,,		Olding, C.		
11662	,,		Offley, E.T.		
3473	,,		Page, B.		Hospl.
3682	,,		Pardoe, H.		
928	,,		Payne, A.		
610	,,		Pennell, F.		
133	,,		Perks, S.		Hospl.
1093	,,		Pither, C.		
1407	,,		Pike, E.		
420	,,		Pickford, J.		Hospl.
12681	,,		Phillips, A.		
772	,,		Phillips, E.		
12471	,,		Powell, T.		(Wounded)
3348	,,		Potts, G.		Hospl.
6723	,,		Preston, R.		
6033	,,		Pryor, E.		Hospl.
1083	,,		Payne, A.		
721	,,		Prosser, W.H.		
254	,,		Peach, H.		
557	,,	(L/C)	Pegg, R.		
3682	,,		Payne, H.		
1335	,,				

Regl.No.	Rank		Name	Remarks	Sheet 12.
12930	Rifleman		Pragnall. E. C.		
11939	,,		Parsons. J.		
7180	,,		Pengelly. E. G.		
7094	,,		Pinder. C.		
14188	,,		Porter. J. H.		
6237	,,		Pybus. R.		
6840	,,		Perry. R.		
724	,,		Parrott. C.		
431	,,		Pilling. W.		
3378	,,		Parker. J.		
1757	,,		Payton. C.		
1756	,,		Payton. A.		
1962	,,		Potter. J.		
2613	,,		Power. C.		
3242	,,		Prosser. H.		
719	,,		Piper. H.		
419	,,		Rice. C.		
449	,, (L/C)		Richardson. F.		
1670	,,		Rose. E.		
6672	,,		Read. A.		
12137	,,		Reynolds. J.		
13267	,,		Rhodes. J.		
448	,,		Rimmer. J.		
14487	,, (L/C)		Rose. G.		
xxxxx	xxxxxxxxxxx				
13816	,,		Rafferty. T.	Hospl.	
444	,,		Randall. P.		
2884	,,		Roper. W.		
xxx	,,		xxxxxxxxxxxx		
14024	,,		Randall. J.		
3383	,,		Rastall. H.		
3676	,,		Read. J.		
1281	,,		Richards. V.		
11114	,,		Richards. F.		
13846	,,		Riddell. A.		
532	,,		Rhodes. A.	Hospl.	
11498	,,		Rhodes. F.		
992	,,		Robinson. S.		
552	,,		Rodwell. R.	Hospl.	
8071	,,		Roscoe. G.		
8070	,,		Roscoe. P.		
3753	,,		Rowles. J.	Brig.Ord.	
7043	,, (L/C)		Ringrose. H.		
642	,,		Rowley. J.		
574	,,		Roberts. F.	Wounded.	
1650	,,		Richards. F. F.		
11883	,,		Royston. C.		
13457	,,		Richardson. J.		
xxxx 1010	,,		Ryan. W. T.		
436	,,		Ranger. A. B.		
833	,,		Rogers. T.		
641	,,		Richardson. J.		
11258	,,		Roberts. H. P.		
10696	,,		Ramsey. V.		
12050	,,		Reynolds. J.		
270	,,		Saunders. F.		
302	,,		Saunders. W.	Hospl.	
103	,,		Scheltz. E.		
2	,,		Speake. R.		
49	,,		Smith. A.		
521	,,		Smith. G.		
728	,,		Smith. G.		
6141	,,		Smith. C.		
8341	,,		Southward. G.		
10704	,,		Sawyer. F.		
3400	,,		Stuart. J.		
1550	,,		Staniford. C.		
13830	,,		Shaw. S.		
3450	,,		Salmon. R. G.		
12380	,,		Sarter. F.		

Sheet 13

Regl.No.	Rank.	Name	Remarks.
11076	Rifleman	Savage, W.	
11585	,,	Shaw, W.	Hospl.
10862	,,	Sheery, S.	
355	,,	Shire, C.	
8998	,,	Simpson, J.	
6586	,,	Singleton, L.	
978	,,	Slim, T.	Hospl.
2565	,,	Small, L.	
12250	,,	Smith, A.H.	
1103	,,	Smith, J.	
12489	,,	Smith, T.	
13499	,,	Smith, A.W.	
8501	,,	Speakman, F.	
1120	,,	Starr, C.	
5992	,,	Storey, A.	
874	,,	Strain, H.	
735	,,	South, C.	
6097	,,	Sullivan, W.	
1023	,,	Starnes, H.	
9490	,, (L/C)	Smith, R.E.	
10863	,, (L/C)	Sorrell, W.	
939	,,	Schleich, J.	
1448	,,	Scandred, F.	
3757	,,	Sargent, A.	
1294	,,	Sharples, G.H.	
3533	,,	Shaw, F.	
1385	,,	Smith, R.A.	
8362	,,	Smith, A.	
8060	,,	Smalwood, F.E.	
12496	,,	Sandles, J.	
10701	,,	Scheran, J.	
12605	,,	Simpson, F.	
12057	,,	Smith, J.	
12562	,,	Smith, H.	
1162	,,	Smith, W.	
11104	,,	Steward, F.	
1443	,,	Smart, C.H.	
781	,,	State, A.	
7081	,,	Saddington, C.	
8353	,,	Snow, G.T.	
8340	,,	Stevenson, E.N.	
3182	,,	Smith, W.H.	
2625	,,	Smith, G.	
838	,,	Smith, A.G.	
8351	,,	Salisbury, J.	
2862	,,	Savin, T.B.	
2237	,,	Sayers, G.	
3374	,,	Shorthouse, A.	
3046	,,	Simms, S.J.	
3293	,,	Smith, W.	
3381	,,	Smith, B.	
3226	,,	Stagg, A.J.	
1656	,,	Stephens, T.	
3232	,,	Staines, W.	
3029	,,	Swindells, E.	
3237	,,	Sullivan, J.	
6964	,,	Skidmore, J.	
7238	,,	Smith, G.	
12163	,,	Styche, H"	
12599	,,	Smith, L.	
12737	,,	Sayers, G.	
618	,,	✗ Taylor, T.	
1011	,,	Thomas, E.	
316	,,	Tucker, J.	✗ 4302 Rfn.Tonkin, T.
185	,,	Turner, T.	
2960	,,	Tyte, W.	
3033	,,	Trueman, H"	
7945	,,	Taylor, E.	
10896	,,	Turner, W.	
576	,,	Timche, C.	Hospl.

Sheet 14.

Regl.No.	Rank.	Name	Remarks.
7235	Rifleman	Thorpe, F.	
3546	,,	Taylor, T.	
6402	,,	Taylor, C.	
12479	,,	Taylor, S.	
3762	,, (L/C)	Tedstone, H.	
1231	,,	Thatcher, H.	
1252	,,	Thomas, J.	
12468	,,	Thomas, H.	
944	,,	Thompson, H.	
3542	,,	Thornton, J.	
3600	,,	Turner, F.	
3390	,,	Taylor, J.	
11483	,, (L/C)	Taylor, C.G.	
1645	,,	Taylor, J.	
1644	,,	Townsend, J.T.	
11171	,,	Turner, S.	
12510	,,	Timms, A.	
12054	,,	Tagg, A.	
1284	,,	Tate, E.A.	
1596	,,	Thorley, T.	
3201	,,	Thistlewood, W.	
3395	,,	Tookey, S.G.	
3239	,,	Turney, C.	
2971	,,	Tildesley, G.E.	
8440	,,	Thomas, D.W.	
6787	,,	Thornton, F.	x991 Rfn.Upton, R.
11638	,,	Venables, T. x	
11522	,,	Veitch, J.	
3453	,,	Vaughan, J.	
232	,,	Whitehead, H.	
338	,, (L/C)	Whitmore, C.	
218	,,	Whiter, F.	
3114	,, (L/C)	Wakeford, H.	
5986	,,	Wright, H.	
11437	,,	Wood, S.	
12043	,,	White, W.	
11233	,,	White, J.	
556	,,	Whitmore, W.	
11997	,,	Walton, J.	
8308	,,	Waters, E.	
1199	,,	Walker, J.	Ypres Police.
6837	,,	Walton, E.	Hospl.
6923	,, (L/C)	Weatherley, W.	
~~2745~~	,,	~~Welsh, J.~~	
12927	,,	Welch, A.	
1380	,,	Weskett, A.	
875	,,	Westbury, N.	
943	,, (L/C)	White, H.	Hospl.
8370	,,	White, C.	
1469	,,	Whittington, D.	Hospl.
~~++++~~	,, (L/C)	~~Wheatley~~	
631	,,	Wicketts, G.	
9294	,, (L/C)	Wilding, J.	
11930	,,	Williams, A.	
1179	,,	Williams, J.	
12904	,,	Wood, R.	
2381	,,	Wright, G.	
10661	,,	Wright, W.	
11876	,,	Wright, W.	
971	,,	Waterman, J.	
1659	,,	Williams, W.	
1653	,,	Wilkins, B.	
3117	,,	White, G"R.	
3295	,,	Wilkinson, C.	
3296	,,	Wilkinson, A.	
1748	,, (L/C)	Williams, W.	
2888	,,	Woods, J.W.	
7242	,,	Walton, R.	
7297	,,	Webster, F.	
6747	,,	Wenlock, W.	
6747-8073	,,	Williams, S.J.	

Sheet 15.

Regl.No.	RANK	Name	Remarks.
8407	Rifleman	White, J.	
12058	,,	White, W.	
1041	,,	Wood, G.J.	
11471	,,	White, J.	
880	,,	Witbread, A.	
3463	,,	Wilman, J.	
3619	,,	Wood, R.W.	
7086	,,	White, C.	
7115	,,	Williams, R.S.	
8301	,,	Weston, D.	
12159	,,	Whittaker, H.	
10688	,,	Wakefield, C.W.	
6409	,,	Waddington, J.	
14048	,,	Whitehouse, F.	
2039	,,	Yates, J.	
12848	,,	Yardley, J.	
5304	,,	Young, E.A.	
13174	,,	Young, H.	
1464	Armourer Sgt.	Ganderton, B. (A.O.C.)	Attached

41st Inf.Bde.
14th Div.

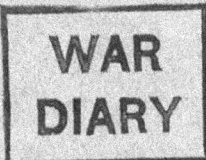

WAR DIARY

8th BATTN. THE KING'S ROYAL RIFLE CORPS.

A P R I L

1 9 1 8

WAR   DIARY

OF

8th. BN. KING'S ROYAL RIFLE CORPS.

From. 1st. APRIL. 1918.

To. 31st. APRIL. 1918.

VOLUME XXXIII

Army Form C. 2118.

WAR DIARY
or
INTELLIGENCE SUMMARY

9ᵗʰ KRRC

April '18 Sheet 1.

(Erase heading not required.)

Instructions regarding War Diaries and Intelligence Summaries are contained in F.S. Regs., Part II. and the Staff Manual respectively. Title Pages will be prepared in manuscript.

Place	Date	Hour	Summary of Events and Information	Remarks and references to Appendices
BACOUL	1ˢᵗ		Bᵗ. left BACOUL at 7AM & proceeded by on foot & by lorry to ST NICHOLAS. At 1. P.M. moved up into support in front of MOURGES under command of Capt TETLEY. (Strength of Bᵗ. 30 Officers & 80 O.R. 2 Lt. JEFFERIES rejoined.	E. Beauclerk Capt
MOURGES	2ⁿᵈ		During the afternoon the position was heavily bombarded for about an hour. At 11.45 P.M. the Bᵗ. was relieved by the French & proceeded to BOIS BLANZY.	E. Beauclerk Capt
BOIS BLANZY	3ʳᵈ		Bᵗ. left at 6. P.M. to take up support position in a quarry in front of BOIS de VAIRE. 2 Lt. NEILSON rejoined.	E. Beauclerk Capt
BOISdeVAIRE	4ᵗʰ		About 4 A.M. report of a probable attack was received shortly after the position was heavily shelled for four hours owing to the nature of the position our casualties were slight during this bombardment. At the end of this time the hoboken the left fell back soon followed by the troops on the right. Owing to the danger to the right flank CAPT. TETLEY formed a defensive flank with 2 Lewis guns & 30 men under 2 Lt NEILSON. About 9AM CAPT. TETLEY was wounded in the head & arm, he insisted on making his position secure before going back to the dressing station. At 10AM Lt NEILSON reported that his position was being enfiladed & was becoming impossible to hold, the garrison having been reduced to 10 men. MAJOR YOUNG of the 7ᵗʰ RB took charge of the situation & ordered to withdraw to ridge Nᵒ of BOIS de VAIRE. In the evening the Bᵗ. (2 Officers & 30 OR)	

Army Form C. 2118.

WAR DIARY
or
INTELLIGENCE SUMMARY
(Erase heading not required.)

J. KERR
Sheet 2.
April '16

Place	Date	Hour	Summary of Events and Information	Remarks and references to Appendices
AUBIGNE	5, 6, 7.		Moved to support line in front of AUBIGNE remained there until evening of 7th when they were relieved & marched to ST. FUSCIEN.	Radcliff Capt.
ST FUSCIEN	8, 9.		Stayed at ST FUSCIEN. CAPT MORSON returned to 14 D.O.B. LT HARRIS rejoined	Radcliff Capt.
	10.		Left ST FUSCIEN at 4.15 P.M. marched to SAHEUX, thence by train to GAMACHES from there marched to BUISNY. CAPT C.E. SCOTT & SJT McKEAN rejoined with men from leave.	
BUISNY	11.		Marched to EU entrained at midnight.	Radcliff Capt.
"	12/13		Detrained at HESDIN about 7AM & marched to FRUGES where baths were at once got going. Tales of a reorganisation abroad	
FRUGES			Marched from FRUGES to MENCAS. Particulars of reorganisation arrived. The three Bns of Rifles of the 14th Divn are to form a composite Bn to such Bn are being formed out of whole Divn. These are formed as the 4.3rd Bde. The Rifle Bn being under command of Lt Col Durham. Peace to send all men other than details & they will form the Bn on the march. The greatest feeling is prevalent in the 13th about the breaking up of one of the original Bns, nobody wishes to leave us.	
MENCAS	14.			
	15.		The people detailed moved to AIRES en route to Base forming Col Carley's following "C" Bn. Details & transport stay behind under CAPT C.E. SCOTT proceeding	Radcliff Capt.

Army Form C. 2118.

WAR DIARY
or
INTELLIGENCE SUMMARY
(Erase heading not required.)

8th K.R.R.C.

April 18

Sheet 3

Instructions regarding War Diaries and Intelligence Summaries are contained in F.S. Regs., Part II. and the Staff Manual respectively. Title Pages will be prepared in manuscript.

Place	Date	Hour	Summary of Events and Information	Remarks and references to Appendices
			Later in the day to LISBOURG.	Buckshott Capt
MOHINGHEM	27.		From this time "C" By was at work daily round MOHINGHEM near ISBERGUES & the transport was doing nothing except marring to get out of the way of the troops. It left LISBOURS to SAINS LES FRESSIN & later went to FRESSIN where we were told of another scheme of forming the whole Division into a skeleton for training Americans, each By to consist of a cadre of 10 Officers & 45 O.R. Great heart-burnings trying to include everyone in the 45 O.R. The composite By was broken up, the personnel other than the 10 officers & 45 O.R. transport were used to the base to go as reinforcements to other By's. Col Curling delivered a lecture on esprit de Battalion & saying that it is much finer than esprit de Battailon, older members of By's very inclined to disagree.	Buckshott Capt
CREPY	28.		Party from "C" B. moved to CREPY.	Buckshott Capt
FRESSIN	29.		Training personnel & transport all at FRESSIN	J Buckshott Capt
	30.		A Col Curling has orders to proceed to command the 16th By.	

Army Form C. 2118.

6th KRRC

April '18.

WAR DIARY
or
INTELLIGENCE SUMMARY
(Erase heading not required.)

Place	Date	Hour	Summary of Events and Information	Remarks and references to Appendices
			The chief feature of the month has been the extraordinary amount of apathy displayed by the men about the breaking up of the old Battalion. One felt that some of the men who have been with the B[attalio]n since its formation lost all interest in life now as soon as they heard the B[attalio]n was to be broken up. They regarded it & seemed to think that their officers showed as much grief about need a calamity as the disbandment of one of the decrease of the "First Hundred Thousand". The general feeling was that "Why didn't the regiment go up altogether with a pretty good fight". It is one of the minor tragedies of the war.	Eaglestott Capt

EXTRACT FROM THE KING'S ROYAL RIFLE CORPS CHRONICLE.

8th Battalion War Records.

1918.
April.

During the early part of April the remnant of the Battalion continued to occupy various defensive positions in conjunction with other Units, until April 14th, when the three Rifle Battalions of the 14th Light Division were formed into a composite Battalion; four such Battalions being formed from the whole Division, and then known as the 43rd Brigade.

The newly formed Rifle Unit was under the command of Lieut. Col. Curling D.S.O., a Rifleman.

This composite Battalion was again broken up on April 27th, and Lieut.Col. Curling proceeded to the Command of the 16th Battalion K.R.R.Corps.

May.

All except 10 Officers and 45 other ranks were sent to the Base. This cadre, during May, took over the administration of an Irish Battalion of the 16th Division, and was commanded by Lieut. Col. Crocker, of the Welsh Regiment, and worked on a line of trenches near the village of Thiennes.

They were relieved by the training staff of the 7th Bn. Royal Irish Rifles on the 27th June, and then divided into four cadre training Companies, and attached to the 314th and 315th Americal Machine-Gun Battalions and the 317th and 320th Machine-gun Companies at Frenc.

The last chapter in the history of the 8th Battalion was closed on 31st July 1918, when orders were received that the Battalion, with other, was to be "broken up". The Battalion was disbanded on August 1st, and the majority of Officers and other ranks proceeded to join the 12th Battalion K.R.R.C.

Our story is now ended. All ranks felt most deeply the tragedy of the situation, and were loud in their protests, which were, nevertheless, unavailing. As a Unit we pass into history. We had performed our task and had endeavoured to uphold the standard of those who had gone before us and died so gloriously at Hooge on that day of trial in July 30th - 31st, 1915.

Certified true extract.

[signature]
Colonel.
Officer i/c Rifle Records.

Winchester.
30th October 1923.

WAR DIARY

of the

8th. Bn. KING'S ROYAL RIFLE CORPS.

From, 1st. May, 1918.

To. 31st. May, 1918.

VOLUME XXXVII

May '18
Army Form C. 2118

WAR DIARY or INTELLIGENCE SUMMARY

8th K.R.R.C. Page 1.

(Erase heading not required.)

Place	Date	Hour	Summary of Events and Information	Remarks and references to Appendices
FRESSIN	1		Training, staff fitting into unit. Lt. Col. Cuening left to take command of the 16 KRR.	Beaufort Camp
EMBRY	2		Bn. moved to EMBRY. Comfortable billets, the cadre of the Bde. are all in the village.	Beaufort Camp
"	3-12		Nothing of interest during this time, training of specialists & cadres, ranges, cleaning up.	Beaufort Camp
"	13/14		Transport personnel (surplus to establishment of cadre B.) left to go to C.S.Q. Great heart burnings over Nellie the Bn. mascot, the transport who bought her out three years ago trying to take her with them, the R.Q.M.S. retained her until some time. Nothing of interest.	Beaufort Camp
AIRE	15		The training staff moved by lorry to L 19 b 4 (Sheet 36 AS) to take over the administration of the great reinforcement	Beaufort Camp

WAR DIARY
or
INTELLIGENCE SUMMARY

(Erase heading not required.)

Army Form C. 2118

May 1918

8 RWF

Page 2

Place	Date	Hour	Summary of Events and Information	Remarks and references to Appendices
NAIRE	16 / 17 / 18		Bn. of the 16th Divn. The Bn. works on a line of trenches around the edge of THIENNES. They work from 9 AM to 4 PM. Lt-Col Crocker of the Welsh Regt took over command of the Bn.	Bacchus Col.
	19		Spent by reinforcements working. The training staff (seconded) positions to be occupied in case of a gas attack & routes to those positions.	C Bacchus Capt.
	20		Bn works in morning. Voluntary service for R.C. at 7 AM. Largely attended.	
	21/ 23/31		Practice manning of Battle Stations, uneventful. Work, only carried out by summary competitions in the canal.	C Bacchus Col.

C Bacchus Lieut Col.
Capt.
Commanding 8th R.W.R.

1875 Wt. W593/826 1,000,000 4/15 J.B.C. & A. A.D.S.S./Forms/C. 2118.

EXTRACT FROM THE KING'S ROYAL RIFLE CORPS
CHRONICLE.

8th Battalion War Records.

1918

April.

During the early part of April the remnant of the Battalion continued to occupy various defensive positions in conjunction with other Units until April 14th, when the three Rifle Battalions of the 14th Light Division were formed into a Composite Battalion; four such Battalions being formed from the whole Division and then known as the 43rd Brigade.

The newly formed Rifle Unit was under the command of Lieut. Col. Curling D.S.O. a Rifleman.

This Composite Battalion was again broken up on April 27th and Lieut. Col. Curling proceeded to the Command of the 16th Battalion K.R.R. Corps.

May.

All except 10 Officers and 45 other ranks were sent to the Base. This cadre, during May, took over the administration of an Irish Battalion of the 16th Division, and was commanded by Lieut. Col. Crocker of the Welsh Regiment, and worked on a line of trenches near the village of Thiennes.

They were relieved by the training staff of the 7th Bn. Royal Irish Rifles on the 27th June, and then divided into four cadre training Companies and attached to the 314th and 315th American Machine-Gun Battalions and the 317th and 320th Machine-Gun Companies at Frenq.

The last chapter in the history of the 8th Battalion was closed on 31st July 1918, when orders were received that the Battalion, with others, was to be "broken up". The Battalion was disbanded on August 1st and the majority of Officers and other ranks proceeded to join the 12th Battalion, K.R.R.C.

Our story is now ended. All ranks felt most deeply the tragedy of the situation, and were loud in their protests which were, nevertheless, unavailing. As a Unit we pass into history. We had performed our task and had endeavoured to uphold the standard of those who had gone before us and died so gloriously at Hooge on that day of trial in July 30th - 31st 1915.

Certified true extract.

G.N. SALMON, Colonel,
Officer i/c Rifle Records.

Winchester.
30th October.

EXTRACT FROM THE KING'S ROYAL RIFLE CORPS CHRONICLE.

8th Battalion War Records.

1918

April.

During the early part of April the remnant of the Battalion continued to occupy various defensive positions in conjunction with other Units until April 14th, when the three Rifle Battalions of the 14th Light Division were formed into a Composite Battalion; four such Battalions being formed from the whole Division and then known as the 43rd Brigade.

The newly formed Rifle Unit was under the command of Lieut. Col. Curling D.S.O. a Rifleman.

This Composite Battalion was again broken up on April 27th and Lieut. Col. Curling proceeded to the Command of the 16th Battalion K.R.R. Corps.

May.

All except 10 Officers and 45 other ranks were sent to the Base. This cadre, during May, took over the administration of an Irish Battalion of the 16th Division, and was commanded by Lieut. Col. Crocker of the Welsh Regiment, and worked on a line of trenches near the village of Thiennes.

They were relieved by the training staff of the 7th Bn. Royal Irish Rifles on the 27th June, and then divided into four cadre training Companies and attached to the 314th and 315th American Machine-Gun Battalions and the 317th and 320th Machine-Gun Companies at Frenq.

The last chapter in the history of the 8th Battalion was closed on 31st July 1918, when orders were received that the Battalion, with others, was to be "broken up". The Battalion was disbanded on August 1st and the majority of Officers and other ranks proceeded to join the 12th Battalion, K.R.R.C.

Our story is now ended. All ranks felt most deeply the tragedy of the situation, and were loud in their protests which were, nevertheless, unavailing. As a Unit we pass into history. We had performed our task and had endeavoured to uphold the standard of those who had gone before us and died so gloriously at Hooge on that day of trial in July 30th - 31st 1915.

Certified true extract.

G.N. SALMON, Colonel,
Officer i/c Rifle Records.

Winchester.
30th October.

EXTRACT FROM THE KING'S ROYAL RIFLE CORPS CHRONICLE.

8th Battalion War Records.

1918

April.

During the early part of April the remnant of the Battalion continued to occupy various defensive positions in conjunction with other Units until April 14th, when the three Rifle Battalions of the 14th Light Division were formed into a Composite Battalion; four such Battalions being formed from the whole Division and then known as the 43rd Brigade.

The newly formed Rifle Unit was under the command of Lieut. Col. Curling D.S.O. a Rifleman.

This Composite Battalion was again broken up on April 27th and Lieut. Col. Curling proceeded to the Command of the 16th Battalion K.R.R. Corps.

May.

All except 10 Officers and 45 other ranks were sent to the Base. This cadre, during May, took over the administration of an Irish Battalion of the 16th Division, and was commanded by Lieut. Col. Crocker of the Welch Regiment, and worked on a line of trenches near the village of Thiennes.

They were relieved by the training staff of the 7th Bn. Royal Irish Rifles on the 27th June, and then divided into four cadre training Companies and attached to the 314th and 315th American Machine-Gun Battalions and the 317th and 320th Machine-Gun Companies at Prenq.

The last chapter in the history of the 8th Battalion was closed on 31st July 1918, when orders were received that the Battalion, with others was to be "broken up". The Battalion was disbanded on August 1st, and the majority of Officers and other ranks proceeded to join the 12th Battalion, K.R.R.C.

Our story is now ended. All ranks felt most deeply the tragedy of the situation, and were loud in their protests which were, nevertheless, unavailing. As a Unit we pass into history. We had performed our task and had endeavoured to uphold the standard of those who had gone before us and died so gloriously at Hooge on that day of trial in July 30th - 31st 1915.

Certified true extract,

G.B. BALECH, Colonel,
Officer i/c Rifle Records.

Winchester.
30th October.

Army Form C. 2118.

WAR DIARY
or
INTELLIGENCE SUMMARY
(Erase heading not required.)

June
8 E.P.R.R.C. Sheet 1
Vol 33

Place	Date	Hour	Summary of Events and Information	Remarks and references to Appendices
BOESINGHEN	1/26		Continuation of work except such reinforcement as time & weather permitted. Troops all had an extraordinary hard day, being of unknown origin the Regiments under the B'n escape for a very few cases.	Valuable
	26		Orders received for B'n to prepare to hand over to Treloain Staff of 7 E.R.R., some little orders about 6 P.M. in early hard rain, and completes before midnight when limos and poses.	
FRENCQ	27		B'n proceeded by lorry to FRENCQ taking over billets there by 7 E R.I.R. taking on their got of training American. Lt Colhacker + Capt C.E. Scott proceeded to PARENTS to be attached to 159 American Infantry Regt. laying the 4 Coys. Coys under Capt HEM? loan to be attached to 319 American M.G. B-n + 317 - 320 M.G. Coys at FRENCQ.	Venture

WAR DIARY
or
INTELLIGENCE SUMMARY

Army Form C. 2118.

June '12 8th KRRC

Place	Date	Hour	Summary of Events and Information	Remarks and references to Appendices
FRENCQ			The scheme of attestation is One Centre Coy, consisting of 1 O.C, 6 Sgs, 1 CSM, & 6 9 O.Rs, was to attacked to an Opponent Bt. to shoot as for as possible in the morning. The idea is to make suppression rather than to lay down a barrage. Chief work is Musketry, Lewis guns, & Bayonet fighting. The Americans make a great point of fire. here is in arms against all men, no matter what they are & have to bear their punishment from 11 to 12 (noon) daily.	
	29.		The Americans arrived out to learn.	
	30.		The Duke of Connaught inspected the 159 A.I.B. at AUBERSENT. New Bdr in between 7000 & 8000 strong. Training.	

www.ingramcontent.com/pod-product-compliance
Lightning Source LLC
Chambersburg PA
CBHW080851010526
44117CB00014B/2232